TEACHING

WITHOUT

TENURE

TEACHING WITHOUT TENURE

Policies and Practices for a New Era

Roger G. Baldwin
Jay L. Chronister

The Johns Hopkins University Press
Baltimore and London

To Peggy and Shirley
and our lifelong tenure

The Johns Hopkins University Press
2715 North Charles Street
Baltimore, Maryland 21218-4363
www.press.jhu.edu

Library of Congress Cataloging-in-Publication Data
Baldwin, Roger G.
    Teaching without tenure : policies and practices for a new era / Roger
G. Baldwin, Jay L. Chronister.
        p. cm.
    Includes bibliographical references and index.
    ISBN 0-8018-6502-6 (alk. paper)
    1. College teachers—Tenure—United States.   2. College
teachers—Selection and appointment—United States.   I. Chronister, Jay L.
II. Title.
    LB2335.7.B36 2001
    378.1'21—dc21   00-008845

A catalog record for this book is available from the British Library.

Contents

List of Figures and Tables   vii

Preface and Acknowledgments   ix

I   Introduction   1

2   The Context for Change   13

3   The Terms and Conditions of Full-Time Non-Tenure-Track
Faculty Employment   31

4   Who Are the Full-Time Non-Tenure-Track Faculty?   77
Bruce M. Gansneder, Elizabeth P. Harper, and Roger G. Baldwin

5   Consequences of Employing Full-Time Non-Tenure-Track
Faculty: Institutional and Individual Experiences   114

6   Exemplary Policies for Full-Time Non-Tenure-Track
Faculty   146

7   The Future: An Action Agenda   173

APPENDIXES

A   Colleges and Universities Participating in the Institutional
Survey and Site Visits   193

B   Institutional Survey Concerning Non-Tenure-Track
Faculty   197

C   Site Visit Interview Questions   202

D   Topical Areas Addressed in the Review of Institutional Policies
Affecting Full-Time Non-Tenure-Track Faculty   205

E   A Framework for Institutional Self-Assessment of Personnel
Policies and Practices Affecting Full-Time Non-Tenure-Track
Faculty   206

References   211

Index   215

Figures and Tables

FIGURES

4.1   Full-Time Faculty within Rank, by Tenure Status   83

4.2   Full-Time Non-Tenure-Track Faculty, by Type of Institution   84

4.3   Full-Time Non-Tenure-Track Faculty, by Program Area   85

4.4   Primary Activity of Full-Time Faculty, by Tenure Status   86

TABLES

3.1   Level of Instruction for Which Full-Time Non-Tenure-Track Faculty Are Hired, by Type of Institution, Fall 1996   32

3.2   Comparability of Average Salaries of Full-Time Non-Tenure-Track and Tenure-Eligible Faculty with Comparable Qualifications, by Type of Institution   50

3.3   Institutions at Which Full-Time Non-Tenure-Track Faculty Are Eligible to Participate in Campus Governance   58

3.4   Survey Institutions Offering Support to Full-Time Faculty for Selected Professional Development Activities and Functions   66

4.1   Demographic Characteristics of Full-Time Faculty, 1992   78

4.2   Full-Time Faculty with Doctorate and Time in Current Position   80

4.3   Teaching Productivity, by Tenure Status   88

4.4   Last Two Years' Productivity, by Tenure Status   89

4.5   Career Productivity, by Tenure Status   89

4.6   Mean Satisfaction with Job and Career Opportunities,
by Tenure Status   91

4.7   Mean Satisfaction with Institutional Support,
by Tenure Status   93

4.8   Some Characteristics of the Four Types of Full-Time
Non-Tenure-Track Faculty   98

4.9   Teachers' Job Satisfaction, by Educational
Attainment   100

4.10   Researchers' Job Satisfaction, by Educational
Attainment   104

4.11   Administrators' Job Satisfaction, by Educational
Attainment   107

4.12   Other Academic Professionals' Job Satisfaction,
by Educational Attainment   110

6.1   A Best Practices Model for the Employment of Full-Time
Non-Tenure-Track Faculty   171

Preface and Acknowledgments

The academic profession is in the midst of a major transition. This change has consequences and implications for relationships between an institution and its faculty and for faculty careers as well. Fundamentally, the nature and quality of higher education are affected as the roles and functions of professors evolve in response to changing conditions on campus and in the larger world. As institutions hire more faculty members who are not on the traditional tenure track, they must carefully design policies and practices that will maintain educational quality. These policies and practices must also provide a supportive work environment and career advancement opportunities for the faculty hired into what have become known on many campuses as *contingent positions*.

Educational quality, efficiency, and cost are widely discussed in the media as major problems and issues facing higher education. Academic tenure is also a controversial subject in many state capitols and in the media. Many proposals for change in academic management practices and academic staffing have been advanced from within and outside higher education. Efforts to redefine the mission and functions of colleges and universities, including the nature of faculty work, need to be carefully examined and discussed. The growing use of part-time and full-time temporary or contingent faculty represents a major change in the staffing pattern of colleges and universities. The part-time faculty issues have been systematically examined in several key publications in recent years. In contrast, the increased use of full-time non-tenure-eligible faculty has not been the subject of a systematic and comprehensive assessment. This book has been designed to bring together a wealth of factual information and diverse perspectives on this growing segment of the faculty in American higher education.

This publication is addressed to institutional policymakers who plan and manage faculty staffing. This includes trustees, presidents, provosts, deans, and department chairs in all types of higher education institutions. In addition, faculty interest groups (e.g., senates, assemblies, professional associations, unions), faculty development specialists, and individual faculty will find the book useful. Governmental policymakers (e.g., state legislative committees, agency heads, coordinating and governing boards) will find the book relevant to their oversight and planning functions. The book also can serve as a text in courses on contemporary issues in higher education, higher education policy, and the academic profession.

We are indebted to a large number of persons and organizations that supported this effort. A special statement of appreciation goes to the Andrew W. Mellon Foundation, the Teachers Insurance Annuity Association–College Retirement Equities Fund (TIAA-CREF), and the Office of Higher Education of the National Education Association for their financial support of the national study that formed the heart of this book. At the outset of the study, we convened a national advisory committee that assisted us in designing the research project. The members subsequently responded to our data collection plans and provided guidance in developing the focus of our site visits. It is with a deep sense of gratitude that we extend thanks to Patricia Hyer, of Virginia Polytechnic Institute and State University, David Leslie, of the College of William and Mary, Christine Maitland, of the National Education Association Office of Higher Education, Jack Schuster, of Claremont Graduate University, and Joan Stark, of the University of Michigan, for their wise counsel and advice. We also extend thanks to John Vaughn, of the Association of American Universities, for assistance during our site visit phase of the study.

There are more faculty members and administrators at our survey and site visit institutions than we can possibly acknowledge personally. Their participation was the foundation upon which this publication is based. We benefited from the institutional policy documents they shared, the surveys they completed, and the many hours that faculty and administrators took from their busy schedules to talk with us during our site visits. To all of these professionals we extend appreciation. At each of our twelve site visit campuses a staff member served as coordinator for the visit, providing the detailed logistical support needed to make our brief visits productive. The interview phase of our study would not have been possible without the coordinators' willingness to do all of the behind-the-scenes work to make our trips successful. To them we extend heartfelt thanks.

On our respective campuses, we received valuable support and assistance from graduate assistants Elizabeth Harper, a contributing author of Chapter 4, William Haarlow, at the University of Virginia, and Anthony Foster and Marc Gingerelli, at the College of William and Mary. Members of the office staffs at our two institutions were indispensable colleagues in completing the task of research and writing. A sincere thank-you to Paula Price and Peggy Powell, at the University of Virginia, and Kerry Evans and Kaffi Williams, at the College of William and Mary. Two colleagues at the University of Virginia must be recognized. David W. Breneman, dean of the Curry School of Education, provided continued encouragement and support to us as a behind-the-scenes member of the research team. The second colleague is Professor Bruce M. Gansneder, who is a contributing author of Chapter 4. His contributions went far beyond data analysis and contributing to the writing of that chapter.

We would also like to acknowledge the contributions made by the external reviewer for the Johns Hopkins University Press and by Jacqueline Wehmueller, editor-in-chief of the Press. Their insightful and incisive comments and recommendations strengthened the contributions we hope this book will make toward understanding the significant changes taking place in the relationship between institutions of higher education and their faculties.

Finally, we want to recognize our wives, Peggy Baldwin and Shirley Chronister, who became partners in this venture. For their steady encouragement and willingness to allow this project to consume valuable family time, we extend our heartfelt thanks. They allowed our travel schedules, concentrated periods of writing, and working visits to each other's homes to impinge on time that we should have spent with them. This endeavor was not just a collaborative venture between two authors but between their families as well.

TEACHING

WITHOUT

TENURE

1 Introduction

Higher education institutions are no longer cozy sanctuaries somewhat removed from the realities of a dynamic society. Today they are the backbone of our nation's knowledge-driven economy. A college education has become a minimum requirement for entry into most skilled jobs and for membership in the upwardly mobile American middle class. In this way, higher education has moved from the periphery to the heart of American society. No longer may it operate purely by its own ancient traditions and arcane decision-making procedures. Like all other sectors of the U.S. economy, higher education exists within a competitive market and must adapt to the rapidly changing environmental forces that alter market conditions.

A variety of concurrent forces account for the rapid transition that colleges and universities are experiencing. Virtually all higher education institutions, even the best endowed, have encountered constraints on their resources as they have tried to respond to seemingly insatiable demands for knowledge and education. Simply put, no institution can operate the way it used to. Adjustments must be made to cut costs and reorder priorities. Advances in technology have likewise altered the way colleges and universities do business. The traditional model of a professor standing in front of a group of live students in real space and time has been called into question as research on the learning process and institutional balance sheets written in red ink encourage educators and administrators to rethink the instructional process.

An increasingly diverse student clientele is another factor challenging traditional practices in higher education. The majority of undergraduates today are over the age of 22 (*Chronicle of Higher Education* 1997, 18). The idea that college is an activity predominantly for youth is now a quaint anachronism. Students are also coming to campus from a wider range of cultures and socioeconomic backgrounds than ever before. More students commute and work off-campus while they attend college than in past decades. Perhaps most significant, many students do not come to campus at all but enroll in college courses through distance learning programs offering higher education through a variety of technological means. It is clear from these patterns that many students have a different relationship to higher education than did their educational predecessors, who viewed college primarily as a four-year residential experience to be completed between the ages of 18 and 22.

Increased competition from other education providers is another key force reshaping higher education. The American college and university system is widely regarded as the best in the world, yet this enviable status does not protect institutions of higher learning from competitors. Higher education is a multi-billion-dollar industry, and many potential players are eager to get on the field and share in the possible profits. Competition among colleges and universities has long been a hallmark of U.S. higher education; however, this once-exclusive league is expanding. New types of institutions such as Western Governors University and for-profit education providers such as the University of Phoenix are entering the game. Their market-sensitive programs and state-of-the-art technologies are forcing traditional institutions to rethink and reconfigure their educational programs, modes of delivery, and, inevitably, staffing practices.

The academic profession is not immune to this rapidly changing context. Certainly, a core component of instructional staff, the tenure-eligible faculty, live within the standard procedures established by the American Association of University Professors in 1940. This academic personnel system imposes a rigorous six-year probationary period followed by the award of tenure and long-term employment security. This core group of tenured faculty is now increasingly supplemented by contingent faculty members who play very important instructional, scholarly, and service roles but who may not earn a long-term employment commitment from their institutions. Contingent faculty may be either full-timers with limited term contracts or part-time faculty. The part-time faculty phenomenon has been the subject of much dialogue and debate in the higher education community. Works such as Gappa and Leslie's *Invisible Faculty* (1993) explore the part-time faculty issue in depth. Our book performs a parallel function by investigating all dimensions of the full-time non-tenure-track phenomenon.

We examine the process of transition going on within the U.S. professoriate by focusing specifically on a growing component of the profession, full-time faculty who are not eligible for tenure. These academic staff members have varying titles on different campuses. Officially they are known by titles such as term faculty, adjunct professors, visiting professors, and lecturers. Unofficially, they are sometimes referred to by facetious but telling labels like "bullpen faculty," "workhorse faculty," and "subfaculty." Although these full-time academic positions are packaged in many ways, the absence of access to tenured status is their one universal attribute. This significant departure from the traditional faculty employment pattern—a pattern that most colleges and universities have followed since the early part of the twentieth century—may be quietly changing the academic profession and the American higher education system. For this reason, it is time to examine it closely.

The Growth of Full-Time Non-Tenure-Track Appointments

Data on faculty staffing patterns confirm that full-time non-tenure-track appointments have been increasing across higher education. For example, Ernst Benjamin (1997), in a report prepared for the American Association of University Professors Executive Committee, shows that between 1975 and 1993 the proportion of tenured faculty declined only slightly but the proportion of untenured but tenure-track faculty declined from 29 percent to less than 21 percent of the full-time faculty. In contrast, non-tenure-track faculty across all higher education institutions (two-year colleges as well as four-year and graduate institutions) grew from under 19 percent to more than 27 percent of the full-time faculty nationwide. According to U.S. Department of Education (1997a) data, between 1987 and 1992 the proportion of full-time faculty not eligible for tenure rose from less than 21 percent to over 24 percent (18). Proportions may vary due to different definitions of non-tenure-eligible faculty. The important finding, however, is the consistent upward trend in full-time non-tenure-track hiring in recent years.

Appointment patterns by academic field and type of institution show similar trends toward more hiring of full-time faculty in non-tenure-eligible positions. All academic program areas except business and engineering experienced growth in the proportion of their full-time faculty who were in non-tenure-track positions during the 1987–92 period. A similar pattern holds true when we compare the academic staffing trends of various types of higher education institutions. The U.S. Department of Education data for 1987–92, cited above, show that all types of colleges and universities except public research universities increased their proportion of full-time but non-tenure-eligible faculty during that time period.

The number of full-time non-tenure-track faculty positions has grown in recent years for a variety of reasons. Those cited frequently by faculty and administrators include the need to employ limited financial resources effectively, the desire to preserve staffing flexibility in a time of rapid change, and the opportunity to hire valuable professionals who may lack the credentials traditionally required for a tenure-track appointment. Sociological changes such as increased numbers of single-parent families and dual-career marriages are also stimulating the expansion of academic positions off the tenure track, as individuals seek alternate forms of academic employment. The varied forces behind the growth of full-time non-tenure-track appointments are explored in detail in Chapter 2.

Two Faculty Views

Full-time non-tenure-track faculty come in a wide variety of forms. Their positions and professional experiences in higher education vary by academic field, institutional type, gender, age, and geographic location. This list of variables is by no means comprehensive but demonstrates that superficial generalizations about faculty off the tenure track can be both inaccurate and misleading. The list suggests that it is necessary to look beneath the surface of generic titles or simplistic labels to comprehend fully the wide variety of persons who work in full-time non-tenure-eligible posts. Similarly, it is necessary to study such positions carefully to understand the rich diversity of roles and experiences that fall under the heading of non-tenure-track appointments.

Later in this book we attempt to portray the full range of types of non-tenure-track faculty currently working full-time in senior institutions of American higher education. Here, two women we met at a major research university help to illustrate the diverse nature of the non-tenure-track faculty experience. Although not completely representative, their stories serve to frame the boundaries within which we find most full-time non-tenure-eligible faculty at the beginning of the new century. With each subsequent chapter, we paint a more colorful and comprehensive portrait of full-time non-tenure-track faculty.

MARILYN THOMPSON

Marilyn Thompson* holds a unique, hybrid position that reflects the distinctive culture and mission of her university. She is part administrator and part professor and has worked at her institution for eleven years. Her title is

*Names used are pseudonyms.

dean of the Class of 2000 and adjunct associate professor. She serves as an academic administrator and study-abroad adviser while also teaching large introductory-level courses in a science-related department. She finds this blended position very appealing. It enables her to combine her interest in science education with her duties as an academic dean. In her discussions with us, she noted how her teaching keeps her in touch with undergraduate concerns and stimulates ideas for curricular reform.

Marilyn followed a traditional path into academic life, earning a Ph.D. from a prestigious research university. She entered the employment market "at a bad time" for her specialty, however, and moved to a location where her husband got a nonacademic appointment in an applied field. A series of events gradually moved Marilyn away from a traditional research-oriented academic career. Temporary appointments at a comprehensive university, as well as time off to have children and geographic constraints, led Marilyn to a full-time appointment at a teaching-oriented undergraduate college. Eventually, she took on administrative duties as a department chair. She came to her current institution on a special program to restart the research careers of liberal arts college professors. By this time, however, Marilyn was committed to teaching in her field and opted not to return to a research track.

Marilyn's distinctive position has enabled her to balance family obligations with her career interests. She readily admits, "I had no interest in the tenure track. I did not want to do what needed to be done to play the tenure game." On balance, Marilyn views her position at her university positively. She sees it as a viable alternative to the tenure track and believes that she can build a fulfilling career within academe following her nontraditional path.

JOYCE SZABO

Joyce Szabo is a visiting assistant professor in her seventh year at the same university. She teaches both in a social science field and in modern languages. Her primary teaching assignment is in languages, although her doctorate is in her social science teaching area. Her appointment has evolved from year to year, gradually moving from a primary emphasis in the social science field to the current concentration in languages. She teaches at all instructional levels, conducts research, and serves on students' committees. She is permitted to chair committees in one department but not the other. In most respects, Joyce functions as a regular faculty member, but she is not on the tenure track. "I do everything you would expect from a tenure track faculty member," she observed, "but [my] university makes no commitment to me."

Joyce followed a traditional path early in her career, earning a doctorate at an Ivy League university followed by a series of postdoctoral appointments at prestigious universities and an internationally renowned research institute in Europe. Her career diverged from the standard pattern when she moved with her husband when he was offered a tenure-eligible post. Since then she has had a series of temporary appointments at the same institution. These have left her feeling exploited by the university. With much emotion, she described herself as "a captive." She noted that academic deans are extremely aware of her position as part of a dual academic career couple. "By definition it is exploitative," she asserted, "because they know I will stick around." She supported her case by noting that she has no voting rights at the college level. She is not eligible for computer upgrades, which tenure-track faculty receive. And after seven years of full-time service, she is not sure that she will be awarded a sabbatical. She asserted that the university will not do anything to improve her situation unless she gets another job offer. Joyce is concerned about the long-term impact of her temporary status on her career. "It begins to look strange to be a visiting professor for seven years," she said. "In my case, it is detrimental." She argued that her situation is debilitating to her students as well as to herself. "I cannot tell them if I will be here next year."

Joyce's view of her non-tenure track status contrasts sharply with Marilyn's. Their differing views emerged in a vigorous group discussion where Joyce tried to convince Marilyn that the university was exploiting Marilyn and other faculty off the tenure track. While Marilyn appreciates the opportunity for an alternative academic career not defined by the demands of the tenure system, Joyce feels that her career has been put at risk by her temporary status and the absence of a long-term commitment to her by the university.

In spite of their differing views on their non-tenure track positions, Marilyn and Joyce agreed that faculty in these types of posts perform valuable work that is critical to the mission of higher education. The university "needs people to do teaching as well as the hot shots," Joyce argued. The university "benefits from non-tenure track positions and should give people in these positions something back" for what they provide to the university. Marilyn essentially concurred with this view. The university "needs to get honest with itself," Marilyn suggested, to "get out of its fantasy world. Students come here, and they and their parents expect good teaching."

Key Themes

The dialogue between Marilyn and Joyce highlights five overarching themes that emerged during the course of our study. These themes evolve through the pages of this book. They carried us, and we hope will carry our readers, to firm conclusions concerning the full-time non-tenure track faculty issue and specific recommendations for action.

The traditional full-time tenure-track faculty model is no longer adequately meeting the educational needs of a complex, dynamic society. Many institutions have designed full-time nontraditional (i.e., non-tenure-eligible) faculty positions to meet specific instructional, research, and/or service obligations or to preserve institutional flexibility in a period of rapid change. Based on faculty appointment patterns over the past several years and our research across the country, we believe that full-time non-tenure-eligible faculty appointments are here to stay. Faculty with these types of appointments are providing many types of essential services and meeting long-term needs at the institutions where they work. We expect that full-time faculty positions off the tenure track will remain a part of the higher education landscape for the foreseeable future.

A two-class faculty system has emerged in American higher education. Although the experience of full-time non-tenure-track faculty varies considerably by disciplinary field and institution of employment, as a general rule these members of the academic profession occupy a disadvantaged status when compared to their tenured and tenure-eligible colleagues. Whether the issue is workload, compensation, professional development support, or some other matter, full-time faculty on term contracts are usually in a less favorable situation than their tenure-class counterparts.

At present, many institutions with long-term needs are treating full-time non-tenure-track faculty as short-term solutions who are expendable and easily replaced. Often full-time faculty off the tenure track are hired only on one-year or even one-semester contracts, which provide little career stability. As important resources hired to address many continuing institutional needs, however, full-time faculty in non-tenure track positions should be treated in a manner consistent with the significant roles they fill and the services they provide. They deserve support for their professional development, equitable compensation for equivalent work, a predictable work life, and opportunities for career advancement.

No consensus has yet emerged within higher education on the terms and conditions of employment of full-time non-tenure track faculty. A few institutions have developed progressive policies that enable faculty off the tenure track to stay current in their fields, grow professionally, and build stable careers. These policies have also minimized the status differences between tenure-eligible faculty and full-time faculty in positions not eligible for tenure. For most institutions, however, the approach to non-tenure track faculty has been ad hoc and inconsistent.

The quality of students' educational experience and the overall health of our higher education system depend on a vigorous academic profession—including faculty in non-tenure-track positions. The complex educational and personnel issues raised by the growing cadre of full-time term-appointment faculty must be addressed in order to respond adequately to society's growing demand for high-quality higher education.

Why This Book?

At many higher education institutions today, many teaching and other critical functions are fulfilled by full-time faculty members who are not eligible for tenure. This complex and growing component of the American professoriate has received little attention from administrators, policymakers, and higher-education scholars. The number of non-tenure-track faculty has increased gradually and, at many institutions, almost unconsciously, as colleges and universities have made necessary adjustments to shifting enrollment patterns, economic circumstances, and technological advances. Now many institutions have become dependent on a core group of academic staff that we know very little about. The purpose of this book is to introduce the full-time non-tenure-track faculty, to clarify the roles they play in higher education, and to identify policies and practices that can support their work and careers as they, along with their tenure-eligible colleagues, serve the nation's growing need for knowledge and for well-educated citizens.

The academic profession has received much attention from researchers and policymakers in recent years. Beginning with Bowen and Schuster's (1986) *American Professors: A National Resource Imperiled,* a series of books and national reports has raised concerns about the state of the faculty in colleges and universities. Both inside calls to arms and external critiques have focused attention on the condition and performance of the chief laborers in the nation's knowledge production enterprise. Some authors have narrowed their focus to specific elements of the professoriate. Bowen and Sosa (1989), for example, attended to faculty in traditional arts and sciences disciplines. Gappa and Leslie (1993), in *The Invisible Faculty,* centered attention on the growing use of part-time instructional staff. *The New Academic Generation: A Profession in Transition* (Finkelstein, Seal, and Schuster 1998) examines the new generation of faculty and compares them with their senior colleagues on a wide range of variables. The authors' purpose is to assess changes in the demographics and responsibilities of these two cohorts of faculty.

Only a few of the recent works on faculty issues have looked in depth at the full-time non-tenure-track faculty phenomenon, however. Gappa's *Off the Tenure Track: Six Models for Full-Time, Nontenurable Appointments* (1996) is part of the American Association for Higher Education's (AAHE) New Pathways Working Paper Series which looks at emerging trends in the academic profession. Her report focuses primarily on non-tenure-track faculty employment policies in a sample of medical and other professional schools. The American Association of University Professors (AAUP) has led in raising questions about the potential impact of the increased use of both full-time and part-time non-tenure-eligible faculty. In 1986 and again in 1993 the organization issued reports on the status of non-tenure-track faculty. In its reports, the AAUP raised concerns about the impact on the careers of non-tenure-track faculty of the lack of job security, inadequate protection of academic freedom, and inequitable compensation. It also raised questions about the impact of using term faculty on the quality of educational programs on campus. In its 1993 report, "The Status of Non-Tenure-Track Faculty," the association included a set of guidelines for good practice for institutions to implement in the employment of full-time and part-time non-tenure-track faculty (AAUP 1995b).

Clearly, the process of looking systematically at the growing use of full-time non-tenure-track faculty has just begun. Our book advances this initiative by taking a comprehensive, data-based look at the non-tenure-track faculty issue. Along with part-time faculty, this other nontraditional type of faculty must be studied carefully to clarify major changes that are under way in college and university staffing.

The full-time term-appointment faculty issue is emerging within the larger context of questions about the academic tenure system, which has structured faculty careers and academic employment practices for nearly a century. For more than a decade a debate has been raging both within and outside higher education concerning the value of the dominant tenure system. Books and reports such as Chait and Ford's (1982) *Beyond Traditional*

Tenure ignited a national dialogue on tenure that has continued into the new century. Potential alternatives to the tenure system have been recommended or at least examined in many of these documents. The contrasting perspectives on this supercharged issue represented by AAHE's New Pathways Project (1996–present) and Matthew Finkin's (1996) edited collection, *The Case for Tenure,* help to set the stage for the specific questions raised in this book:

1. What factors account for the growing use of full-time non-tenure-track faculty?
2. Who are the full-time non-tenure-track faculty?
3. How are full-time non-tenure-track appointments structured? What is the range of non-tenure-track models currently in use?
4. What are the perceived costs and consequences of employing full-time faculty in non-tenure-eligible positions for institutions? for individual careers?
5. What are the characteristics of effective policies and programs to support full-time non-tenure-track faculty?

Each of these questions is addressed in detail in this book.

Method

This book draws from many sources to paint a clear and comprehensive picture of full-time non-tenure-track faculty. We conducted an extensive review of the literature on the academic profession as well as related topics to build a foundation for our study of non-tenure-eligible faculty. Relevant data were selected from the 1988 National Survey of Postsecondary Faculty (NSOPF-88) and the 1993 National Study of Postsecondary Faculty (NSOPF-93). These data bases draw on representative samples of eleven thousand and twenty-five thousand faculty, respectively. They provide information specifically on full-time non-tenure-track faculty in all types of higher education institutions and set that distinctive population in the larger context of the entire American academic profession.

We supplemented these sources with an original research project focusing specifically on full-time non-tenure-eligible faculty and the institutions that employ them. This project included three principal elements:

1. a survey of a cross-section of U.S. higher education institutions about their use of full-time non-tenure-track faculty and the policies that regulate these appointments (see Appendixes A and B);

2. a review of institutional policy documents that structure the work and career development of full-time faculty in non-tenure-track positions (see Appendix D); and

3. campus visits to twelve institutions that represent the major types of senior-level (four-year) colleges and universities in the United States (see Appendixes A and C). Baccalaureate, master's-level, doctoral, and research institutions are included in the sample. Both public and private institutions are represented.

The institutions we visited are widely dispersed geographically. On each campus we interviewed full-time faculty in non-tenure-track, tenured, and tenure-track positions, department chairs, faculty leaders (e.g., president of the faculty senate, chair of the promotion and tenure committee), and various administrators (e.g., deans, provosts, directors of faculty development) with oversight responsibilities that include non-tenure-track faculty. Over the course of a year we interviewed approximately 385 people.

Our interviews were semistructured in order to gather consistent information on different campuses while also retaining the flexibility to learn about issues and practices distinctive to the conditions and culture of each unique institution. Generally, we conducted separate focus group interviews for full-time non-tenure-track faculty, tenured and tenure-track faculty, and department chairs. Usually we interviewed key faculty leaders and central administrators individually, although there were some exceptions to this pattern. Interviews typically lasted between one and one and one-half hours. Our campus visits usually lasted between two and three days, depending on the size and complexity of the institution. An on-site coordinator, usually appointed by the institution's chief academic officer, selected the persons we interviewed and set up our daily schedule. This person followed selection guidelines we developed to make sure that we would meet with a cross-section of faculty and staff at each institution.

We personally transcribed all interview sessions after our return home. We believe that this process ensured the most accurate record of the sessions. Following transcription, each session record was entered into a computerized qualitative data base set up to identify common themes and patterns and to enable us to retrieve illustrative comments and quotes to supplement related quantitative data.

Although together our sources paint the clearest picture currently available of an increasingly significant component of the academic profession, we wish to add a caveat: We have tried to be as objective as possible in reporting our findings and drawing conclusions from them. Our account, of course, is based on the data we had access to, the institutions we visited, and the persons we interviewed. Other researchers who study this topic from different vantage points may draw somewhat different conclusions. Furthermore, our use of multiple data sources required a complex interpretive task that can never be totally objective. We did our best to report our findings in an impartial, nonjudgmental manner. Nevertheless, other observers looking at the same information may reach different conclusions about the full-time non-tenure-track faculty issue.

Our goal is to inform readers within and outside higher education of a major shift in the staffing of American colleges and universities. We have tried to draw valid conclusions about the nature and consequences of this shift. Our book will fulfill its purpose if it informs its readers and stimulates lively discussion and a variety of proposals for supporting the performance of faculty who serve higher education without benefit of tenure.

Terminology

Throughout this publication we use a variety of terms interchangeably to refer to full-time non-tenure-track faculty. In addition to full-time non-tenure-track, these include non-tenure-eligible full-time faculty, full-time term-appointment faculty, full-time faculty in non-tenure-track positions, full-time faculty in non-tenure-eligible positions, and full-time contract faculty. We also use the abbreviation FTNTT faculty. When referring to tenured or tenure-track faculty we also use tenure-eligible, ladder, tenure-class, or career faculty. These terms reflect the variety of designations in use in policies we studied and the institutions we visited.

2 The Context for Change

The increased use of [full-time] non-tenure-track faculty at [this master's-level institution] has been largely due to 3 factors: declining enrollment; an increased percentage of faculty who are retirement age, but have not retired; and an institutional tenure cap of 66 percent. (From a master's-level institution)

[This research university] has a lid on how much the legislature will increase the university budget but the institution must increase enrollment to [a number x% greater than current levels] by 2010. We must think of how to use resources in the most effective manner. Departments recognize the benefit of bringing in people to teach large lecture courses. Lecturers are appreciated on campus. (Research university administrator)

The need for flexibility drove [the institution's] policy on [full-time] non-tenure-track faculty. [The] long-term renewable contract system is better for the college and for the academics. The college also has a tenure cap. (Administrator of a liberal arts college)

The past decade has been an especially trying time for higher education. In examining the factors that have been stimulating changes in faculty staffing, it is necessary to look beyond the financial stress and program changes that individual colleges and universities have faced. It is also important to examine key developments in the broader context within which institutions have been functioning. In this chapter we attempt to answer the following questions:

— What is the environment of the past two decades within which the changes in faculty employment patterns have been taking place?
— What are the major factors that have motivated colleges and universities to increase the use of full-time non-tenure-track appointments instead of continuing to rely on the traditional tenure-track employment pattern for faculty?

— Which of these factors are external to the institution and which are internal?

It is not possible to understand the increased use of full-time non-tenure-track faculty in recent years without examining the broader social, economic, and political context within which colleges and universities function. Changing conditions within higher education and in the country at large have led government officials, corporate executives, and concerned citizens to encourage higher education to "get its house in order." This includes the policies and practices that regulate faculty employment.

American colleges and universities have traditionally been autonomous in pursuing distinctive missions. Recent decades have witnessed the gradual erosion of that autonomy, especially among public institutions. External expectations and demands have focused on (1) the need to reduce the costs of institutional operations, (2) controls on spiraling tuition charges, (3) increasing emphasis on undergraduate education—especially at graduate institutions, (4) increased accountability with regard to faculty workload and productivity, and (5) challenges to the concept of tenure as an employment strategy. We turn now to a close look at the external and internal factors that have provoked calls for reform in higher education and its faculty employment practices, including the increased use of full-time faculty in non-tenure-track positions.

External Factors

LOSS OF PUBLIC CONFIDENCE AND TRUST

For many decades higher education enjoyed a special status among American institutions. The public generally held colleges and universities in high esteem, trusted their leaders, and valued their products. Above all, there was a sense that higher education was worth its price and represented a good long-term investment. In recent years, however, many public officials and education consumers have begun to doubt higher education's merits. A number of higher education analysts (e.g., Bok 1992; Fairweather 1996; Winston 1992) have discussed the decline of public trust in higher education from a variety of perspectives. The loss of trust has been attributed to a number of factors, including a perceived decline in institutional commitment to undergraduate education (Bok 1992, 15) and the perception that colleges and universities maximize revenues through spiraling tuition charges, aggressive pursuit of grants and contracts, and overhead income at rates that exceed their legitimate educational needs (Winston 1992).

In Fairweather's opinion, the two largest sources of public mistrust are the belief that faculty are protected from the vagaries of the marketplace by a tenure system that immunizes them from the reality of rapidly changing employment and economic conditions and the perception that too much faculty time is spent on their own research and scholarly pursuits rather than teaching (1996, xii). Fairweather views the restoration of trust to be a function of returning teaching and public service to a valued place among faculty roles. Boyer (1987) has argued that the restoration of public trust in higher education depends on institutional renewal of its investment in undergraduate education.

The loss of public confidence in higher education has taken place at the same time that other social issues such as public safety, corrections, and health care were ascending in priority and in their access to government subsidy at the state and federal levels (Levine 1997, 1). Compounding the problem for colleges and universities was the loss of public confidence in the outcomes of higher education at a time when tuition levels were rising sharply to meet growing operating costs (Zumeta and Looney 1994, 79). Many observers of the higher education scene believe that funding for colleges and universities will be tighter as we move into the twenty-first century than at almost any time since the Great Depression. Even as state funding resources improve, higher education will not be at the top of state funding priorities, nor is it likely to move up in the near future (Heydinger and Simsek 1992, 14). Under these circumstances, the use of non-tenure-track faculty who are hired with a full-time responsibility to teach undergraduates may be an institutional attempt to show the public that colleges and universities do have a commitment to undergraduate education and thereby to regain a measure of the previously lost trust.

DECLINE IN GOVERNMENT SUPPORT

During the late 1980s and the 1990s, government financial and political support for higher education decreased at the federal and state levels. Prior to that period, the federal government had for several decades been a major influence in shaping the mission and scope of institutional initiatives. Grant support fostered the development of the research mission of many institutions, especially the research and doctoral universities. Government funding facilitated the construction of research facilities, the acquisition of additional faculty members skilled in and committed to research, and the development and significant growth of graduate programs, especially in the sciences. In addition, government-funded student financial aid was a major factor in the democratization of postsecondary education, making it more financially accessible to previously underrepresented student populations. Research support and financial aid also facilitated the growth of enrollment in graduate programs that had the preparation of future faculty members as a major mission. Each of these factors raised the sensitivity of the federal government to the size of its investment in higher education and the relationship between that investment and the efficiency of institutional operations, perhaps especially as reflected in escalating prices paid by students and parents.

As America entered the early 1990s, the economy was in an uncertain state after a period of recession and slow, erratic growth. Adding to the financial problems caused by the recession was the burgeoning federal deficit, which cast a cloud over the ability of the federal and state governments to fund important social initiatives adequately, including higher education (Zumeta and Looney 1994, 79). Between 1990 and 1993 federal funds for higher education grew from about eighteen billion to about twenty-one billion in current dollars. In constant dollars this was a loss of about 14 percent, including a decline of over 8 percent in financial aid support (Honeyman and Bruhn 1996, 2). This constant decline leveled off from 1993 to 1997, especially in terms of research dollars. Although calls for increased higher education funding at the federal level seem to be gaining renewed momentum, few observers expect the national government to expand its financial support of colleges and universities to the generous pre-1980s levels.

For public colleges and universities, reductions in state funding have been among the most significant factors affecting institutional operations. In 1991–92, state governments decreased funding for higher education from the previous year's level for the first time in about thirty-three years (Jaschik 1991). A further reduction for 1992–93 provided for the first two-year reduction in memory (Jaschik 1992). In 1991–92, midyear budget cuts affected 73 percent of public two-year institutions, 61 percent of public four-year institutions, and 35 percent of independent institutions (El-Khawas 1992, 20). Declines in government aid shifted responsibility for funding from state and federal sources to students and institutions (Massy and Wilger 1992, 365). After the decline in funding from 1990–91 through 1993–94, state appropriations for higher education began to recover, showing a two-year gain of 9 percent (3 percent when adjusted for inflation) from 1994–95 to 1996–97 (Academe Today 1996).

For both public and private institutions, tuition and fees, gifts and grants, and endowment income became the primary sources of financial support to meet rising costs and to offset some of the loss of government funding (El-Khawas 1995, 27–28). According to an American Council on Education survey of institutional leaders, as recently as 1996, only 40 percent of all institutions were in very good to excellent financial condition, and 25 percent of public institutions were in fair or poor financial condition (El-Khawas and Knopp 1996, 9).

In order to accommodate the loss of state funding, many public institutions reacted by reducing staff or freezing faculty and staff hiring. Private institutions attempted to respond to criticism of their growing tuition charges and increasing costs by reducing programs and controlling staff size and expenses. Between 1987–88 and 1992–93, nearly 40 percent of higher education institutions offered early or phased retirement options to encourage the retirement of permanent full-time instructional faculty and staff, with between two-thirds and three-quarters of public and private research and public doctoral institutions utilizing the options (U.S. Department of Education 1996, 16). In those same intervals, the proportion of instructional faculty and staff who were employed full-time decreased from 67 percent to 58 percent, while the size of the part-time employment force increased from 33 percent to 42 percent. Among full-time faculty, the proportion of non-tenure-track faculty increased from about one in five to one in four (U.S. Department of Education 1997a, 14, 18). The growth of full-time term-appointment faculty is in part a response to the uncertainty generated by fluctuating government financial support of higher education.

FEDERAL POLICIES INFLUENCING FACULTY PERSONNEL POLICIES

Several pieces of federal legislation in the late 1970s and the 1980s contributed to the increase in the hiring of full-time non-tenure-track faculty in the 1980s and 1990s. The Employees Retirement Security Act of 1974 (ERISA) and the 1978 amendments to the Age Discrimination in Employment Act (ADEA) raised questions about the management of faculty resources. ERISA restricted the ability of colleges and universities to alter their pension plans in order to influence the retirement decisions of faculty (Holden 1985). The amended ADEA raised the then-allowable mandatory retirement age from 65 to 70, with tenured faculty exempted from the retirement age change until July 1, 1982. These changes stimulated the development of incentive-based early retirement programs to encourage faculty to retire at or before the "normal" retirement age (65).

Amendments to ADEA in 1986 abolished mandatory retirement and raised questions on a large number of campuses about the potential effects on institutional finance, program quality, and faculty vitality of having large cohorts of tenured faculty continuing employment beyond age 70. With a mandatory retirement age of 70, tenure had always had an end date that institutions could use for planning for staff turnover and recruiting new faculty. In the absence of a mandatory retirement age, effective January 1, 1994, tenure could be viewed as a lifetime appointment, severable primarily at the discretion of the individual faculty member. In anticipation of a lack of normal turnover in faculty based upon retirements at the traditional retirement age of 65, many institutions once again turned to incentive retirement options to encourage early retirement (Chronister and Kepple 1987; U.S. Department of Education 1996).

A 1990 report on the potential consequences of the uncapping of the mandatory retirement age concluded that based on trends in faculty retirement ages, only research universities would probably be adversely affected by the abolition of the mandatory retirement age by having a significant number of faculty continue employment beyond age 70 (Hammond and Morgan 1991). In addition to implementing incentive retirement plans to encourage faculty departures, institutions have increased the use of full-time and part-time faculty not eligible for tenure to compensate for the increase in the number of faculty aged 70 and older.

THE RISE OF NEW TECHNOLOGIES

The past twenty years have seen an acceleration in the use of new technologies on college and university campuses. The impact of user-friendly, high-capacity information technologies at ever-declining prices has been felt in administrative, research, and instructional contexts on campus (Van Dusen 1997, 4). The challenges and opportunities of the new technologies, as well as the rapid pace of change in technologies, have introduced a heightened sense of uncertainty into the lives of individual faculty members and the operations of institutions in general. The need to introduce and utilize new technologies posed critical opportunity cost decisions for institutions during the severe financial constraints of the late 1980s and early 1990s. To remain competitive in the student marketplace, institutions must provide educational opportunities and programs that prepare students for lives in an information technology–based society. Decisions about adding information technology systems were being made at the same time that many institutions found it necessary to reduce staffing at both the faculty and support staff levels. Full-time non-tenure-track appointments, when used judiciously, can help colleges and universities compensate for the increased costs of building a state-of-the-art technology infrastructure.

The increase in the use of new technologies has brought to the campus at least two additional cohorts of professional staff with whom faculty interact. The first are the technical staff who provide logistical support to maintain new hardware and information systems. The second are personnel who specialize in providing support in instructional design of courses and programs to enhance student learning through evolving technology (Van Dusen 1997). These new types of personnel are cost drivers that also have the potential of diverting institutional resources from traditional faculty positions to full-time and part-time non-tenure-eligible positions.

The infusion of new technology into college classrooms, libraries, and dormitories has taken place during a period when many educational authorities were calling for a shift from a teaching-centered to a learning-centered paradigm on college and university campuses. The new technology is seen as one means of making that shift efficiently, at an anticipated cost savings to institutions. Increased emphasis on the use of technology has cast faculty in the role of facilitators of learning rather than solely as lecturers and dispensers of knowledge (Van Dusen 1997, iii). Such a change requires faculty to learn to work with the new technology and to develop the educational products that are delivered utilizing technology.

At the same time there has been an increased emphasis on using new technology to provide distance learning opportunities for an ever more diverse student population (Van Dusen 1997, 24). In the fall of 1995, 30 percent of higher education institutions offered distance education courses, with another 25 percent planning to do so in the next three years (National Education Association 1998, 1). In addressing distance learning opportunities, many institutions are attempting to cultivate new and different student populations. The uncertainties of these new educational markets encourage institutions to hire full-time and/or part-time faculty on term rather than tenure-track appointments.

In multiple ways, the increased application of technology to the teaching-learning process calls for faculty to assume different roles than they have traditionally filled. To utilize technology effectively to support the classroom and laboratory, faculty must invest increased time and energy in the instructional role, to the possible detriment of other professional obligations. Hiring full-time faculty in non-tenure-track positions to take on specialized roles, for example, in large introductory-level courses or in language, laboratory, or other skill-based subjects, where technology applications are increasing rapidly, can free tenure-track faculty to concentrate on preferred roles such as working with majors and scholarship.

NEW, MORE AGGRESSIVE COMPETITORS

Competition has always been a key attribute of the American higher education system. Until relatively recently, however, competition occurred primarily among campus-based, nonprofit postsecondary education providers. Most of these institutions shared basic educational principles and adhered to many common educational traditions and practices.

New communication and instructional technologies have now made it possible to reach much larger populations of potential students than before. Coupled with society's growing demand for lifelong education, the new technology has dramatically expanded the education marketplace. In the process, education has become an attractive enterprise for nontraditional education providers such as corporate subsidiary Motorola University and for-profit proprietary institutions like the University of Phoenix. Even traditional institutions like Old Dominion University have moved aggressively to serve new populations of students through such technology-based distance learning programs as Teletechnet. In addition, "virtual universities" such as Western Governors University are being created not only to reach out to underserved populations but also to provide higher education in a more efficient and cost-effective manner. The competitive potential of these new types of education providers is readily apparent. In the United Kingdom, for instance, the distance learning–based Open University is the largest educational institution in the country, enrolling 160,000 students (*Introduction to the Open University* 1998). The University of Phoenix, founded in 1976, now claims to be the second largest private university in the United States (Traub 1997).

Chester Finn (1998) refers collectively to these new types of higher education providers as "convenience institutions." Many have a different vision of higher education and structure their programs accordingly. Finn notes that convenience institutions are often more user-friendly and market-responsive. In his view, they typically are more flexible and often cost less than traditional colleges and universities. They rely heavily on technology to cut the delivery costs of education and to reach out to widely dispersed clientele wherever they happen to be. Convenience institutions are especially attractive, Finn argues, to "job-minded students [especially adults] for whom liberal-arts degrees hold scant appeal" (2). The adult market, of course, is where most of higher education's growth has occurred in recent years (Frances 1998, 5).

Highly responsive, technologically advanced, sometimes profit-driven competitors provide yet another incentive for increased use of full-time and part-time non-tenure-eligible faculty. In a turbulent environment, institutions are reluctant to lock up limited resources for long periods by granting tenure employment status to large portions of their faculty. As Finn sees the situation, "Tenure-track faculty members in traditional fields won't be flexible enough to adapt to changing market requirements, so more part-timers and non-tenure-track instructors will be taken on to handle the niche teaching—the evening and summer courses, the non-degree programs, the mid-career refreshers, the distance-learning courses, the branch-campus offerings" (1998, 4). National data reveal that full-time contingent faculty are also teaching a large portion of the traditional undergraduate curriculum at many colleges and universities (U.S. Department of Education 1997a). The increased competition that is challenging most types of higher education institutions undoubtedly will make full-time non-tenure-track faculty more attractive into the foreseeable future.

TRANSFORMATION IN THE WORKPLACE

Significant transformations have taken place in recent years in the American workplace as well. In response to a series of economic pressures beginning in the mid-1980s, companies have altered their methods of doing business and their relationships with their employees. Increased competition, changing markets, the emergence of new management techniques, mergers and takeovers, and investor pressures have led many companies to undertake significant downsizing and restructuring (Capelli et al. 1997). Between 1979 and 1995, more than forty-three million jobs were cut from the labor market (*New York Times* 1996, 27). In addition to downsizing and restructuring jobs, there has been a significant increase in the use of contingent and contract workers, with 25 percent of the civilian labor force in 1988 being contingent personnel (temporary workers, either full-time or part-time). Employment through temporary help agencies, for example, increased by 21 percent between 1993 and 1994 (Capelli et al. 1997, 17, 18).

The experiences of the constituents of higher education, whether students, parents, legislators, or individuals from the corporate world who are serving on college boards of trustees, have caused them to raise questions about the nature of faculty-institutional employment arrangements and faculty workload. If the corporate world has dealt with financial constraints, changing market conditions, and increased competition by restructuring employee-employer relationships and downsizing, many of higher education's constituents ask why colleges and universities should not make the same types of adjustments.

CRITICISM OF TENURE

In a period of financial constraint and rapid change, a large portion of college and university resources is intractable, since it is tied to faculty salaries. This inflexibility is cemented by tenure—the ultimate buffer against the uncertainties of the academic job market. Higher education's patrons, including legislators, parents, and the corporate world, began to raise questions over the past decade about the viability of tenure as the standard employment strategy for faculty. As part of this process, various alternatives to tenure have been considered (Gumport 1997, 125).

Although tenure has been viewed as the linchpin of the academic profession by many faculty since at least the 1940 statement on academic freedom and tenure drafted by the American Association of University Professors (AAUP) and the Association of American Colleges (AAC), it has faced continued challenges. Because tenure was developed to provide freedom in teaching, research, and extramural activities, as well as a sufficient degree of economic security to make the profession attractive to men and women of ability (AAUP 1995a), tenure's defenders state that it has frequently been misinterpreted by critics both within and external to institutions of higher education.

To many within higher education, tenure serves as a lifetime assurance that faculty members will receive due process within the context of the academic institution when their competence or the quality of their performance is challenged (Hutcheson 1998, 310). Due process, according to the proponents of tenure, provides the protection necessary to the continued viability of the concept of academic freedom. In contrast, advocates of alternatives to tenure indicate that academic freedom no longer requires the defense of tenure, since there are constitutional and contractual safeguards that can protect faculty. Another common charge against the tenure system has been that it protects faculty "deadwood" from expulsion from the academy and shields all faculty from demands of accountability and responsiveness to changing institutional circumstances.

Also, an increasing proportion of the professoriate sees tenure as an exclusionary process. A 1995 national survey of full-time faculty who spend at least a portion of their time teaching undergraduates found that slightly more than one-third of the respondents agreed "strongly" or "somewhat" that "tenure is an outmoded concept," slightly higher than in 1989 (Leatherman 1996). Much of the disaffection was found among faculty under 35 years of age, although the segment with the largest increase in skepticism was faculty aged 45 to 54. Many institutions have increased their requirements for achieving tenure in response to the perceived lack of flexibility of a tenured professoriate. Fifty-four percent of full-time faculty participating in a 1989 survey of nearly ten thousand faculty "agreed strongly or with reservations" that it was more difficult to achieve tenure than five years earlier (*Almanac of Higher Education* 1991, 52). This concern with tenure requirements appears to have become more pronounced among young faculty during the 1990s when financial constraints and increased emphasis on the teaching role, but no reduction in the expectations for research and scholarship for receiving tenure, caused stress and anxiety for many just beginning faculty careers.

What has been the magnitude of the "tenured-in" condition of the professoriate? According to a 1980 estimate, approximately 63–68 percent of full-time faculty had tenure, up from approximately 50–55 percent in the 1960s (Bowen and Schuster 1986, 44–45). In 1987–88 approximately 59 percent of full-time faculty were tenured, with that percentage declining to 54 percent in 1992–93 (U.S. Department of Education 1997a, 18). In the fall of 1995, about 52 percent of full-time faculty were tenured (U.S. Department of Education 1998, 2–11). Hence, in recent years higher education has become slightly less tenured-in.

Tenure status among faculty varies by institutional type and disciplinary area as well as by age. In the fall of 1992, public research (65.4%), public doctoral (53.6%), public comprehensive (60.7%), and public two-year institutions (52.7%) had tenure rates well above 50 percent. Tenure rates were somewhat lower at their private sector counterparts (U.S. Department of Education 1997a, 18). By disciplinary area, tenure rates were highest in agriculture/home economics (75.3%), humanities (68.7%), social sciences (67.9%), and natural sciences (63.3%).

Some of the current disaffection with tenure can be attributed to a growing concern over the past two decades that institutions are heavily tenured-in at a time when increased flexibility in staffing is needed. In a time of financial constraints and dynamic change, the employment of full-time non-tenure-eligible faculty gives institutions a flexibility not provided by the continued tenuring of faculty.

Internal Factors

RISING COSTS

Increasing costs have been a multidimensional problem for higher education for several decades. The most visible cost to the public is the price of tuition that students and parents must pay. Between 1980 and 1990 the price of tuition and fees for attending college in the United States increased by an average of slightly more than 9 percent annually, nearly double the rate of inflation (Massy and Wilger 1992, 361). Between 1976 and 1996, the average tuition increased from $642 to $3,151 at public universities and from $2,881 to $15,581 at their private counterparts. Over the same period the average tuition at public two-year colleges increased fivefold, from $245 to $1,245 (National Commission on the Cost of Higher Education 1998, 1).

The increase in tuition price, although the most visible issue, is only part of the cost problem that institutions have been forced to face since the early 1980s. As tuition has increased, legislators and other policymakers have asked why the costs to educate a student have increased at a rate that has exceeded inflation. Massy and Wilger identified five causes of the cost escalation in institutional finance: (1) regulation, micromanagement, and cost shifting; (2) the cost disease; (3) the growth force; (4) the administrative lattice; and (5) the academic ratchet (1992, 364–65). As the authors state, the first factor occurs partially in response to increased state and federal agency reporting requirements. These requirements are outside the control of the institution and contribute to increased costs by necessitating the employment of additional staff. In addition, shifting costs to students and parents has often occurred in response to reduced state funding of higher education and has frequently been initiated with the blessing of state government. The last four items on Massy and Wilger's list are a function of institutional choice and can therefore be addressed by colleges and universities.

The "cost disease" is a function of the labor intensiveness of higher education and the resulting growth in compensation costs not offset by a comparable increase in productivity. For example, between 1972–73 and 1996–97 there was a 260 percent increase in average faculty salaries in current dollars (Clery and Lee 1998, 12). There is no evidence of an increase in productivity in terms of credit hours produced or students educated that offsets that increase in salary, even with the infusion of technology into the teaching function. The "growth force" relates to institutional striving for quality and the increased expenditures that accompany the addition of new courses, new disciplines, and new technology. The "administrative lattice" refers to the significant increase in the size of the administrative staff on the vast majority of campuses as reflected in the 60 percent growth of administrative staffs between 1975 and 1985 (Grassmuck, as cited by Massy and Wilger 1992, 366). The "academic ratchet" describes the gradual shift in institutional output, primarily at research and doctoral institutions, from teaching and its products to research and scholarship as outputs. This gradual shift in emphasis is reflected in the devotion of increased faculty time and rewards to research, scholarship, and participation in professional organizations (Massy and Wilger 1992, 367). Each of these four factors has contributed to the increased employment of full-time non-tenure-track faculty on college and university campuses. The lack of increased productivity in relation to growth in salaries of "regular" (tenure-eligible) faculty, the growth in administrative staff, and the academic ratchet have led many campuses to hire full-time faculty off the tenure track. These faculty often carry a heavier teaching load than their tenure-track colleagues, frequently at somewhat lower salaries.

ISSUES OF FACULTY WORKLOAD AND PRODUCTIVITY

In the face of financial constraints, critics have raised concerns about inefficiency in the operation of colleges and universities. Faculty have increasingly been viewed as either the source of institutional inefficiency or the obstacle to this problem's solution, with the tenure system being targeted for much of the blame. In the late 1980s and early 1990s, when a poor job market for college graduates and corporate downsizing led to high white-collar unemployment, the tenure system for faculty seemed to the public and to legislators to be anathema. Many of higher education's patrons were asking why, if colleges were facing financial deficits, faculty were protected from layoffs or from significantly increased teaching loads by tenure, an apparent anachronism.

The nature of faculty work has been a related concern. A recent study has shown that full-time faculty, on average, work from forty-six to fifty-eight hours per week depending on their discipline and type of institution of employment (U.S. Department of Education 1997a, 37). These hours have increased over figures from a report for the 1978–79 academic year, when the average for faculty was forty-six hours per week (Bowen and Schuster 1986, 73). But much of the criticism of faculty work during the past decade has not been over the number of hours worked but how faculty spend their time. Faculty members are largely autonomous in their use of time, with the exception of their scheduled hours in the classroom, and these hours vary widely by type of institution, discipline, faculty rank, and primary faculty assignment. State governments, coordinating agencies, and boards of trustees became increasingly reluctant to recognize institutionally funded research as an effective use of faculty resources during times of financial constraint and rising costs.

In response to questions from constituents about professors' work and productivity, legislators and trustees began to take actions to exert some level of control over faculty. Among public institutions, responses to economic and political challenges meant changes in institutional practices that directly altered the expectations of faculty work (Russell 1992, 35). One of the changes made in response to legislative directives to improve undergraduate education was to increase the amount of time faculty spend on undergraduate instruction (Gumport 1997, 125). Likewise, on an increasing number of campuses in the late 1980s and early 1990s, institutions began to hire more faculty in short-term non-tenure-track contract positions (U.S. Department of Education, 1997a, 18). Many of these faculty were hired specifically to teach undergraduates, primarily at the lower-division level (Harper 1997, 10). This strategy represented an effort to enhance the quality of undergraduate education. It was also another means to exert more control over faculty work.

During the 1990s, the need for flexibility in faculty staffing in response to budget shortfalls was joined with the desire to make staffing commitments to new degree programs or modifications of existing programs in response to changing student interests and enrollment patterns. In this dynamic context, many institutions have not been willing to make long-term faculty commitments until student enrollments stabilize in new or restructured degree programs. Hiring full-time and part-time faculty off the tenure track gives institutions more opportunities to regulate professors' work assignments and the distribution of their time. In the process, it gives institutions more control over their destiny.

ENROLLMENT AND THE CHANGING CHARACTERISTICS OF STUDENTS

Changing student demographics over the past several decades also have impacted institutional plans for faculty staffing. Enrollment is the main force driving faculty staffing decisions on college and university campuses, and we anticipate that the enrollment influence will continue over the next decade. In 1995 there were approximately 14,262,000 students enrolled in higher education. Frances estimates that at current enrollment rates and in view of the increase in the number of 17-year-olds due to the "echo [baby] boom," college enrollment may increase by almost 1.5 million students (7%) to 15,700,000 by 2005. If the attendance rate increases slightly for younger age groups, the increase could be almost 2.5 million (14%) more students for an overall enrollment of 16.7 million by 2005 (1998, 21).

For the past twenty years a major share of the growth in enrollment has resulted from the matriculation of nontraditional students. Half of the added students have been 25 years of age or older, nearly 75 percent female, and about 55 percent part-time. Only about 20 percent of undergraduates are 18- to 22-year-olds attending full-time and living on campus (Levine 1997, 6). The older, nontraditional student presents institutions and faculty with different challenges than the traditional student does. These students are more likely to drop in and drop out of college for personal and professional reasons, complicating institutional planning. The unpredictable enrollment patterns of nontraditional students, of course, make non-tenure-track positions (full-time and part-time), as a flexible resource, more appealing to institutions.

Nontraditional students will also affect enrollment patterns in the foreseeable future. Between 1970 and 1990 overall college enrollment increased about 54 percent, with approximately 80 percent of that growth attributed to students aged 35 and older. Between 1990 and 1995, with an increase of about 7 percent in total enrollment, around 30 percent of the growth was among the 35 and older population (Frances 1998, 5, 6). As education becomes increasingly important to career advancement and economic well-being, chances are that the enrollment of nontraditional age students will continue to grow. It is important to monitor students from older age cohorts. Not only do they increase enrollments, they also make distinctive demands on institutions to provide client-centered programs involving retraining and skill enhancement at times convenient to the consumer.

Adding to the challenge of nontraditional students is the increasing proportion of traditional college students who are not as well prepared as their predecessors. A 1997 study found that about 75 percent of institutions experienced an increase in the proportion of students requiring remedial or developmental education assistance (Frances 1998, 7). These underprepared students present faculty with differing instructional challenges and institutions with the need for faculty with flexible teaching styles and special pedagogical expertise. Traditional faculty, complying with the demands to earn tenure, often cannot, or choose not to, provide the type of intensive support needed by developmental and other students with special needs. For these reasons, some institutions have begun to staff these positions with full-time instructors who are not eligible for tenure and who can concentrate primarily on these distinctive instructional duties and develop expertise and skills that enhance their effectiveness with students needing special types of support.

In the face of projected enrollment growth, institutions will be required to adjust faculty staffing to accommodate the added students. Decisions about the numbers of faculty needed to meet enrollment demand depend on institutional policies on student-faculty ratios and teaching loads. Frances found that in spite of demands for increased productivity and constrained financial resources during the period from the early 1970s until 1995, student-faculty ratios declined slightly (12, 13). Whether this decline continues will influence the demand for faculty through the year 2005. If the demand for increased teaching loads for faculty continues with mandates from legislative bodies or other significant stakeholders, an increased number of institutions may choose to utilize more full-time non-track faculty who carry heavier teaching loads than their tenure-eligible colleagues to accommodate increased enrollment. The long-range plans of at least one large institution we visited are to employ this strategy to accommodate a large mandated enrollment increase.

Frances has estimated that an additional 135,000 to 197,000 new faculty will be needed to meet her projections for enrollment growth for the year 2005. In addition, she anticipates that institutions will need 148,000 faculty to replace retirees over the same period (12, 13). The data suggest that enrollment patterns for both traditional and nontraditional students are likely to remain fluid and not entirely predictable. With a need for more faculty and uncertainty about student demands, non-tenure-track appointments will remain attractive to colleges and universities and may actually increase on many campuses.

AGING OF THE FACULTY

Significant changes in the age distribution of the full-time faculty have occurred over the past two decades. In the fifteen-year period from 1977–78 to 1992–93, the mean age of the professoriate increased from 44 to 48. Highlighting the change was a decline of 17 percent in faculty aged 44 and younger and an increase of 9 percent among faculty aged 55 and older. This aging trend gains increased significance in the absence of a mandatory retirement age. Among tenured faculty in 1992–93, nearly 20 percent expected to work to age 70 or beyond (U.S. Department of Education 1997b, 24).

The aging and retirement patterns of faculty vary by institution type and discipline area. This has implications for the degree of flexibility that an institution may have in recruiting new faculty. These patterns also affect an institution's ability to shift resources in response to changing financial circumstances and students' program choices. For example, in the fall of 1992 the average age of full-time faculty at four-year institutions in education, agriculture/home economics, and humanities was approximately 50, while the average age for business, engineering, fine arts, social sciences, and natural sciences faculty was less than 48. Faculty at public and private comprehensive institutions (48.6) tended to be, on average, older than their colleagues at the other types of institutions (average ages for other types of institutions ranged from 46.7 to 47.8) (U.S. Department of Education 1997a, 22–23). One projection anticipated that by the year 2000, 51 percent of the full-time faculty would be 55 years of age and older, and only 20 percent of that cohort would retire in that year (Bland and Bergquist 1997, 7). Full-time non-tenure-track faculty appointments are perceived to address the staffing uncertainties accompanying an aging faculty with no mandatory retirement age.

THE ACADEMIC LABOR MARKET

On many of the campuses we visited, we often heard that hiring faculty off the tenure track was a function of the academic labor market—that the surplus of Ph.D.'s and other qualified candidates in many academic fields has made it possible for colleges and universities to fill academic positions off the tenure track with relative ease. We view this labor market condition as an internal issue, since universities control the majority of the flow of new talent through graduate study enrollment.

Full-time non-tenure-track positions would almost certainly be more difficult to fill in an academic labor market where jobs were plentiful or the number of qualified candidates had decreased. But such has not been the case in recent years. For example, at the 1997 meeting of the American Historical Association, faculty job openings increased 23.5 percent from the previous year. Yet, there were still 777 applicants vying at the conference for only 220 positions (Magner 1997). Headlines such as "Shrinking Job Market for Ph.D.'s" (Magner 1998b) and "'Postdocs' Seeing Little Way into the Academic Labor Market" (Magner 1998a) have reflected conditions of the faculty labor market for the past decade. Although the job market for academic posts has not been uniform, it seems likely that a continuing surplus of Ph.D.'s in many fields in the near future will maintain a climate conducive to making full-time non-tenure-track faculty appointments.

Summary

A host of external and internal forces is encouraging colleges and universities to rethink their faculty staffing policies and practices. These forces include rising costs, perceived declines in faculty workload and productivity, projected increases in student enrollment, a diversifying student clientele, the shifting popularity of academic fields, an aging faculty, and a favorable academic labor market. Collectively, these factors have required colleges and universities to look at new ways to utilize limited resources more effectively to fulfill their multiple missions. As institutions try to cope with demands for greater accountability and responsiveness, new technologies and competitors, and strident criticism of the tenure system, faculty appointments off the tenure track have become increasingly attractive.

Developing alternatives to traditional tenure as a means of assuring some degree of staffing flexibility has become a more and more common faculty employment strategy. At many institutions this has meant limiting faculty appointments to fixed or renewable term contracts and in some cases narrowing these positions to specialized or single-function roles rather than the traditional multiple-function faculty position. In a transitional period, full-time non-tenure-track positions buy institutions time and flexibility to respond to the diverse forces that are reshaping higher education.

3 The Terms and Conditions of Full-Time Non-Tenure-Track Faculty Employment

This chapter examines the terms and conditions of employment for full-time non-tenure-track faculty on four-year college and university campuses. Our goal is to provide an overview of the employment policies and practices we found through three investigatory routes: our institutional survey, analysis of faculty handbooks and other institutional policy documents, and our discussions with administrators and faculty at twelve colleges and universities. Comparisons with employment policies and practices affecting tenure-eligible faculty are presented where appropriate, as are examples of selected policies included in collective bargaining agreements.

We have attempted to identify similarities and differences between the roles of full-time non-tenure-track faculty and those of tenure-eligible faculty; how the hiring of the former is designed to assist the institution in achieving its mission; and whether the role expectations and terms and conditions of employment of FTNTT faculty vary by discipline and type and control of institution. In analyzing policies, we focus attention on faculty role definition, length of contracts, renewal notification policies, workload, compensation, participation in governance, support for professional development, and academic freedom. (Chapter 6 presents exemplary policies and programs we have identified that support the performance of and enhance the professional lives of full-time non-tenure-track faculty.)

Roles of Full-Time Non-Tenure-Track Faculty

Few of the institutional policies that we reviewed contained language that clearly defined roles for full-time non-tenure-track faculty. The following quotes illustrate the widely varied ways institutions define the roles of these faculty:

> to fill vacancies created by leaves, to staff instructional programs supported by time-limited funds, or to respond to particular enrollment or curricular needs. (From the policy statement of a liberal arts college)

> Persons who teach or assist with specified courses but carry no faculty responsibilities beyond their course-related duties are appointed to the rank of lecturer. (From the policy statement of a liberal arts college)

> In order to maintain the quality, flexibility, and continuity of the activities of [the] University in all their aspects (instructional, scholarly, professional, and artistic), the work of the regular faculty may be complemented by the services of other qualified persons engaged in educational activities in positions that confer faculty status . . . This document concerns the full-time teaching positions of Lecturer, Senior Lecturer, and Principal Lecturer (referred to collectively as the Lecturer track). These positions confer faculty status but are subject neither to the Appointment and Tenure policy of [this] University, nor to the Policy on research faculty, nor to the Policy on Special Faculty Appointments. (From the policy statement of a research university)

Some institutional policies define a clear distinction between full-time non-tenure-track faculty and tenure-eligible faculty. Except for four-year undergraduate colleges, the majority of institutions hire FTNTT faculty to teach lower-division undergraduate courses only (table 3.1). For example, a policy document at a research institution states that the role of lecturers (full-time faculty not eligible for tenure) is "to complement regular faculty by teaching introductory courses" and goes on to say that "the main criterion for appointment will be teaching excellence." In this case the non-tenure-track faculty role is defined as different from the requirements for "regular" faculty, who are expected to produce scholarship. At another re-

Table 3.1   Level of Instruction for Which Full-Time Non-Tenure-Track Faculty Are Hired, by Type of Institution, Fall 1996

Type of Institution	N	Lower Division Only (%)	Upper Division Only (%)	Upper & Lower Division (%)	Graduate (%)
Research	15	73.3	0.0	26.7	0.0
Doctoral	6	83.3	0.0	16.7	0.0
Master's	6	83.3	0.0	16.7	0.0
4-Year undergraduate	32	6.3	0.0	93.7	0.0

Note: Only 59 of 86 institutions responding to the survey answered this item.

search university the policy states that full-time non-tenure-eligible faculty are "not expected to perform the same range of duties" as regular faculty.

It became evident from our interviews with full-time faculty in non-tenure-eligible positions and their department chairs that tenure-track and tenured faculty are expected to fulfill responsibilities that include research, teaching, and service. In contrast, the vast majority of full-time non-tenure track faculty hired at research universities have a much more restricted role definition, one primarily focused on teaching. Consistent with this pattern, at several of the research universities we visited, FTNTT faculty members coordinated the work of teaching assistants in their department or program area in addition to their instructional duties.

Institutional policy statements concerning the role of FTNTT faculty at doctoral-level and master's-level institutions vary between no formal definition and, at one institution, a comprehensive definition, which is: non-tenure-track faculty "teach courses, conduct research, direct students, assist with student research, direct student field work, or provide consultation on research or instructional projects." This particular university restricts faculty in full-time non-tenure-eligible positions to lower-division undergraduate program responsibilities. Among the policies from master's-level institutions, one defined the role for these faculty as essentially equivalent to that for tenure-eligible faculty. The only difference was the nature of the contractual relationship with the institution. Most of our doctoral-level and master's-level institutions indicated that they hired full-time non-tenure-track faculty to teach primarily at the lower-division undergraduate level.

At several institutions, although the policy states that the full-time non-tenure-track faculty are to teach only at the lower-division level, if a chair felt that the faculty member was well qualified, he or she periodically provided the opportunity to teach upper-division or graduate courses. Among the doctoral- and master's-level institutions, the role definitions and actual role implementation of tenure-track and non-tenure-eligible faculty sometimes varied based on the specific institutional needs being met by the full-time faculty in non-tenure-eligible positions. Distinctive circumstances within the institutions or specific academic units generally dictated how much difference there was between the functions of tenure-eligible and non-tenure-eligible full-time faculty. In several instances, it was difficult to discriminate between the roles of the full-time non-tenure-track and tenure-track faculty.

At many of the four-year undergraduate colleges we visited, full-time term-appointment faculty appear to function in roles that are comparable to those of tenure-eligible faculty, although the institution may restrict the disciplines or program areas in which such personnel are hired. A large number of the baccalaureate institutions utilize full-time non-tenure-track faculty in dual capacities such as instructor and coordinator of a science laboratory or teacher and coordinator of a writing program or language laboratory.

No consistent definitions of roles for full-time non-tenure-track faculty emerged from our study. Some institutions restrict these faculty members primarily to teaching-related duties. Indeed, some limit them to teaching only introductory and intermediate-level courses. Institutions also have developed hybrid full-time non-tenure-eligible positions to fill needs not adequately addressed by traditional tenure-track positions. These hybrid posts usually involve some combination of classroom teaching with clinical/field supervision or administrative work. At the opposite extreme are institutions where full-time faculty in non-tenure-track positions function similarly to their tenure-track colleagues. They perform the same teaching, research, and service roles as their tenure-eligible colleagues. How an institution defines and restricts its non-tenure-track positions appears to depend on the mission, culture, and, especially, academic personnel needs of the institution.

Why Employ Full-Time Non-Tenure-Track Faculty?

The varied roles of faculty hired into full-time non-tenure-track positions relate closely to the reasons institutions have for creating such positions. These reasons also directly influenced the various policies we found that control the terms and conditions of employment affecting these faculty. These policies are discussed in later sections of this chapter.

TO PROTECT TENURE-TRACK FACULTY

Deans and chairs at many of the interview institutions stated that they hire full-time non-tenure-track faculty to fill specific roles and responsibilities that they consider inappropriate for tenure-track faculty. In summarizing why there was such a large proportion of non-tenure-track faculty in her college, a dean of humanities stated that "[in] the humanities, you have disciplinary norms. Teaching of writing and languages within [this college] is deemed not the domain of ladder faculty. TAs and lecturers do this teaching." In the sciences and modern languages, where laboratory instruction involves a large expenditure of effort, these non-tenure-track faculty are often deemed the most appropriate personnel to coordinate laboratory schedules, oversee laboratory instruction, and ensure that supplies and equipment are available when needed. This arrangement protects tenure-track faculty, who can more effectively utilize their time on research.

TO MEET INSTITUTIONAL NEEDS ECONOMICALLY

The need for staffing flexibility and cost control were often cited as reasons for hiring faculty into full-time non-tenure-eligible positions. The flexibility issue was highlighted by a senior administrator who cited the need for a "safe zone" in finance and faculty staffing during a period of recovery from enrollment decline and the implementation of new programs. The utilization of yearly contracts did not commit this institution to faculty beyond the length of their contract if enrollments declined in continuing or new degree programs. This administrator viewed full-time term-appointment faculty as a short-term solution but not a long-term option. A number of other institutions also cited the need for staffing flexibility because of unpredictable enrollments. Some also stated that they needed flexibility during the transition from the extensive use of part-time faculty to an increase in full-time tenure-track faculty.

In addition, a large number of institutions cited cost and budgetary considerations as important reasons for employing full-time non-tenure-track faculty. Some institutions reduced costs by hiring these faculty at lower salaries than they paid to tenure-track faculty. They cut personnel costs by employing individuals with lesser degree qualifications than would be required to fill tenure-track slots. In most cases this meant hiring individuals who did not hold the terminal degree in their discipline, although we did find institutions with lower salary scales for these types of positions regardless of degree qualifications. At several institutions, administrators indicated that the use of full-time non-tenure-track faculty contributes to budgetary efficiency because faculty in such positions tend to carry heavier teaching loads than tenured or tenure-track faculty. For example, at many institutions we studied, FTNTT faculty often teach at least one more course per term than their tenure-eligible colleagues. The faculty hired at the majority of campuses to teach first-year writing courses and lower-level language courses were prime examples of such appointments.

TO ENRICH THE ACADEMIC COMMUNITY

The term *specialized hires* refers to those personnel who are appointed because they have the desired experience, knowledge, and skills but do not have the traditional qualifications deemed necessary for access to or success on the tenure track. This was a common reason given by deans of business, law, education, and health sciences for non-tenure-track appointments.

Such appointments were also identifiable in some of the traditional arts and sciences disciplines. One example is the hiring of retired corporate leaders—practitioners—who do not have terminal degrees in business but bring a wealth of corporate experience not typically available among traditional tenure-track faculty. An academic vice-president at a research university described the use of these nontraditional faculty in some disciplines as "a way to enrich the academic community."

Another type of specialized hire is the full-time term-contract research faculty member. They are most evident on the campuses of institutions actively involved in sponsored research endeavors. These faculty are found across a variety of disciplines on university campuses, with the heaviest concentrations in the natural sciences, engineering, and medicine. Typically referred to as assistant, associate, or research professors, these full-time faculty usually commit 100 percent of their efforts to research activities and research laboratories.

The need for supervisors with clinical experience is another rationale for appointing full-time faculty who are not eligible for tenure. These types of hires are often found in the field of education, where, for example, former teachers, administrators, or new doctoral graduates are used to supervise students in their field placements in schools. Likewise, medical schools utilize physicians in clinical teaching experiences for medical students. Such practices may also be found in sociology, social work, psychology, and other programs that include internship experiences as part of the undergraduate degree program.

TO CHANGE STAFFING PATTERNS

Administrators at several of the institutions we studied indicated that they use full-time non-tenure-track faculty to remedy the excessive use of part-time faculty, especially in specific disciplines. For example, a dean of business told us that he was in the process of replacing part-time faculty with full-time non-tenure-track faculty in order to comply with professional accreditation standards. Several department chairs in arts and sciences at institutions that had gone through enrollment fluctuations in recent years stated that they also had replaced part-time faculty with full-time term-appointment faculty.

Hiring Practices

The search process for [full-time] non-tenure track faculty shall follow the same procedures as those for tenure-track faculty. Searches may be either national or local, depending on the nature of the position to be filled and the discretion of the Department Chair/Dean/ Director. (Policy statement from a doctoral institution)

Most [full-time] non-tenure-track faculty are local. It's a mechanism to take advantage of local talent. They are not recruited nationally. (A social science department chair at a baccalaureate institution)

Policies affecting the hiring of full-time non-tenure-track faculty vary across institutions and among departments within institutions. Depending on the nature of the position the institution is attempting to fill, recruiting may be national, regional, or local in its emphasis. We learned from our site visit interviews that the recruitment process is influenced by several factors: the program area (discipline) for which a candidate is being sought, qualifications required, geographic location of an institution, and the proximity of other institutions. For example, an institution located in a metropolitan area might recruit locally for candidates to teach lower-division writing courses or introductory language courses, positions for which they do not require the terminal degree. An institution that is geographically more isolated, however, might need to recruit regionally or nationally for candidates to fill full-time non-tenure-track positions.

Similarly, in disciplines for which the institution is seeking candidates who have qualifications comparable to their tenure-track faculty, the recruiting is most likely to be national in scope. This is especially true if the program area is in high demand and candidates are at a premium. We identified some institutions where specific disciplines were forced to change their recruitment strategy from a regional to a national focus and from non-tenure-track to tenure-track appointments in order to hire the high-quality individuals they were seeking. Such changes to meet staffing needs were more likely to occur in natural sciences disciplines than in the humanities or social sciences. All the institutions we visited assured us that they complied with affirmative action and equal opportunity guidelines regardless of whether their recruiting emphasis was local, regional, or national.

Cost is another factor that influences the scope of non-tenure-track recruitment. Some institutions told us that they recruited mostly locally for full-time term-appointment faculty positions because it would be too expensive to advertise nationally for short-term appointments and to bring candidates to campus from distant locations. Some deans and department chairs also mentioned that it made little sense to move people across the country for appointments that are conceptually and contractually temporary.

Many institutions also use full-time non-tenure-eligible positions to accommodate the employment aspirations of an accompanying spouse or partner in a two-career marriage or relationship. We learned that it is common, especially among research and doctoral universities, for administrators to create full-time non-tenure-eligible positions for the partner of a faculty member whom the institution is aggressively recruiting for a tenured or tenure-track position. This often occurs when the institution has no tenure-eligible position available for the partner or there is no such position available at a neighboring institution. The ability to create such positions was identified as especially critical for colleges and universities that are geographically isolated.

A number of the institutional policies we studied did address the eligibility of full-time non-tenure-track faculty for tenure-track appointments. For example, a doctoral level institution states that "no person in a specified-term appointment may receive a tenure-eligible or tenure-track appointment unless he or she is selected as a result of a formal search to fill such an appointment." This type of statement clearly indicates that non-tenure-track faculty typically do not receive favored treatment when competing for a tenure-track position.

The feasibility of using a full-time non-tenure-track appointment as an avenue for subsequently acquiring a tenure-track or tenured position at the same institution is viewed with skepticism by many non-tenure-track faculty members. A full-time faculty member in a non-tenure-track position at a research university summed up his feelings (and those of many others we interviewed) about the possibility of qualifying for a tenure-track position at his institution. "It is a dead end situation," he observed. "You are where you are. It is not a ticket to anything. [You are] not able to negotiate for a tenure-track post."

Employment Qualifications

The extent to which qualifications for full-time non-tenure-track positions are spelled out in institutional policy documents varies considerably across institutions. The following policy statements reveal how differently institutions specify required credentials for appointment to a non-tenure-eligible post. The first example from a research university does not specify minimum degree requirements for lecturer or artist-in-residence positions but does indicate that such personnel have special roles. For senior ranks the holders of the positions must be highly trained and experienced in their discipline.

1. Lecturer and artist in residence are instructional titles that may be conferred on persons who have special instructional roles. Appointments may be renewed pursuant to Section . . .

2. Senior lecturer and senior artist are instructional titles that may be conferred on persons who have special instructional roles and who have extensive training, competence, and experience in their discipline. Appointments may be renewed pursuant to Section . . . (From the policy document on Qualifications for Appointment at Specific Ranks and Titles of a Research I University)

In contrast, the policy statement from a liberal arts college sets degree expectations or an equivalent.

Lecturer. A position requiring the standard degree commonly expected of specialists (Ph.D., M.F.A., or other degree) or prior equivalent experience in teaching. (From the policy statement of a liberal arts college setting forth the qualifications necessary for appointment to a continuing non-tenure-track appointment in the arts)

With a few exceptions, institutional policy documents tend not to set forth the minimum degree qualifications necessary for full-time non-tenure-track faculty appointments. It appears that many of the decisions about qualifications are made within the context of the role to be filled and the abilities and knowledge required to perform the job effectively.

At many of the institutions we visited, we learned that the qualifications sought in FTNTT faculty were those required of tenure-eligible faculty. In these cases the candidates were expected to hold the terminal degree or to have other necessary qualifications. For positions that were primarily instructional in nature, the terminal degree in the discipline with a commitment to teaching rather than to research was often the discriminating factor. The emphasis on teaching for the full-time non-tenure-track lecturers at one research university is clearly set forth in the following policy statement: "Lecturers are responsible for classroom teaching and its related activities. The position is based on professional qualifications in teaching." In institutions where the role of the non-tenure-track faculty is similar to that of the tenure-track faculty, desired credentials typically included scholarly interest and skills.

A major exception to the terminal degree requirement was evident at many institutions hiring faculty to teach writing and lower-division language courses. In these cases, the master's degree was acceptable at most institutions. Similar exceptions were granted at most institutions for non-tenure-track faculty hired in the performing arts program areas.

Institutions that employ experienced practitioners to enhance their educational programs in professional areas were often more interested in the experience, knowledge, and skills that were gained by those professionals in the "real world" than in their traditional faculty qualifications. We learned from conversations with deans of professional schools that many of these faculty are retired from business, government, education, or industry and are comfortable with term appointments.

In sum, the qualifications required for appointment to full-time non-tenure-track positions differ considerably. Minimum credentials seem to vary, especially by discipline, level or type of instruction, and labor market conditions. The more closely the functions of a non-tenure-track position parallel a traditional tenure-track post, the more likely a terminal degree and comparable professional experience are required. In a labor market where a surplus of candidates is available, the qualifications expected for appointment to a non-tenure-track post also tend to parallel those of tenure-track faculty. Full-time non-tenure-track faculty who are hired to teach introductory, intermediate, or developmental courses often do not need a terminal degree. Similarly, full-time faculty in non-tenure-track positions who bring extensive experience as practitioners in a professional area frequently are not required to hold a doctoral or other terminal degree. These institutional practices may influence the caliber of the faculty who fill these posts. When compared with their tenure-track colleagues, locally recruited full-time term-appointment faculty, who often come from a smaller talent pool, may bring less experience or fewer academic credentials to their posts. This may partially account for the lower status that these faculty possess on many campuses.

What Percentage of the Faculty May Hold Full-Time Non-Tenure-Track Appointments?

No more than 50% of untenured full-time academic faculty shall be on the non-tenure track. (From the policy statement of a private baccalaureate college)

Term appointments shall be limited to no more than ten percent (10%) of the total number of tenured and tenure-track faculty in the bargaining unit. (From a public doctoral institution's collective bargaining agreement)

Research universities will not be well served if they create an imbalance in the numbers of these (NTT) positions. [A] one in four principle may be O.K. At the 50% level you get into cultural problems. (Comments by a research university provost about the issues faced in the employment of a growing number of full-time non-tenure-track faculty)

At a number of the institutions that participated in this study, concerns about tenure ratios and the need for program and financial flexibility were a primary motivation for employing non-tenure-track faculty in full-time positions. Although the institutions' attempts to reduce or control their tenure ratios did not specify a limit on the proportion of full-time non-tenure-track positions, the ratios did appear to set employment targets for non-tenure-eligible faculty. For example, in order to maintain a specified degree of freedom in staffing, one state system established a target of 85 percent as the maximum proportion of the total full-time equivalent (FTE) faculty that could be tenured or tenure-eligible. This created a 15 percent target for the hiring of non-tenure-track faculty, full-time or part-time. At a master's-level public institution, at which the overall tenure figure had reached about 90 percent, the board of trustees began raising questions about the reasons for having tenure. It subsequently set a tenure cap of 75 percent for the institution. In order to comply with this target, the institution developed a three-year full-time revolving term-appointment plan as an alternative to making all new hires tenure-track appointments. Both of these examples represent institutional attempts to control tenure ratios and preserve the degree of freedom deemed necessary to maintain flexibility in faculty staffing.

The three quotations introducing this section raise concerns about the excessive use of full-time non-tenure-track faculty. Or, stated another way, if an increasing number of non-tenure-eligible full-time faculty are hired at an institution with a faculty culture based on the principles and practices of tenure, at what ratio of non-tenure-track to tenure-track faculty does the culture of the institution change, if at all? It became clear during our site visit discussions that there are serious concerns on nearly all campuses among both tenure-track and non-tenure-track faculty that two classes of faculty will develop. The degree of class distinction that arises between full-time tenure-track and non-tenure-track faculty tends to be a function of the nature of the contract system under which the full-time non-tenure-track faculty work, the general culture of the institution, the attitudes and actions of academic leaders, and the proportion of non-tenure-track faculty among all full-time faculty. One dean summarized this situation when he voiced his concern with the possibility of having two faculty cultures that have distinct and conflicting professional expectations of the institution.

Specifying a maximum proportion of the full-time faculty who may be in non-tenure-eligible positions is also a way of controlling the loss of tenure-eligible positions to non-eligible appointments. This appears to be the motivation for setting non-tenure-track ratios for full-time faculty in collective bargaining agreements. For institutions with a commitment to instruction, research, and service, setting maximum ratios of full-time non-tenure-track faculty is also a way of preserving a large enough core of "regular" faculty with instruction, research, governance, and other service role commitments to fulfill the multiple responsibilities inherent in their mission statement.

Length of Contract and Contract Renewal Policies

Non-tenure-track appointments are on year-by-year contracts. The timing of renewal letters shall follow the same procedures as timing for renewal letters for untenured tenure-track faculty. (From the policy statement of a doctoral institution)

Appointments to the position of lecturer are for terms of three years. Initial appointments as, or promotion to, Senior Lecturer is [sic] also for a three-year term, but subsequent appointments as Senior Lecturer are for five-year terms. Senior Lecturers are expected to demonstrate exceptional mastery in teaching with a substantial impact on the university's educational mission.

Appointments as Principal Lecturer are for five-year terms. Appointments at this rank are made only for extraordinary accomplishment in teaching and fundamental contributions to the university's educational mission. (From the policy statements of a research university that has a career ladder for full-time non-tenure-track faculty)

The most common contract length across all institutions responding to our survey was one year, but multiyear contracts are prevalent at the majority of our site visit institutions. The use of one-year contracts varies by institution and according to the rationale for hiring full-time non-tenure-track faculty. Many institutions limit their contracts for these faculty to one year, renewable indefinitely or for a specified maximum number of years. In addition to their use in providing a temporary substitute for an individual on leave or sabbatical or in providing temporary coverage for positions that become vacant on short notice, a series of one-year contracts may serve as a probationary period for full-time non-tenure-track faculty before they are awarded multiyear contracts.

Fifty-eight percent of our survey institutions, including 78 percent of the research, 44 percent of the doctoral, 67 percent of the master's, and 41 percent of the baccalaureate, indicated that they provide for unlimited renewal of their full-time term-contract faculty. The remaining 42 percent of the institutions set a limit on the number of years a full-time non-tenure-track faculty member may remain employed in term-contract status. In some cases the institutions set a maximum number of years as a means of preventing full-time non-tenure-track faculty from reaching a de facto tenure status. At some other institutions the reason for renewal limits is to create and maintain an infusion of new faculty or to control instructional costs. The policy statement set forth in the bargaining agreement of a doctoral institution captures the concern about the relationship between a limit on the number of years in non-track status and tenure.

> Term appointments are full-time appointments and are normally made for no more than one (1) academic year, but may be granted for up to two (2) consecutive academic years. Such appointments are terminable or renewable for up to a total of six (6) consecutive academic years by the Dean of the College. Neither the initial term appointment, nor any renewals thereof, leads to or grants tenure or promotion.

The following excerpt from the policy statement of a research university provides a contrasting perspective on term limits for full-time non-tenure-track faculty:

> [A] senior lecturer . . . shall be appointed by the President for a term not to exceed five years, renewable indefinitely . . . and [a] lecturer . . . shall be appointed by the President for a term not to exceed three years, renewable indefinitely.

Among institutions that have formalized multiyear full-time non-tenure-eligible career tracks as alternatives to tenure-track appointments, the one-year appointment is often used as a probationary period. To some extent, this practice parallels the six one-year term appointments used as the probationary period in a tenure system. Some combination of one-year appointments is often used prior to the issuance of multiyear term contracts. Common combinations of contract progression for full-time non-tenure-track faculty who require successful periodic evaluations include

— six one-year contracts, a three-year contract, and then five-year contracts
— three one-year contracts, then a three-year contract followed by five-year contracts
— two three-year contracts, followed by five-year contracts

In each of these cases the contracts are for a specified number of years and must be renewed prior to or during the final year of the contract period. Otherwise, the contract lapses or is terminated. From our interviews we learned that the establishment of a standard contract progression around which faculty can plan a secure and predictable career is often very important to persons under a contract system. Whether the faculty personnel system involves annual renewal of yearly contracts or renewal of a three- or five-year contract in the last year of the contract period, many full-time term-appointment faculty wish to have the opportunity for predictable and stable employment within which they can advance professionally and build a stable life for themselves and their family members.

An alternative to the strategy of using discrete annual or multiyear contracts is the use of "rolling" contracts, or "revolving term" appointments. Under a rolling contract system a full-time faculty member is evaluated at the end of each year, and, if a satisfactory evaluation is achieved, the contract is extended for another year. Therefore, if a three-year contract is initially awarded and the faculty member receives a satisfactory evaluation at the end of the first year, the contract is automatically extended for a year to maintain the three-year employment security. Similar arrangements are in place at some institutions for five-year rolling contract appointments.

A master's-level institution that has a tenure system and a modification of a full-time rolling contract system describes its "revolving term appointment" (RTA) contract system as follows:

> The RTA is intended to meet long-term staffing needs. Through the RTA the University attempts to provide appointees with a degree of job security while retaining the ability to shift resources as programmatic needs fluctuate. RTA contracts are non-tenure track. The initial appointment is for a three-year period with an extension decision made in the second year of the contract and annually thereafter.

According to the multiyear rolling contracts at many institutions, if a less than satisfactory evaluation is received at the conclusion of a year the contract will not be rolled forward for the additional year. The second year becomes a probationary period during which improvement to a satisfactory level must be achieved for the contract to be extended to the original length. Failure to achieve the satisfactory level then becomes grounds for termination of employment at the end of the contract period.

The master's-level institution with the revolving term appointment system clearly spells out for faculty how contracts are extended or allowed to lapse.

Although it is anticipated that supervisors and RTA faculty will be in communication regarding the possibilities of extension, no separate notice of non-extension is required. Any extension must be in writing; if there is no written extension, an RTA will automatically expire at the end of the initial three year period or extended term, whichever is applicable.

Several institutions' policies include provisions for contract termination prior to the end of the contract due to an enrollment decline or financial constraints. In such cases the institution has the right to buy out the contract, without prejudice to the faculty member. The policy of a baccalaureate college that provides for seven-year contracts and that conditions renewal on performance and institutional need for the position contains these provisions:

(1) If, prior to commencement in any year during the seven-year term of appointment, the Chancellor, in consultation with the Dean, decides that this position is no longer needed, you will be given, at the College's option, either notice of nonrenewal at the end of the next academic year or notice of immediate nonrenewal with a lump sum payment equal to 125% of your then current salary.

(2) If, during the annual evaluation process or in any year of the seven-year appointment, it is determined that your performance falls below expectations, you will be placed on conditional status for a twelve-month period and notified that nonrenewal without compensation from the College may result if the performance does not rise to the level specified by the end of the conditional period, i.e., by the time of the next year's annual evaluation process.

This particular policy clearly articulates the conditions under which nonrenewal may take place and the implications of such actions for planning on the part of faculty whose contracts may not be renewed.

The time frame under which contract renewal notification operates is of concern to faculty, whether they are serving under single- or multiyear contracts. We heard several stories during our campus interviews in which full-time faculty on single- and multiyear contracts were not notified of contract renewal or nonrenewal until one or two months prior to the beginning of the new academic year. These shortcomings were the exceptions, however. Many of the institutional policies we reviewed included provisions that comply with the contract renewal standards advocated by the American Association of University Professors. These standards specify that faculty in their first year be given three months' notice; second-year personnel receive six months' notification, and individuals with three or more years of service receive a one-year notice. An alternative at one research university is three months' notification for faculty in the first year and six months' notification for anyone in their second year or beyond.

A key issue with regard to notification of renewal or termination revolves around full-time personnel on a series of one-year "temporary" contracts that are renewed each year. Does the three-month notification standard apply at the end of each year, or is the accumulation of years the standard that should be applied? This is not addressed in the policies of many institutions.

The significant role sometimes played by department chairs in the renewal process was highlighted by several of the full-time non-tenure-track faculty with whom we spoke. In each of these cases the faculty members, at research universities, had held three- or five-year contracts, but their renewal of contract review and reappointment coincided with the appointment of a new department chair. In each case, although they had received satisfactory evaluations, they were reappointed for only one year and were in that year at the time of our interviews. Each of these cases was at an institution that has a multiyear contract system for their full-time non-tenure-track faculty. Situations like this raise questions about consistency in the application of the policy and the integrity of the contract renewal process. If a multiyear contract system is in effect for full-time faculty in non-tenure-track positions, it is critical that the policies be administered consistently and equitably across changes in departmental or college leadership. The experience of one of our interviewees at a liberal arts college highlights the problem of inconsistency, which full-time non-tenure-track faculty sometimes encounter, when she stated, "You can have a five-year contract followed by a one-year contract. [Full-time non-tenure-tracks] seem to be in the dark on how the system works and what policies are (if they exist)."

Policies guiding contract length and renewal have evolved in a variety of ways at institutions that employ faculty in full-time non-tenure-track positions. Some combination of probationary single-year contracts followed by multiyear contracts seems to represent a more mature level of policy development for FTNTT appointments. This type of arrangement preserves institutional flexibility while providing some career stability for long-serving full-time term-appointment faculty. We found, however, that contract length and renewal policies are not always applied consistently. This was particularly common in large, decentralized institutions. Departmental and college autonomy in complex universities sometimes leads to variation in the dissemination, interpretation, and application of these policies. In the process, some full-time non-tenure-eligible faculty benefit and some are disadvantaged.

A full-time non-tenure-track faculty member in business summed up the concerns expressed by many others about the lack of clarity and consistency in the policies and practices that govern their employment. He recommended that his institution "clarify it [the non-tenure-track status] for us and treat us fairly. What are the parameters within which we walk?" In Chapter 7 we make specific recommendations about how to deal with the need for consistency in policy interpretation and implementation.

Ranks, Titles, and Promotion

Ranks and titles are viewed as an inherent part of the traditional faculty career in higher education. The career progression from assistant to full professor serves both as a measure of academic achievement and as progression up the career ladder for tenure-track faculty. For full-time faculty in non-tenure-track positions, the availability of a career ladder with clearly defined titles, ranks, and promotion criteria is not as common. At some of the institutions we studied, a full-time non-tenure-track faculty member may serve for many years but never progress above the title of lecturer, for example. One doctoral university we visited currently has no consistent set of ranks for its non-tenure-track faculty. The following proposed policy at this institution is intended to address the promotion issue, but in a very decentralized and potentially inconsistent manner:

> Each College/Unit [of the doctoral institution] will determine any process, criteria, timing, titles, and other specifications for promotion within the non-tenure track.

In contrast, the two following policy statements highlight the provision of a career ladder utilizing two different sets of titles and ranks. The research university employs a lecturer track, which distinguishes the full-time non-tenure-track faculty from the tenure-track ranks and titles. The baccalaureate college includes term-appointment faculty within the traditional career ladder titles and ranks.

> The designations Lecturer, Senior Lecturer, and Principal Lecturer are specific to Lecturer Track positions and may not be used for any other positions in the University, unless preceded by distinguishing qualifiers such as visiting, special, part-time, or adjunct. (From the policy statement of a private research I university)

> Titles of full-time members of the Faculty, including full-time term appointments, normally come from the following list: Professor, Associate Professor, Assistant Professor, or Instructor. Generally, the terminal de-

gree for the field is necessary for the rank of Assistant Professor and above. (From the policy statement of a private baccalaureate college)

Discussion about rank and titles arose in a number of our sessions with the non-tenure-track faculty. The nature of the titles and chance for career progression that is reflected by advancement in rank is a serious consideration for many members of the professoriate, whether they be tenure-track or non-tenure-track. It was common for the full-time non-tenure-track faculty at institutions with the traditional rank ladder of assistant professor, associate professor, and professor to question their professional status if they were not eligible for that standard progression in rank. Many full-time non-tenure-eligible faculty perceived the title of lecturer as one that does not carry prestige in the traditional professorial career.

Among our survey institutions, 35 percent stated that their non-tenure-track faculty were eligible for the traditional professorial ranks, while 26 percent assigned their full-time non-tenure-track faculty a special title such as lecturer. At many of the institutions using the lecturer designation there was a chance to progress to the rank of senior lecturer. This arrangement provides the opportunity for career advancement, albeit with one less step than the traditional academic ranks provide. For faculty in the arts, the special designation for non-tenure-track faculty was often artist-in-residence or resident artist. At 24 percent of the institutions, full-time faculty in non-tenure-eligible positions could be assigned either to one of the traditional ranks or to a special title and rank.

At a number of institutions that utilized the traditional faculty ranks, a prefix such as "clinical," "visiting," "research," or "adjunct" was assigned to differentiate among the types of full-time non-tenure-eligible faculty on campus. It was common to find the title of lecturer being used on a campus to designate full-time non-tenure-track faculty who had primarily instructional responsibilities while a research faculty member had the label "research" as the prefix to professor. This reflects the latter's responsibilities primarily in some area of scholarly inquiry. Many of the institutions with lecturer titles for their full-time multiyear term-appointment instructional faculty assign the prefix "visiting" to the standard professorial ranks to represent a full-time one-year faculty member whose primary responsibility is teaching.

Some institutions we studied have thus far failed to develop clear, systematic, and consistent promotion policies. For example, at a research university we visited there were no common criteria by which lecturers are evaluated and no standard criteria by which they are promoted to senior lecturer. In fact, at this institution we found great variation in terms of when and on what basis lecturers are elevated to senior status. These decisions seem to occur at the discretion of departments and sometimes at the whim of department chairs. This is not an isolated example. At another major university where a senior lecturer rank appeared in university policy, there was much uncertainty among lecturers about how they could be promoted. Promotions did not occur within a standard time frame, and even long-term full-time lecturers we interviewed did not know how to qualify for promotion to the senior level. A similar situation prevails at a doctoral university we visited. We found no clear or codified evaluation and promotion policy for full-time non-tenure-track faculty. Unless these faculty, who often play different roles than tenure-track faculty, can comply with the research expectations held for tenurable faculty, they probably will not be promoted under current policy at this institution.

Non-tenure-track faculty holding full-time appointments complained that not having a career ladder similar to that available to the tenure-track faculty was discriminatory, demeaning, and demoralizing. Some observed that the lack of a career ladder with a respected set of titles is an example of their status as second-class faculty. To carry the development of distinctions between non-tenure-track and tenure-track faculty to an extreme, one institution does not classify FTNTT personnel as "faculty" within the institutional environment.

Obviously, the ranks and titles that institutions apply to full-time non-tenure-eligible faculty vary considerably. Even within the same institution we found that the non-tenure-track faculty sometimes had different titles in different academic units. The situation with regard to promotions is similar. Across the institutions we studied, a lack of consistency seems to prevail. While some institutions have clear policies for assigning titles and ranks and for awarding promotions, many operate on a more inconsistent, ad hoc basis. In these situations, decisions about title, rank, and promotion may vary with the traditions of a discipline, the customs of an academic unit, or the personal inclination of deans and department chairs. The lack of adequate policies affecting the terms and conditions of employment for full-time faculty in appointments that are not eligible for tenure is demoralizing for many faculty, but having policies that are not consistently and equitably applied is equally dispiriting.

Salary and Benefits

Discussion of compensation for full-time non-tenure-track faculty is most meaningful when salary and benefits are described separately and when compared with compensation for tenured and tenure-track faculty on the same campuses.

SALARY

Data from the 86 institutions that responded to our question about comparability of salaries of full-time non-tenure-track and tenure-eligible faculty are shown in table 3.2. Comparability of salaries between the tenure-eligible and non-tenure-eligible full-time faculty with comparable qualifications varies by type of institution.

The majority of research and doctoral institutions pay lower salaries to their full-time non-tenure-track faculty than to their tenure-track faculty. In contrast, master's and baccalaureate institutions are more prone to pay comparable salaries when non-tenure-track and tenure-track faculty have similar qualifications. Our institutional survey also revealed that a larger proportion of the public institutions (50%) were likely to offer lower salaries to FTNTT faculty than were private institutions (26%), whereas the private institutions (68% vs. 47%) were more likely to offer comparable salaries. It is evident that very few institutions offer higher salaries to comparably qualified full-time non-tenure-track faculty than to tenure-eligible personnel.

A liberal arts college that views its long-term renewable appointments for full-time faculty as a viable career alternative to tenure provides a salary and benefit package designed to enhance the attractiveness of the renewable appointments. The following statement sets forth the institution's policy on benefits and salary.

> Faculty hired on this type of appointment [NTT] receive the same fringe benefits as full-time, tenure-track faculty, and they are eligible for professional travel and research funds on the same basis as tenured and

Table 3.2   Comparability of Average Salaries of Full-Time Non-Tenure-Track and Tenure-Eligible Faculty with Comparable Qualifications, by Type of Institution

	Salaries of Non-Tenure-Track Faculty Are		
Type of Institution	Lower (%)	Comparable (%)	Higher (%)
Baccalaureate	24	73	3
Master's	29	71	0
Doctoral	55	36	9
Research	52	44	4

Source: Survey data from 86 four-year colleges and universities.

tenure-track faculty. However, faculty hired on this type of appointment are paid a salary that is *somewhat higher* than the salary that would be offered to someone hired on the tenure track.

The rationale for the use of higher salaries and enhanced benefits for FT-NTT faculty is discussed in more detail in Chapter 5.

A contrasting philosophy is in place at a master's-level institution at which the full-time non-tenure-track positions "cost the institution about 85 percent of what a tenure-track position costs," the chief academic officer explained. The rationale for paying these non-tenure-track faculty less varies by institution. Some are paid less because their role at the institution (primarily teaching) is more limited than the duties of their tenure-track colleagues. Some full-time non-tenure-eligible faculty do not have the same qualifications as tenure-track faculty and, for that reason, are paid lower salaries. In other cases, these faculty receive lower salaries because of an oversupply of qualified candidates in their fields. This favorable market situation makes it easy for colleges and universities to recruit well-qualified full-time faculty off the tenure track for lower-paid positions.

At approximately 80 percent of the institutions we surveyed, the full-time non-tenure-track faculty are eligible for merit salary increases, with slightly fewer private institutions awarding such increases than public institutions (76% vs. 86%). In the area of merit salary increases, the non-tenure-track faculty members often do not fare as well as their tenure-track counterparts. Faculty at a number of the site visit institutions reported that the salary pool from which their merit increases is drawn is not equivalent, on a per faculty member basis, to that for the tenured and tenure-eligible faculty. At one of the institutions this discrepancy was verified by an academic administrator.

FRINGE BENEFITS

An important aspect of the total compensation package for non-tenure-eligible full-time faculty members is the availability of fringe benefits and the eligibility criteria for such benefits. The fringe benefit policy at a liberal arts college reads:

> The College will provide the standard fringe benefits for full-time faculty, and you will be eligible for professional travel and research funds on the same basis as other full-time faculty. In addition, the College will pay up to $1,500 of the cost of your move to [this institution].

This statement describes the benefit package of an institution that treats full-time non-tenure-track faculty essentially the same as tenure-eligible faculty. The fringe benefits include the full range of pension, health insurance, and life insurance that is normally included in a typical benefits package. The eligibility for professional travel, research funds, and moving expenses is not typical of the professional support provided to full-time non-tenure-track faculty at most institutions.

Ninety-three percent of the institutions we surveyed provide full-time non-tenure-track faculty with full fringe benefits, with little difference between public and private colleges and universities. Fringe benefits, particularly health coverage, are very important to faculty in what many individuals on campus feel are full-time temporary positions. One university we visited provides benefits to all faculty who work more than half-time. This requirement leads to interesting and complex permutations from term to term as the institution tries to balance its staffing and budgetary circumstances with the needs of term-appointment faculty for various fringe benefits.

Institutions with collective bargaining agreements are very likely to have benefit eligibility requirements and the nature of the fringe benefits provided spelled out in detail. For example, an agreement specifically for full-time non-tenure-eligible faculty members at a public research university states: "The University shall provide members of the bargaining unit hospitalization, medical and life insurance benefits as are provided to other full-time University employees." The benefits under this agreement include a pension, health insurance, coverage of preventive services, life insurance, a prescription drug benefit, a dental benefit, vision care, and fee remission (instructional and general). This level of specificity concerning benefits is not common in most institutional policies affecting non-tenure-eligible full-time faculty.

Compensation policies, like other policies affecting the terms and conditions of employment of full-time faculty not eligible for tenure, seem to defy standardization. Considerable variation occurs across institutions and sometimes even across disciplines within the same institution. Some institutions pay their full-time non-tenure-track faculty salaries comparable to tenure-eligible faculty with similar qualifications. Other colleges and universities, especially public institutions, typically pay their non-tenure-track faculty less than tenure-track faculty. On the other hand, these FTNTT faculty have essentially the same access to fringe benefits such as life insurance, health coverage, and pension plans as do tenure-track faculty at the vast majority of institutions.

Teaching and Related Workload Issues

> Term appointees shall normally be assigned teaching duties only at the introductory level of instruction in the various academic disciplines, and shall normally be assigned between 12 and 16 credit hours of instruction per quarter. (Policy statement from a doctoral institution)

> The teaching load for our tenure-track and tenured faculty is normally 5 courses per academic year while our full-time non-tenure-track [faculty] normally are responsible for 6 courses. (Dean at a liberal arts college)

> NTT faculty carry a heavier teaching load than do tenure-track faculty but the load for both classes of faculty varies by disciplinary field. (Report from a research university)

The statements above provide a brief introduction to the diverse nature of the teaching loads of full-time faculty in non-tenure-track positions. Forty-six percent of the institutions responding to our survey indicated that their full-time term-appointment faculty generally carry teaching loads equivalent to that of the tenured and tenure-track faculty. In many of those cases the full-time non-tenure-track faculty are carrying out the same range of duties and responsibilities (instruction, research, and service) as their tenure-track colleagues. The difference between the two faculty groups generally rests almost solely on the fact that one group is tenure-eligible and the other is not. On the other hand, it was not uncommon to find full-time non-tenure-track faculty with teaching loads equivalent to their tenure-eligible colleagues who were responsible for and committed to administering lower-division instructional programs rather than committing time to research and service.

For example, a lecturer in languages we interviewed at a research university pointed to another subtle difference between her and her tenure-eligible colleagues in the following statement: "I teach two large lecture classes per quarter. Tenured colleagues automatically receive TAs to assist with large classes. I do not. There is no TA budget for full-time lecturers." This faculty member also coordinates an academic program, serves on departmental committees, and is active in scholarly activities. Her formal teaching load may be comparable to her tenure-track colleague's assignments, but her other responsibilities are considerably different from theirs and her teaching support is less.

At 44 percent of the institutions we surveyed, the full-time faculty off the tenure track carry heavier teaching loads and generally are hired just to teach. In these cases, no workload time is allocated or released to support research, service, or governance activities. Research universities were more likely to report heavier teaching loads for their full-time non-tenure-track faculty than were the other types of higher education institutions. The master's-level and baccalaureate-level institutions were more likely to indicate that teaching loads of their full-time tenure-track and non-tenure-track faculty were equivalent or comparable.

Data from our site visits revealed substantial differences in teaching arrangements between large and small institutions. At the smaller institutions, the availability of a college-wide policy often led to a degree of uniformity in the teaching loads of FTNTT faculty across disciplines. At the larger institutions in which the department is a base of power for personnel decisions and, therefore, has a large degree of autonomy in how faculty resources are utilized, less uniformity in workload was evident. In several cases the faculty or chair in one department would indicate that his or her department was operating according to institutional policy on teaching load while personnel from a sister department in the same institution cited the lack of such a policy. The lack of consistency in how workload was determined and assessed appeared to be a significant issue when discussing morale problems with full-time non-tenure-track faculty at the larger and more complex institutions. This lack of consistency in policy or policy implementation is one of the key issues that arises repeatedly in discussions of the terms and conditions of employment of full-time non-tenure-track faculty.

Whether or not full-time non-tenure-track faculty have teaching loads similar to those of tenure-eligible faculty, the nature of the teaching experience itself is often different. The more circumscribed teaching experiences of the non-tenure-track faculty can have a negative impact on their professional growth opportunities, status, and morale. As stated previously, some of these full-time term-appointment faculty are restricted to lower-division (introductory- and intermediate-level) instruction. We found numerous cases where they were excluded from teaching upper-division courses for undergraduate majors or courses for graduate students. A full-time lecturer in a scientific field, for example, told us she teaches only laboratory courses and has a great deal of intensive contact with students. She stated that there is a "monotony aspect" to her job. She has taught the same course for eight years and asks herself, "Can you do this for thirty years?" In many of these cases, full-time non-tenure-track faculty are also forbidden to chair thesis and dissertation committees. These types of restrictions are often imposed at the departmental rather than the institutional level. For example, the non-tenure-eligible faculty in English composition frequently are banned from teaching English literature courses. Not surprisingly, enterprising faculty and flexible department chairs sometimes find creative means to subvert such rigid policies. One non-tenure-track professor at a research university told us he "operates in a state of criminality," because his chair has occasionally permitted him to teach an upper-division literature course.

Being restricted to teaching only lower-division courses is a professional issue, especially for full-time non-tenure-track faculty who have qualifications comparable to their tenure-eligible colleagues and who may aspire to a tenure-track position in the future. Some term-appointment faculty believe that the lack of opportunity to teach advanced courses places them at a disadvantage in the academic labor market. Many full-time non-tenure-track faculty feel that being restricted to lower-division courses reinforces their second-class status on campus when tenure-eligible faculty have the opportunity to teach across the breadth of the curriculum. The level of teaching responsibility also arises as an issue when the policy or policy implementation varies significantly across departments in the same institution. Consistency is a major problem within the institutional context in terms of its impact on morale.

During our site visits it was not uncommon to have full-time non-tenure-track faculty who were hired with the understanding that their role was solely instructional express concern about the lack of time they had for research or involvement in governance. In a contrasting position were the faculty who acknowledged they were hired just to teach, and with a heavier teaching load than their tenure-track colleagues. Some noted they were happy that no other expectations of campus involvement were held for them. A large proportion of the non-tenure-track faculty we interviewed saw themselves as committed to teaching and felt that although their load was heavy, it was consistent with their strengths as faculty members. Those who aspired to a tenure-track position were the most likely to express dissatisfaction with their heavier instructional load, seeing it as an impediment to competing for the elusive tenure-track positions.

We learned that the responsibilities and workload of faculty in full-time positions off the tenure track often change over time. Many of the faculty hired primarily to teach a heavy load eventually became program or laboratory coordinators. Some became trainers and supervisors of graduate teaching assistants. Others were given assignments as advisers to large groups of lower-division students in addition to their teaching loads. In assuming these duties some were given slightly reduced teaching loads, while for others no adjustments were made. In many cases it appears, based on comments from both tenured and full-time non-tenure-track faculty, that the FTNTT faculty are given assignments that do not interest tenured faculty. One full-time term-appointment faculty member has had colleagues tell her that "no one with tenure would ever do what we [full-time non-tenure-track faculty] do." Another female full-time term-appointment faculty member attributed the distribution of loads among tenured and non-tenure-track faculty in her department to the "TOTAL" principle. If tenured faculty did not want to do something, the department chair would "Turn it Over To A Lecturer [TOTAL]." It seemed, from many of our site visit interviews, that this is how the job descriptions of numerous non-tenure-track faculty have developed or evolved over time.

Tenured faculty also expressed some concerns about the impact that hiring full-time non-tenure-track faculty was having on their workloads. Some reported that the use of these faculty required tenure-track faculty to carry heavier student advising loads because advising was not defined as part of the non-tenure-track faculty role at their institution. Others felt that the lack of involvement in governance by the non-tenure-eligible faculty placed a greater burden on them. A tenured faculty member at a liberal arts college voiced this common concern. "Lecturers will always be vulnerable," she observed. "It seems there will always be more for tenured faculty to do because lecturers will avoid controversial/power committees." The issue of how much of an additional load the employment of non-tenure-track faculty places on tenured or tenure-track faculty because of the nature of their differentiated assignments has not been adequately addressed as a policy issue at most of the institutions we studied.

No consensus has emerged on the appropriate workload for full-time non-tenure-track faculty. Some institutions have devised clear workload policies, while others set workload on an ad hoc, case-by-case basis. In either situation, workload decisions appear to be based primarily on the staffing needs of the institution or academic unit involved. Some workload restrictions prevent full-time non-tenure-track faculty from teaching specialized courses to majors and graduate students, the sacred domain of the tenured and tenure-track faculty. The workload assigned to full-time non-tenure-track faculty is often the work that tenure-eligible faculty have neither the time nor the desire to perform.

Participation in Governance

Lecturers and senior lecturers, and those bearing the adjunct title shall be nonvoting members, except as stated in the paragraph below, or unless given the right to vote by the particular faculty in circumstances defined by that faculty.

Lecturers and senior lecturers shall participate fully in those decisions that are directly related to their roles within the college or school and within the department. (From the policy statement of a research university)

Each College/Unit shall determine the voting privileges, the eligibility for committee assignments, and other responsibilities of non-tenure-track faculty. Non-tenure track faculty participate in University, College, Department, or School ceremonies. (From the policy statement of a doctoral institution)

They [NTT faculty] also are eligible for appointment to university, college, and department/school committees, as well as membership on the faculty senate. They enjoy the same voting rights as tenured/tenure track faculty. (From the policy statement of a master's-level institution on the voting rights of full-time non-tenure-track faculty)

Participation in campus governance is one of the cherished traditions of the American professoriate. For full-time non-tenure-track faculty on many campuses, eligibility to participate actively in the governance process is limited or lacking altogether (table 3.3). Eighty-four percent of the survey institutions permit non-tenure-track faculty who work full-time to participate in departmental committees, with 49 percent providing eligibility for service in the faculty senate or its equivalent. The eligibility for participation varies by type of institution. In addition to the institutional variation shown in table 3.3, our survey revealed that private institutions were more likely than public institutions to permit departmental committee participation (89% vs. 77%) and participation in the senate or its equivalent (51% vs. 47%) by full-time non-tenure-track faculty.

In addition to data regarding the eligibility of full-time faculty off the tenure track to serve on committees, we found that voting privileges on department and institution matters also varied by type and control of institution. Private institutions were more prone to provide voting privileges on departmental matters (82% vs. 58%). Seventy-eight percent of the private institutions and 55 percent of the public colleges and universities permit non-tenure-track faculty to vote on institutional matters. According to our

Table 3.3   Institutions at Which Full-Time Non-Tenure-Track Faculty
Are Eligible to Participate in Campus Governance

Type of Institution	N	Department Committees (% institutions)	Faculty Senate (% institutions)
Research	26	84.0	46.0
Doctoral	11	46.0	10.0
Master's	17	82.0	65.0
Four-year undergraduate	32	97.0	59.0

Source: Survey data from 86 four-year institutions.

survey results, baccalaureate institutions are more likely to permit term-appointment faculty to vote on institutional matters than any other type of four-year institution.

Many institutions have not systematically addressed the governance role of full-time non-tenure-eligible faculty by developing clear-cut policies. As a result, uncertainty and confusion sometimes prevail. Most term faculty we interviewed knew they could not participate in tenure and promotion decisions. Otherwise, many did not know on what academic or organizational issues they could or could not vote in departmental or institutional governance. Awkward moments can result in such situations. We learned of one arts and sciences college where the academic dean must decide in each faculty meeting on which issues non-tenure-track faculty may or may not vote. Although uncertainty about the role of term faculty is common at all organizational levels, it is greatest at the college and institution-wide levels. Perhaps because they are better integrated into the departments where they teach, many of the full-time term-appointment faculty we talked with had a clearer sense of their governance role within their departments than within other areas of the institution.

Full-time non-tenure-track faculty have varied reactions to their governance role. Many we interviewed were happy that they were not expected or eligible to participate because it was not one of their areas of professional interest. Others felt disenfranchised and overlooked. This sense of disenfranchisement becomes apparent when governance decisions directly affect instructional or program areas for which the non-tenure-track faculty have responsibility. A faculty member succinctly summarized this view. "I have a voice but no vote," she stated. "I must operate by persuasion and through the voting privileges of others." This faculty member perceived herself as a fringe member of the faculty in shaping matters that directly affected her and the program area for which she was responsible. We heard a different but complementary message from a senior lecturer who teaches large undergraduate science classes at a research university. "We have a vote but I would say not a voice in the department," she observed. "I would even hesitate to express my opinion at a faculty meeting." A humanities lecturer at the same institution provided a similar assessment of the governance role of term faculty. "We do not have the same kind of voice [as tenure-eligible faculty]. We have a lower voice." In contrast, at some institutions these non-tenure-track faculty play an active and important role in the governance process. For example, on one campus we visited, a full-time non-tenure-track faculty member had served as chair of the faculty senate and was a highly respected campus leader. At a different institution we heard that "a lot of lecturers play major roles on campus. They are actively involved in the life of the campus and in local service."

Several factors seem to account for the varied involvement of non-tenure-track faculty in shared governance. The chair of a major senate committee at a research university noted that "participation [of full-time non-tenure-track faculty] varies greatly by the [academic] unit and person." Some full-time term-appointment faculty wish to be fully involved in the life of the institution where they work. Others wish to restrict their involvement to teaching or other specialized duties. One lecturer described the "freedom to be uninvolved" as a perk of full-time non-tenure-track status. Likewise, the characteristics of an academic unit play a role. We learned that full-time term-appointment faculty in small units or units with a large percentage of these faculty tend to play a larger governance role than the full-time non-tenure-track faculty who are less visible or less essential. The principle appears to be, where institutions or academic units depend heavily on full-time non-tenure-eligible faculty, these faculty play a more substantial role in the governance and decision-making process. A senior lecturer at a different research university attributed some of this variation to the department chair as well. Where clear policies on the governance role of full-time term faculty are not in place, the department chair's views on governance involvement can shape the participation of these faculty. If the chair values participation, it will happen. If the chair does not value their input and involvement, it will not occur.

It is important to distinguish between formal and informal roles in governance. Although some restrictions are placed on the formal governance involvement of most non-tenure-track faculty, many play indirect, sometimes influential roles in curriculum design and policy development. This is especially common at the department level, where contributions of full-time non-tenure-track faculty are more easily recognized and personal relationships reduce status distinctions.

We came away from our discussions on governance involvement of full-time non-tenure-track faculty with the same sense of diversity and dynamism that characterizes so many dimensions of this faculty issue. At one end of the governance spectrum is the university lecturer who complained, "It seems [at my institution] decisions are made at the top and we at the grass roots must make things work. I personally feel out of the loop and out of control of the situation." At the other extreme, some of these non-tenure-track faculty play major governance roles equivalent to their tenure-eligible colleagues. Most full-time term-appointment faculty, however, seem to function somewhere in between. Certainly the governance role of full-time non-tenure-eligible faculty should concern their institutions. The effectiveness of the shared governance system depends on the active participation of all key players in the academic enterprise. Colleges and universities that employ full-time non-tenure-track faculty should facilitate and reinforce the governance involvement of these important members of the academic community. In general, however, we observed a casual neglect of the governance role of these faculty at the vast majority of campuses we visited. This neglect can only weaken academic governance over the long term.

Evaluation of Full-Time Non-Tenure-Track Faculty

The evaluation of full-time non-tenure-track faculty frequently reflects their status and function within the institutions they serve. As the following quote suggests, some evaluation policies treat these faculty primarily as short-term employees and leave considerable room for varied applications of the evaluation process.

> Supervisors are expected to evaluate [revolving term-appointment] faculty in the second semester of the first year and annually thereafter (i.e. in the second semester of the second year). Additional evaluations will be at the discretion of the faculty member's supervisor. (Policy statement from a master's-level institution)

In contrast, as this next policy excerpt demonstrates, some institutions have defined elaborate evaluation procedures for their full-time non-tenure-track faculty.

> Non-tenure-track faculty comply with the same annual evaluation process as tenure-track faculty. Non-tenure track faculty will be subject

to a cumulative review process three years after the initial appointment, three years after the first review, and every five years after the second review. This will be comparable to the "pre-tenure" and "post-tenure" review of tenure-track faculty . . . If a non-tenure track faculty seeks review for promotion within one year of a scheduled review, the periodic review is superseded by the promotion review. (Policy statement from a doctoral institution that utilizes multiyear contracts for full-time non-tenure-track faculty)

Such precise and developmental evaluation procedures to a large extent parallel the evaluation process for tenure-track faculty. By its very nature, this latter type of evaluation system assumes that full-time non-tenure-track faculty are valued and potentially long-term members of the academic community who may build a career at their institution.

THE PURPOSE AND TIMING OF EVALUATION

The value of, and rationale for, annual and periodic evaluations of term-appointment faculty was a topic faculty and administrators at each of our site visit institutions highlighted. Although it was common for institutions to have policies for evaluating full-time non-tenure-track faculty, administrators and faculty within the same institutions often had differing perspectives on the utility and effectiveness of the evaluation criteria or the process itself.

Similarly, the rationale for faculty evaluations varies among the institutional policies that we reviewed. Most seemed to present the process or schedule for evaluation and the sources to be used without providing a clear-cut rationale. In contrast, a few presented a rationale for the process such as the following from a baccalaureate institution.

There are two basic objectives in faculty evaluation and review at [this institution].
   a. To assist in the professional development of the individual faculty through assessment, feedback, and dialogue with reviewers.
   b. To contribute to professional, efficient, and appropriate personnel decisions.

All of the institutions we visited indicated that an annual review of full-time non-tenure-track faculty is conducted as part of the process of decision making about salary increases. For faculty on annual or one-year appointments this evaluation also played a key role in decisions about reappointment. Annual reviews were important at institutions that offered rolling contracts. The review often was the basis for extending the contract for an additional year. For institutions that utilize multiyear contracts, the periodic evaluations (i.e., every three or five years based on the length of the contract) serve as critical data-gathering points for decisions about the issuance of another long-term contract.

THE EVALUATION PROCESS AND CRITERIA

The criteria utilized for the evaluation of non-tenure-track faculty vary across institutions. A common element among the various strategies is reliance on student evaluations of courses and instructors. One institution enumerated the areas of assessment of teaching as follows:

> Consideration will be given to such matters as knowledge of subject matter, effectiveness of course design, clarity of thought and expression, maintenance of fair and appropriate standards, ability to arouse and maintain interest, rapport with students, availability to students, and ability to direct research and non-traditional learning activities.

In contrast to this detailed list of evaluation criteria, a master's-level institution indicated that

> the [committee] will use the following criteria in making the initial status determination and for continuing status periodic reviews.
> *a.* classroom teaching and advising
> *b.* professional development appropriate to the individual's discipline
> *c.* service to the University, academic and professional communities.

Many of the full-time non-tenure-track faculty we interviewed were concerned about the validity of the review procedures and evaluation criteria that their institutions were using. A faculty member at a liberal arts college asserted that his institution placed too much reliance on student evaluation of teaching and therefore placed too much power in the hands of students. Numerous full-time faculty, in non-tenure-eligible positions also complained that they were asked to complete the same faculty assessment forms as tenured and tenure-track faculty even though they were hired primarily to teach and carried heavier teaching loads. Often these forms included questions about research and service. In other words, the criteria for evaluating full-time non-track faculty were not shaped specifically by the functions they performed for their institution.

Evaluation was a topic of major interest on nearly every campus we visited, but for a variety of reasons. For example, a full-time non-tenure-track political science faculty member at a liberal arts college expressed a strong desire to be evaluated by the same standards as tenure-track faculty so that he would not be perceived as second-class. He also wished to be competitive for a tenure slot if one were to open. For many of the non-tenure-track faculty aspiring to tenure-track positions, there was a strong concern that they would be disadvantaged if they were evaluated solely on teaching. However, most had neither the time nor the resources to build a meaningful research and scholarship curriculum vitae.

Full-time non-tenure-track faculty also wanted the evaluation process to be meaningful, not perfunctory. Their attitude was, if it must be done, make it meaningful for both non-tenure-track and tenure-track faculty. This concern was expressed another way by several faculty: "If our jobs and the renewal of our contracts depend on productivity, make the post-tenure review of tenured faculty serve the same purpose." Some tenured faculty were concerned that the quality of continuing full-time non-tenure-track faculty would be lower if they did not go through a stringent probationary review similar to that required for tenure status. This attitude reflects concerns about the development of two classes of faculty on campus based on the nature of the contractual relationship between the faculty member and the institution.

Both faculty and administrators expressed concern about the number and frequency of evaluations. The full-time non-tenure-track faculty on annual contracts and some on rolling contracts are subject to yearly evaluations, while those on longer-term contracts or certain revolving or rolling contracts may be subject to in-depth reviews every three to five years. The number of full-time non-tenure-track faculty in departments, the nature of the evaluation dossier that must be prepared, and the number of individuals involved in the process had a significant impact on how onerous the evaluation task was perceived to be for all involved.

The nature of the materials the full-time non-tenure-track faculty are required to compile as part of the evaluation process varies by institution and, at some of the larger institutions, by department. A liberal arts college we studied requires the faculty who are up for reappointment or promotion to compile a dossier. The dossier is to include the candidate's statement of professional goals and achievements, a complete curriculum vitae, copies of annual faculty reports, the chair or director's evaluation and recommendation, a summary of student evaluations, and any merit evaluations. A master's-level institution with a very strong emphasis on teaching requires an up-to-date c.v., a self-assessment statement, a list of all courses taught, original copies of student evaluations of courses, a list of honors papers and theses supervised, and copies of any publications the candidate has authored. The second institution appears to emphasize the primary instructional role of the faculty in the information considered necessary for reappointment or promotion, although it does not overlook the fact that the non-tenure-track faculty may be involved in scholarly activities.

Research universities are more likely to require their full-time non-tenure track faculty to provide evidence of scholarly productivity in addition to their instructional achievements for evaluation purposes. The research expectations appear to be highest for faculty in certain disciplines who were hired with qualifications deemed to be equivalent to those of the tenure-track hires.

The following policy for evaluation of full-time non-track faculty at one research university also highlights the role that service to the institution may play in evaluation for promotion:

> Evaluation of individual faculty/instructors in the unit for reappointment are [sic]to be made on the basis of demonstrated competence in the field and demonstrated ability in teaching and other assigned duties which may include University co-curricular and community service. Reappointment to the senior rank requires, in addition, service of exceptional value to the University.

We found, however, that most institutional policies do not explicitly address the service role of non-tenure-eligible faculty or how their service is evaluated.

The responsibility for conducting the evaluations of full-time non-tenure track faculty generally falls to department chairs, especially at the time of annual reviews for salary decisions. At several institutions, the evaluations also involve select committees, or all tenured faculty within the department, when the review is for contract renewal or promotion in rank. In one research university the evaluations are conducted by department chairs in conjunction with a faculty review committee. At most research universities the authority for making decisions about reappointing non-tenure-track faculty members resides with the dean but generally requires the concurrence of the chief academic officer. At most smaller institutions the authority rests with the chief academic officer or the president, depending on the academic structure of the institution.

We heard very little during our campus visits about the use of faculty evaluations for professional development purposes. Although several department chairs stated that they utilized the results of evaluations to mentor their full-time non-tenure-track faculty, such efforts appeared to be exceptions rather than the rule.

Our interviews with faculty and administrators revealed that constant attention must be paid to both the criteria used in evaluating full-time term-appointment faculty and the process of evaluation. The full-time non-tenure-track faculty we interviewed consistently stated that the criteria for evaluation for salary increases, reappointment, and promotion need to be directly related to the job for which they have been hired. Many of these faculty criticized discrepancies in the evaluation process, such as being hired to teach a heavy load of lower-division undergraduate courses, with no expectation for research and service, and then being evaluated on the same criteria as tenure-track faculty. Among another cohort of full-time non-tenure-track faculty, concern centered around the perfunctory nature of their evaluations. They believed that this contributed to a lack of respect from their tenured colleagues because it sent the message that term faculty were not important enough to be evaluated rigorously.

Faculty evaluation is an important component of quality control in higher education. The diverse, sometimes erratic, approaches to evaluating the performance of full-time faculty in non-tenure-track positions concern us. We believe that colleges and universities should have in place clear, consistent policies and procedures for the evaluation of all faculty, including those off the tenure track.

Support for Professional Development

Support for continued professional development is a fundamental requirement if faculty are to remain current in their disciplinary fields and continue contributing to the academic vitality of their institutions. Table 3.4 shows the difference in the proportion of institutions that support selected professional development activities and functions for full-time non-tenure-track faculty as compared with their tenured and tenure-track colleagues. Across all areas the tenured and tenure-track faculty have greater access to professional development support than do the non-tenure-track faculty. The largest area of discrepancy is the provision of sabbatical leaves. Only 22 percent of the institutions we surveyed provide sabbatical support for non-tenure-track faculty as compared with 89 percent that provide sabbaticals for tenured faculty.

We believe it is important to point out that the survey data shown in this table are not consistent with the institutional support for the professional development of full-time non-tenure-track faculty described by many of our interview subjects. In our discussions with full-time non-tenure-track

Table 3.4 Survey Institutions Offering Support to Full-Time Faculty
for Selected Professional Development Activities and Functions

Activities	Tenured and Tenure-Track (% institutions)	Non-Tenure-Track (% institutions)
Professional travel	96.4	79.1
Association or conference fees	81.9	75.6
Sabbatical leave	89.2	22.1
Training to improve teaching or research	88.0	79.1
Retraining for high-demand fields	31.4	17.4

Note: Based on responses from 84 (35 public and 49 private) colleges and universities.

faculty and administrators at the majority of campuses, we found less support for professional travel, association dues, and conference fees for non-tenure-eligible faculty than these survey findings suggest is available.

A common complaint from both the tenured and non-tenure-track faculty was that the level of financial support for participation in professional meetings was so low that meeting expenses frequently required a significant personal outlay. We learned that support for the full-time term-appointment faculty to attend professional meetings was often at the discretion of the department chair, while tenured or tenure-track faculty had a guaranteed level of funding. In the case of several site visit institutions, support for full-time non-tenure-track faculty came from the balance in discretionary accounts after the funds for tenured faculty had been allocated.

Eligibility for professional leaves or sabbatical leaves is a "benefit" that differs for full-time tenured and non-tenure-eligible faculty members at the majority of institutions. Among faculty respondents to NSOPF-93, 65 percent of the tenured, 45 percent of tenure-track, and 32 percent of full-time non-tenure-track faculty stated that they were eligible for sabbatical leaves. At many of the institutions we surveyed, full-time non-tenure-track faculty are not eligible for leaves, while at others the number of years of service required for eligibility varies by tenure status. The following policy statement presents a rare leave policy where full-time non-tenure-track faculty actually have a more generous leave benefit than do tenure-track faculty:

> A tenured faculty member is eligible for a one year sabbatical at half salary or a half year sabbatical at full salary in his/her seventh year at [this institution], or in the seventh year since the last sabbatical.
> A faculty member with [Faculty Development Leave] status is eligi-

ble for one semester FDL at full salary or a one year FDL at half salary in his/her fifth year at [this institution], or fifth year since the last FDL. (From the policy statement of a private master's-level institution)

The above policy statement presents a sharp contrast in terms of eligibility for the full-time contract faculty members (FDL faculty) and tenure-track faculty at this institution. The non-track faculty are eligible for this leave opportunity more frequently (every five years) than are their tenured colleagues (every seven years). A dean at the institution sees this program as a commitment to professional renewal of faculty, one that is in keeping with the university commitment to "teaching writ large" as the priority mission.

A more typical policy on the eligibility of non-tenure-track full-time faculty for sabbatical leaves is set forth in the following statement, from the collective bargaining agreement of a doctoral institution:

A full-time faculty member with at least six (6) academic years of teaching service at the University may be granted professional leave with pay not to exceed one (1) year to engage in further education, research, or other program of professional involvement that can contribute directly to the improvement and development of the faculty member and the University.
Eligibility: (a) The faculty member *must have tenure* (emphasis added) effective as of the date of the beginning of the professional leave.

This more traditional practice of making sabbaticals available only to tenure-track faculty appears to reflect a commitment to investing in the professional growth and vitality of long-term faculty rather than of faculty who are viewed more as short-term staff members because of the limited time frame of their contracts.

Access to professional or sabbatical leaves is a point of concern for the majority of full-time non-tenure-eligible faculty with whom we spoke. Support for professional growth is especially important to those who have had long-term employment with their institutions. The fact that a large proportion of these faculty carry heavier teaching loads than their tenure-track colleagues raises their concern with burnout and being able to remain current in their fields. Administrators at the institution that provided the opportunity for a professional development leave every five years for full-time non-tenure-track faculty felt that the institution benefited from its leave program because faculty utilized their leaves for program development and instructional development activities. Most institutions, however, do not invest this heavily in the professional growth of their non-tenure-track faculty.

Support for training to improve teaching for full-time faculty in non-tenure-track positions was most often provided through campus teaching centers that are open to all faculty. At a number of institutions, special workshops and training sessions on the use of technology are an important part of this effort. In a very few instances, institutions provided financial support in the form of summer grants for full-time non-tenure-track faculty to work on improving their teaching.

An area in which full-time faculty in non-tenure-eligible positions felt a large degree of neglect was the lack of support for research endeavors. The full-time non-tenure-track faculty at research universities were especially troubled by this deficiency when summer research grants were available for tenure-track faculty. Many of the non-tenure-track faculty we interviewed also have research agendas and desire to remain current in their disciplines to benefit the students they teach. In particular, faculty in the sciences were critical of their institutions on this topic.

In general, non-tenure-eligible full-time faculty receive less support for professional development than do tenure-class faculty. Often the funding they receive for professional travel is lower or less reliable than the funding their tenure-eligible colleagues can count on. Much of this support is awarded on an ad hoc, case-by-case basis at the discretion of department chairs. Sabbaticals and research support provide the clearest demarcation between non-tenure-track and tenure-track faculty. With only a few exceptions, most colleges and universities appear to prefer to invest limited resources in the faculty most likely to have a long-term relationship with the institution.

Given that many full-time non-tenure-track faculty work at their institutions for many years, policies and traditions that arbitrarily restrict professional development support are short-sighted, if not downright harmful. We believe that professional development support should be available to full-time faculty off the tenure track. The level of this support, of course, should be consistent with the faculty member's role and period of service to the institution.

Academic Freedom

Every member of the faculty is entitled to due process and academic freedom as established by academic tradition and the constitutions and laws of the United States and the state of [. . .] and as amplified by resolutions of the Board of Regents. (From the policy statement of a research university)

Statements such as the above can be found in faculty policy documents in nearly every American college and university. For most of this century, academic freedom has been protected by a tenure system that guarantees due process to permanent faculty before they can be dismissed for cause. But how comfortable do full-time non-tenure-track faculty feel about their academic freedom? What we found was a diversity of experiences and opinions, not a uniform response. Most of the full-time non-tenure-track faculty we interviewed never raised the academic freedom issue. Hence, we concluded that for most, academic freedom is not a major concern. Of those who discussed the subject, some felt their academic freedom was secure. Others felt vulnerable and hesitant to provoke controversy. A social science faculty member told us that at her liberal arts institution there is no difference in the academic freedom of full-time non-tenure-track and tenured faculty. On the other hand, we talked with numerous non-tenure-eligible faculty who questioned their freedom to act as fully autonomous professionals.

When we broached the question about academic freedom for full-time non-tenure-track faculty, concerns arose in two areas of their professional responsibility. The first was freedom in teaching and scholarship. Second was freedom to participate fully in the shared governance process. A full-time non-tenure-track religion professor at a liberal arts college, for example, described her reluctance to bring up controversial religious issues in class because there might be consequences if she offended religiously conservative students. A professor of theater and dance noted that at her university "academic freedom is a concern in some fields . . . like art, history, and political science [where controversy sometimes erupts]." A lecturer in modern languages at a research university described pressure in his department to employ the instructional methodology of a particular linguist. "I feel paranoid," he observed. To object, he suggested, was to put oneself in a dangerous position. The chair of the English department of a research university described a more subtle impediment to academic freedom. The chair discussed a lecturer he knows who is reluctant to innovate or experiment in the classroom. The lecturer's concern is that if he gets one bad set of evaluations his career will be at risk. By virtue of their permanent status, this is not a concern tenured faculty share with their full-time non-tenure-track counterparts. The incentive for the non-tenure-eligible faculty to behave conservatively can pervade the scholarly domain as well. A full-time contract professor in a professional field is a case in point. "I am going to stay away from religion and ethical issues such as the right to die and the role of religion in parental decisionmaking," she observed. "Scholarship is more apt to be questioned when writing in such areas."

Somewhat surprisingly, academic freedom in teaching and scholarship was noted less frequently than concerns about freedom in the shared governance domain. More of the full-time faculty in non-tenure-track positions that we interviewed expressed concern about their freedom to participate without reservation in the planning, policy development, and politics of their programs and institutions. For example, a full-time non-tenure-track social science faculty member at a master's-level university told us she feels no constraints when speaking within her field, but she does feel that her ability to speak out on her institution's administration is limited. A colleague at the same university supported this observation, noting that "only long-term tenured professors are the ones raising reservations about a new program proposal that is sailing through. Privately, people are expressing a lot of concern [about the proposal]." A senior humanities lecturer (non-tenure-track) at a research university spoke of a similar constraint. She noted that some lecturers are reticent to speak out on some issues, perhaps because their colleagues have to vote on their reappointment. A director of faculty development and humanities professor at a research university captured the plight of many full-time non-tenure-track professors in a succinct but graphic way. "If I know I need to live in [this area], you have tremendous implicit power over me. If you do things 'ass backwards,' I am not apt to tell you. [Essentially,] you muzzle me."

It is a challenge to paint a clear picture of the academic freedom concerns of full-time non-tenure-track faculty. The issues vary considerably with the context and culture of the academic workplace and the different disciplines. We heard relatively few concerns about academic freedom in institutions with a long tradition of protecting free inquiry. With regard to academic freedom, a dean at a research university told us, "We would treat lecturers just as we would other faculty. [This university] has gone the extra mile to defend academic freedom historically." At some institutions where an individual or an influential group can wield great power, the academic freedom situation may be less clear-cut. On some campuses we visited we heard that a powerful president, politically aligned board, or specific religious heritage may place limits on the freedom of faculty in non-tenure-track positions, or at least make them especially cautious.

We did not learn that the academic freedom of full-time non-tenure-track faculty is more sacred in some disciplines than in others. We did learn, however, that some disciplines may, by virtue of their subject matter, provoke more controversy than others and, hence, make faculty in such fields sensitive and anxious. Some full-time term-appointment faculty in the arts, humanities, and social sciences expressed reluctance to address controversial issues in their teaching and scholarship because it might lead to the termination of their contracts. In contrast, some faculty we interviewed in applied and professional fields like business and computer science seemed less concerned about sticking their necks out professionally. The distinguishing factor may be the ready availability of career alternatives. While full-time term-appointment faculty in professional and applied areas may automatically see viable career alternatives outside the academy, faculty with similar appointments in traditional arts and science fields may avoid risks and experimentation, because they feel personally dependent on the non-tenure-track position they hold.

Clearly, the academic freedom issue as it relates to non-tenure-track faculty is neither uniform nor easy to explain. From our conversations on twelve campuses across the country, academic freedom seems to be less of a concern when a culture and tradition that values professional autonomy is coupled with clear policies and procedures to protect the academic freedom of all faculty. Institutional leadership is a key variable in this formula. At two site visit campuses, the full-time non-tenure-track faculty stated forcefully that their level of comfort with institutional support for their academic freedom was directly related to their confidence in the campus leadership, especially the president. Such comfort was tempered by the recognition that a change in leadership would require a reassessment of that comfort level and their satisfaction with their non-tenure-track appointment.

Academic freedom is a fundamental value of higher education. Our investigation revealed that the academic freedom of most full-time non-tenure-track faculty seems to be respected on their campuses. Often, however, it is not buttressed by clear policies and procedures to guarantee the academic freedom of these faculty. All colleges and universities that employ faculty in non-tenure-eligible positions should take steps to ensure that their academic freedom is secure.

Three Models of Full-Time Non-Tenure-Track Faculty Employment

We summarize differing approaches to FTNTT faculty employment with three models. In developing these models we recognize that institutional policies affecting these positions exist on a continuum. At one extreme are institutions that employ faculty in full-time non-tenure-track positions with minimal policies articulating their terms and conditions of employment. At the other extreme are institutions with clearly articulated policies governing such appointments. Typically, these policies are comprehensive and progressive and address the major dimensions of the professional lives of faculty in positions not eligible for tenure. In addition, the policies of some institutions serve to isolate and segregate the non-tenure-track faculty on the periphery of the academic community while the policies of other institutions serve to integrate these faculty and move them into the mainstream of the institution. Most institutions fall somewhere between these two poles. Therefore, our models should not be viewed as completely discrete. There is overlap across their margins.

THE MARGINALIZED MODEL

Under this model the institutional intent is to utilize the full-time non-tenure-track faculty as a cost-saving resource and to maintain maximum staffing flexibility. Faculty hired into positions under this model are not well integrated into the institutional community. As marginalized faculty they have limited status and respect within the institution. Typically, they lack a voice, even at the department level, in governance activities and receive little if any support for professional development. They are expected to fulfill their responsibilities and be satisfied with their role. They are not expected to build a career at the institution. As a number of full-time non-tenure-eligible faculty members at several of the site visit institutions told us, "We are not considered to be real faculty." This model has the following characteristics:

— Faculty are hired on annual contracts, usually renewable for a maximum of four to six years. Some may serve for longer periods but with constant uncertainty about contract renewal.
— One title or rank is utilized, such as instructor or lecturer, with no other ranks available that could provide a reward for professional achievement.
— These faculty members carry heavier teaching loads than tenure-track faculty in the same department or institution and have little time to perform other professional tasks such as research and service.
— There is limited support for professional development in terms of funding for professional travel, leaves, etc.
— These full-time faculty members have limited or no voting privileges on departmental or institutional matters.

— These faculty members often receive lower salaries than comparably qualified tenure-track faculty.
— As full-time faculty they do receive full fringe benefits.
— There is annual evaluation of the teaching effectiveness of the full-time non-tenure-track faculty.

Essentially, these policies for non-tenure-track appointments create a marginalized, disadvantaged, and second-class faculty when compared to the policies affecting tenured and tenure-track faculty.

THE INTEGRATED MODEL

In the integrated model the institutional intent is to use full-time non-tenure-track faculty as a way of maintaining some long-term staffing flexibility, achieving cost control, or accessing specialized faculty resources. This is accomplished by hiring personnel with distinctive skills and interests that will enhance program offerings, complement the efforts and qualifications of tenure-track faculty, and contribute to cost control through filling more limited faculty roles than their tenure-track colleagues. The faculty members hired into positions under this model have the potential to be more fully integrated into the culture of the institution than is possible under the Marginalized Model. Tenured faculty continue to be the dominant faculty cohort on campus, but policies in this model integrate the faculty in full-time non-tenure-eligible positions more readily into the institutional culture because these faculty have the opportunity to be more involved in the institutional community and are valued for their contributions and abilities. Although the professional status and contributions of the full-time non-tenure-track faculty are respected under this model, the primary focus regarding these faculty is on institutional needs and not on the professional career development needs of the faculty member. The following are characteristics of this model:

— Faculty members are hired initially on annual full-time contracts for a probationary period (three to six years). A successful probationary period leads to a series of multiyear contracts. The schedule for notification of reappointment or termination is in general compliance with the practice recommended by the American Association of University Professors.
— Faculty rank and titles may be the same as tenure-track faculty, or a separate set of ranks and titles may be available such as lecturer and senior lecturer. Potential for promotion is available.

— Full-time non-tenure-track faculty may have comparable or heavier teaching loads than tenure-track faculty. Likewise, they may also carry specified administrative duties in their program area.

— Support for professional development is provided in the form of funding for professional travel. In some cases there is eligibility for sabbaticals or professional leaves and funds to support scholarship.

— Voting privileges may be available on departmental and institutional matters. Potential for service on committees is provided at many institutions.

— Salaries may be lower, comparable, or in some cases higher than salaries for tenure-track faculty with comparable qualifications.

— Full fringe benefits are provided.

— Evaluation of faculty is structured and consistent with the nature of the contract system in effect.

Institutions employing the Integrated Model view the full-time non-tenure-track faculty as different from tenure-eligible faculty but attempt to engage them in the full range of faculty activities and treat them as fully functioning professionals.

THE ALTERNATIVE CAREER TRACK MODEL

The Alternative Career Track Model has many of the characteristics of the Integrated Model. The institutional objectives of the model may include cost savings and staffing flexibility but have the potential to go beyond these goals. This model contains policies that potentially offer a complete alternative to tenure. Although a tenure system continues at most institutions employing this model, the contract system is designed to be attractive enough to serve as a viable career alternative at the institution offering the plan. In addition to policies that are designed to meet specific institutional needs, policies within this model address the professional development and career progression of the full-time non-tenure-track faculty. This comprehensive approach to faculty employment has the potential to elevate the respect, status, and influence of the full-time non-tenure-eligible faculty in the eyes of their tenure-eligible faculty colleagues, students, and professional colleagues on other campuses. This model includes the following attributes:

— Full-time non-tenure-track faculty members are initially hired on annual or multiple-year contracts. After successful completion of a probationary period of three to six years, multiple-year contracts are awarded. These contracts may range from three to ten years, based on the system implemented.

— Either the title and rank system is the same as for tenure-track faculty or a separate but clearly articulated career progression is established (e.g., lecturer, senior lecturer, principal lecturer).
— Teaching load and faculty roles are comparable between full-time non-tenure-track and tenure-track faculty.
— There is extensive support for the professional development of non-tenure-track faculty, comparable to or greater than the support for tenure-track faculty (such as eligibility for more frequent sabbatical leaves).
— Full-time non-tenure-track faculty have full voting privileges at departmental and institutional levels (votes on the award of tenure are the only exception.)
— Full-time non-tenure-track faculty have salaries comparable to or higher than tenure-track faculty.
— Full-time non-tenure-track faculty have full fringe benefits.
— Full-time non-tenure-track faculty evaluation procedures are coordinated with contract system renewal decision points.

Faculty employed on the Alternative Career Track Model function as full-fledged members of their institutional community. With the exception of tenure, they are equivalent to their tenured colleagues in all respects. Where this model is fully implemented, full-time term-appointment and tenure-track faculty appear to enjoy equal status, respect, and influence.

These models should be viewed as points on a continuum, since in actuality we found no single institution that offered policies that encompassed all of the characteristics that we attribute to each model. However, several institutions had very comprehensive and supportive policies for full-time non-tenure-track faculty. In Chapter 6 we present examples of policies and programs that we feel have the necessary attributes to regulate and successfully support the employment of full-time non-tenure-track faculty.

A review of institutional policies and discussion with a cross-section of faculty and administrators indicated to us that there is a wide disparity in the completeness and uniformity of policies developed to set the terms and conditions of employment for full-time faculty in non-tenure-track positions. It appears that the hiring of FTNTT faculty at many institutions is not matched by the development of policies to adequately address the implications of such employment conditions for either the institution or the faculty they hire. In many cases, although the institutions have been employing faculty in such positions for a number of years and these personnel are carrying important instructional and related responsibilities for the institution, only passing recognition of the terms and conditions of their employment is set forth in policy documents. In several institutions' policies, for example, reference to the protection of academic freedom is made, but the documents appear to be primarily protective of the rights of tenured faculty rather than pre-tenure and non-tenure-track faculty.

4 Who Are the Full-Time Non-Tenure-Track Faculty?

Bruce M. Gansneder, Elizabeth P. Harper, and Roger G. Baldwin

Stereotypes abound about full-time non-tenure-track faculty: they are underqualified, exploited, underappreciated; they are gypsy faculty who travel from campus to campus, overworked and underpaid; they are professorial "wannabes" who could not quite make the grade. Gappa and Leslie (1993) called part-time non-tenure-track faculty the "invisible faculty"; one of our study participants referred to full-time non-tenure-track faculty as the "ghost faculty."

The purpose of this chapter is to use NSOPF-93 data supplemented by selected other reports, our institutional survey, and interview data collected in site visits to twelve institutions to describe full-time non-tenure-track faculty at four-year colleges and universities. We explore who they are, their educational attainment, where they work, what they teach, their productivity, their professional status, and their job satisfaction. We show that full-time non-tenure-track faculty usually fill one of four different primary roles: teacher, researcher, administrator, or other academic professional. Understanding these four different FTNTT faculty types may provide a truer picture of who they are.

Almost one-fifth of all full-time four-year college and university faculty who teach some credit courses are non-tenure-track. Full-time non-tenure-track faculty differ from their tenured and tenure-track colleagues in several

Bruce Gansneder is professor of education at the University of Virginia. Elizabeth Harper is a doctoral student at the Center for the Study of Higher Education, University of Virginia.

significant ways, but there are also many areas of commonality. In addition, full-time faculty off the tenure track are a diverse group themselves, with striking differences by discipline and type of institution, in their qualifications, in the work that they do, and in their career progression and stability.

According to data from the 1993 National Study of Postsecondary Faculty, in 1992 there were 904,935 higher education faculty in the United States. This number includes both full-time and part-time faculty. Over one-third of these faculty (383,616) were employed full-time in four-year institutions and had at least some instructional responsibility (for credit). The majority of these faculty members (220,609, or 57.5%) held tenured positions. Another one-fourth (93,113, or 24.3%) were in tenure-track positions, and slightly less than one-fifth (69,894, or 18.2%) were in non-tenure-track positions. It is these nearly 70,000 full-time non-tenure-eligible faculty in four-year institutions that we describe in this chapter. These faculty are of special importance because they hold positions that are similar in many ways to those held by tenured faculty. Also, virtually all of these faculty fill important roles and provide vital services to higher education.

Social and Demographic Characteristics

As seen in table 4.1, full-time non-tenure-track faculty were somewhat younger than their tenured colleagues and older than tenure-track faculty. Fewer than half of minority faculty were tenured, and almost one-fourth were full-time faculty in non-tenure-eligible positions. By contrast, almost three-fifths of whites were tenured, with another fifth in non-tenure-eligible positions. Among minority groups, Asians were the most likely to be tenured, while Hispanics were the least likely.

Using NSOPF-88 data, the American Association of University Professors reported that in 1987, 40 to 50 percent of all full-time term appointments were filled by women. The AAUP also reported that from 1975 to

Table 4.1 Demographic Characteristics of Full-Time Faculty, 1992

	Tenured	Tenure-Track	Non-Tenure-Track
Average age	58.2	40.9	44.1
% Female	20.8	39.0	47.8
% Married	80.0	70.0	70.0
% White	90.0	81.0	85.0

Source: NSOPF-93.

1985 the percentage of women on the tenure track rose from 18.3 to 20.7 percent while the percentage of full-time non-tenure-eligible women rose from 33.6 to 40.3 percent (AAUP 1995b).

Cecilia Ottinger and Robin Sikula (1993) reported that almost half the doctorates awarded to U.S. citizens in 1991 went to women, an increase of 25 percent from 1981. This advance is not reflected, however, in the percentage of women holding tenured faculty positions in colleges and universities. Even though the proportion of women faculty rose from 27 to 32 percent during the decade from 1981 to 1991, women were overwhelmingly clustered in the lowest ranks of full-time faculty. The proportion of tenure-track women was almost twice what it was among tenured faculty (suggesting that more women will be tenured in the future), but women still made up only about one-third of the total tenure-track faculty. Although only 30 percent of full-time faculty are women, they hold 48 percent of the non-tenure-track positions. These statistics suggest that women are disproportionately represented among the lower faculty ranks. In particular, women are heavily represented among the full-time non-tenure-track faculty.

Finkelstein, Seal, and Schuster (1998) found that among junior faculty (those hired within the last seven years), men were twice as likely as women to have been awarded tenure. The gender gap in tenure among junior faculty was most pronounced in research, doctoral, and comprehensive universities. Among program areas, the biggest gender differences in tenure rates among junior faculty occurred in the humanities, where 54 percent of new-cohort hires were women, but more than twice as many recently hired men as women were tenured (32% vs. 15%).

Many of the full-time non-tenure-track faculty we interviewed were conscious of the atypically high representation of women. For example, a senior lecturer at a research university noted that her institution has a "gender problem . . . Most lecturers are women." We learned at a doctoral university that most of the people filling full-time term-appointment faculty slots were place-bound, including a number of women whose husbands worked in the university's metropolitan area. A woman we interviewed at a master's-level university described herself as a "trailing spouse." She reported that her husband was here, so she was not going anywhere. A department chair at a baccalaureate institution stated that some women who occupy full-time non-tenure-eligible positions have opted for the "mommy track." In this chair's view, full-time non-tenure-track positions meet the needs of some women. Clearly a variety of reasons account for the larger representation of women in full-time non-tenure-track than tenure-track or tenured positions. Family goals and responsibilities, personal preferences, dual-career constraints, rigid tenure policies, and perhaps male-dominated disciplinary cultures help to account for the overrepresentation of women in full-time positions that do not lead to tenure.

Reflecting the drive for equal employment opportunity in recent decades, there was more racial and ethnic diversity among tenure-track and full-time non-tenure-track faculty than among tenured faculty. In their study of hiring and employment patterns, Deborah J. Carter and Eileen M. O'Brien (1993) found that the growth in full-time non-tenure-track hiring from 1981 to 1991 was greater for faculty of color than for white faculty. While faculty of color increased by 40 percent during the decade among the tenured and tenure-track faculty, they increased by 87 percent in the full-time non-tenure-track cohort. During the same period, the increase for white faculty was 4 percent for tenured and tenure-track faculty and 36 percent for full-time non-tenure-track faculty. Among faculty of color, the non-tenure-track increase was greater for women (93%) than for men (83%). Similarly, the full-time non-tenure-track increase was also larger for white women (59%) than for white men (23%). Like women, minority faculty were clustered in the lowest faculty ranks and were less likely to be tenured than their white counterparts. It is obvious that the percentage of minority faculty in full-time-non-tenure-track positions has increased much more than the percentage of white faculty in these positions. In an era when higher education has been trying to increase the number of minority faculty in traditional positions, the numbers suggest that this effort has not been as successful as we would have liked. The same could be said for higher education's efforts to create gender equity within the faculty ranks.

Degree Status, Career Origins, Rank, and Length of Time in Current Position

According to NSOPF-93, two-thirds of all full-time faculty in four-year institutions held a doctoral degree (table 4.2). Three-fourths of tenured fac-

Table 4.2 Full-Time Faculty with Doctorate and Time in Current Position

	Tenured (%)	Tenure-Track (%)	Non-Tenure-Track (%)
With doctorate	75.0	66.0	33.0
7 or more years	81.6	12.0	36.3
Fewer than 7 years	18.4	88.0	63.7

Source: NSOPF-93.

ulty and two-thirds of tenure-track faculty had the doctorate. In contrast, the highest degrees of full-time non-tenure-track faculty are more varied: about one third have the doctorate; over 60 percent hold a master's or professional degree; 5 percent have only bachelor's degrees.

Using NSOPF-88 data, Gappa and Leslie (1993, 31) found that 28.5 percent of part-time faculty had a doctorate or professional degree, 42.7 percent had a master's degree, and nearly 29 percent had a bachelor's or other degree as their highest degree. As a group, full-time non-tenure-track faculty appear to have somewhat more advanced educational credentials than part-time faculty. (This inference is made cautiously, however, because the comparative data come from surveys taken at two different times.) Full-time term-appointment faculty as a group, however, have lower educational credentials than faculty on the tenure track.

In 1992, most tenured and tenure-track faculty held jobs in a four-year college or university before obtaining their current position, but slightly less than half (46%) of full-time non-tenure-track faculty had a similar background. We learned from our interviews that full-time term-appointment faculty came to their institutions from a wide variety of employment settings. Full-time term-appointment faculty in the traditional arts and sciences most often came to their current position from a temporary teaching appointment elsewhere or a postdoctoral or other type of position within academia. In contrast, full-time non-tenure-track faculty in professional and applied fields came to higher education from more diverse backgrounds. Those who came from outside the academic world were most likely to have worked in health care, business, law, or education.

For example, a senior lecturer in chemistry at a research university had previously worked within higher education as a postdoctoral fellow in chemistry and as director of undergraduate services in chemistry. This rather mainstream academic career path contrasts sharply with the full-time non-tenure-eligible professor of marketing and advertising who came to campus directly from fourteen years in the advertising field, or the full-time term-appointment professor in science and technology who spent ten years in industry to earn credibility in engineering. The backgrounds and credentials of the full-time non-tenure-track faculty we met on our campus visits were more diverse than the standard academic route from graduate school directly to a faculty appointment at a college or university.

With regard to work history, full-time non-tenure-track faculty again seem to fit somewhere between tenure-eligible faculty and part-time faculty. Gappa and Leslie (1993) observed that part-time faculty "come from extraordinarily varied and interesting work lives" (45). Similarly, we found many full-time term-appointment faculty with rich and varied prior employment experiences both in and out of higher education. Many other FTNTT faculty, however, follow traditional academic career patterns as closely as they can, given their lack of a tenurable position.

As would be expected, the NSOPF-93 survey revealed that more than 80 percent of tenured faculty had been at their current institution seven or more years, while 87 percent of the tenure-track faculty had been there less than seven years. Interestingly, the distribution of time in their current position for full-time non-tenure-track faculty was bimodal. More than one-third of full-time non-tenure-track faculty had been in their current position seven or more years, but 42 percent had been there less than three years. Gappa and Leslie (1993) reported a similar bimodal pattern for part-time faculty. According to their analysis of national data, slightly more than half of all part-time faculty had worked fewer than four years at their current institution. On the other hand, one-third had seven or more years of work at their present institution. These figures belie the notion that faculty in non-tenure-track appointments are universally transient or temporary. Clearly, some are, but others serve their institutions for long periods.

Our campus visits uncovered this bimodal pattern as well. Many of the full-time non-tenure-track faculty we met, especially at large universities, had been in their positions relatively briefly. In some cases their positions had a fixed term and were not renewable. Occupants of these positions often viewed them as steppingstones to other academic positions or as way stations until they could find more stable employment. In contrast, we also interviewed a number of full-time non-tenure-track faculty with many years of service to their college or university. We met one FTNTT professor in biology who had been at his institution for thirty-one years. Although he had the longest record of service among the full-time non-tenure-track faculty we interviewed, we met many others with twenty or more years of professional work at their institutions. Clearly, many full-time faculty in non-tenure-eligible positions are filling long-term needs. They play important, although sometimes little-recognized, roles that are not covered by tenured and tenure-track faculty.

Since tenure is often associated with promotion to associate professor, almost all tenured faculty were either associate or full professors, while the majority of full-time tenure-track faculty were assistant professors. About one-third of the full-time term-appointment faculty were either lecturers or instructors, and almost three-fourths held ranks below associate professor (fig. 4.1). It appears that few full-time non-tenure-track faculty progress beyond the rank of assistant professor.

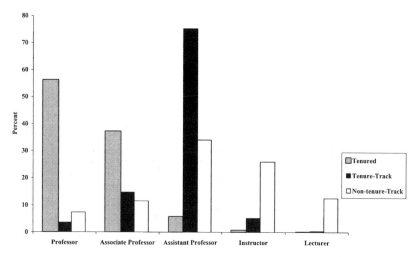

Figure 4.1.   Full-Time Faculty within Rank, by Tenure Status

Our campus visits revealed a wide range of titles for full-time non-tenure-track faculty. In addition to lecturer and the standard ranks of assistant, associate, and full professor, we met full-time non-tenure-track faculty with titles such as visiting professor, adjunct professor, program coordinator, laboratory instructor, and educational specialist.

Where Do Full-Time Non-Tenure-Track Faculty Work?

While non-tenure-track appointments made up 18.2 percent of full-time faculty in four-year institutions in 1992–93, their distribution varied by type and control of institution. Proportionally non-tenure-track faculty made up a smaller share of full-time faculty in public than in private institutions. They were about one-fourth of full-time faculty in baccalaureate and private doctoral and research institutions. Among public institutions, the full-time non-tenure-track faculty were most prevalent at doctoral institutions and less likely to be found at master's-level institutions (fig. 4.2).

These employment patterns are difficult to interpret. In many cases, private institutions may be free to add academic staff without placing them in the tenure stream. In contrast, at some public institutions the hiring of faculty off the tenure track may be restricted by specific personnel policies or political considerations. In addition, the availability of graduate assistants at larger public universities with extensive graduate programs may reduce the need for full-time non-tenure-track appointments. The greater use of

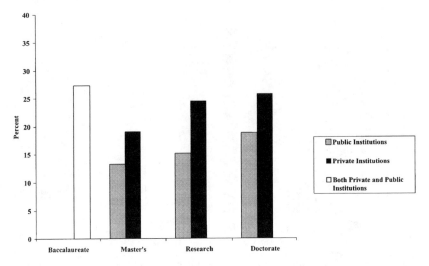

Figure 4.2. Full-Time Non-Tenure-Track Faculty, by Type of Institution

full-time non-tenure-eligible faculty at baccalaureate institutions may reflect the frequent employment of individuals who lack the terminal degree at schools without graduate programs.

What Do Full-Time Non-Tenure-Track Faculty Teach?

The number of full-time term-appointment faculty varies greatly across programs and disciplines (fig. 4.3). Among broad program areas at the time of the 1993 National Study of Postsecondary Faculty, engineering had the smallest proportion of full-time non-tenure-track faculty. Health sciences had both the largest percentage of full-time non-tenure-track faculty and the smallest percentage of tenured faculty. It was the only area in which fewer than half the faculty were tenured. Education was second to health sciences in the percentage of full-time non-tenure-track faculty.

Within program areas some interesting differences emerged among specific disciplines. In health sciences, nursing, traditionally a female field, had a higher proportion of full-time term-appointment faculty than any other field. Within the humanities, English and foreign languages employed approximately twice as many full-time non-tenure-track faculty as did history or philosophy. Anecdotal evidence suggests that this is because of the large

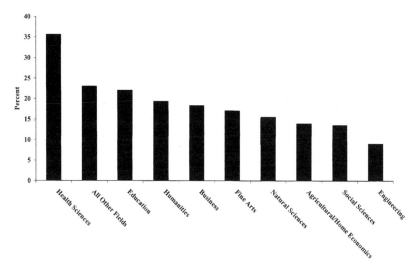

Figure 4.3.   Full-Time Non-Tenure-Track Faculty, by Program Area

numbers of full-time term-appointment faculty who teach beginning composition and language courses and perhaps also because these have traditionally been female-dominated fields. Within the natural sciences, about one-fourth of computer sciences faculty were in full-time non-tenure-eligible positions, compared with less than 10 percent of physical science faculty. Within other fields, about 22 percent of the faculty were in this type of position.

These differential patterns of employing full-time term-appointment faculty reflect distinctive educational arrangements and differing labor market circumstances across various disciplines. In the humanities, where many full-time non-tenure-track faculty teach beginning courses in modern languages and English composition, there is widespread belief that introductory-level instruction does not require a research-oriented degree. Hence, these instructors often lack the terminal degree, which usually is a minimum requirement for a tenure-track appointment at most higher education institutions. Similarly, in very competitive disciplinary fields such as computer science, colleges and universities sometimes must hire master's-level faculty into full-time non-tenure-track positions because they are unable to compete with the salaries that doctorally prepared personnel can command outside of higher education.

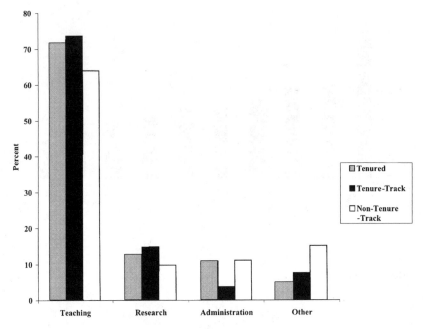

Figure 4.4. Primary Activity of Full-Time Faculty, by Tenure Status

What Is Their Primary Activity?

While two-thirds of full-term non-tenure-track faculty reported teaching as their primary activity, 11 percent of those who taught at least one class described their primary focus as administration and 15 percent described their primary activity as other professional activities* (fig. 4.4). Only 10 percent considered themselves primarily researchers. By contrast, more than 70 percent of tenured and tenure-track faculty reported that their primary activity was teaching, and another 12 to 15 percent classified themselves as primarily researchers. More than 70 percent of full-time non-tenure-track faculty taught only undergraduate students as compared to about 60 percent of tenured and tenure-track faculty.

Full-time non-tenure-track faculty reported that they worked fewer hours a week than tenure-track and tenured faculty; however, they spent

*Other professional activities include technical activities (e.g., programmer, technician, chemist, engineer), clinical service, community or public service, sabbatical leave, and performers and artists-in-residence.

more hours each week teaching than tenured and tenure-track faculty, and they devoted a larger percentage of their time to teaching and advising. This probably reflects the narrower role definition of many full-time non-tenure-track faculty. Frequently they are hired exclusively to teach or to teach and fill other specialized duties. Full-time non-tenure-track faculty may work less than tenure-track faculty because they often are not expected to perform at the level of tenure-eligible faculty in areas like research and service. Most full-time non-tenure-track faculty do not fill the same range of teaching, research, and service roles as their tenure-eligible colleagues.

Tenured faculty taught fewer classes than did full-time non-tenure-track faculty, but their classes tended to be larger. This probably reflects the fact that many full-time non-tenure-track faculty teach intensive language drill courses and writing-intense composition classes rather than large lecture classes. More than one-third of full-time term-appointment faculty reported teaching more than twelve hours per week. They spent a smaller percentage of their time in research (11%) than either tenure-track (23%) or tenured (21%) faculty. Both full-time non-tenure-track and tenured faculty spent about 14 percent of their time in administrative activities, while tenure-track faculty spent only about 8 percent of their time in administrative activities. By contrast, full-time non-tenure-track faculty spent about 16 percent of their time in other professional activities as compared to about 13 percent for tenure-track and tenured faculty.

Senior tenured faculty typically played a larger administrative role in their programs than did junior or full-time faculty in non-tenure-eligible positions. As we learned from our campus interviews, however, full-time term-appointment faculty often assumed administrative responsibilities that tenured and tenure-track faculty did not want. Tenure-track faculty were especially averse to administrative tasks that might divert them from the research and writing so crucial to their promotion and elevation to tenure status. The larger percentage of time that full-time non-tenure-track faculty spent in activities like technical assistance or international student advising also reflects the unique and specialized roles that these faculty frequently play within their program areas.

In short, full-time non-tenure-track faculty generally worked slightly fewer hours per week than their tenure-class colleagues. They spent a larger percentage of their time teaching and carrying out other professional activities than did tenured and tenure-track faculty but devoted less time to research. The findings reported here suggest that many full-time non-tenure-track faculty fill specialized roles and meet distinctive needs at their institutions. Although some faculty off the tenure track do essentially the same work as their tenure-eligible colleagues, many perform important complementary tasks (instructional, administrative, scholarly, technical) that supplement the work that tenure-class faculty perform.

How Productive Are They?

When examining the productivity of full-time non-tenure-track faculty, it is important to keep four variables in mind. First, institutions often hire full-time faculty in non-tenure-eligible positions for different reasons than they hire tenure-track faculty. Full-time term-appointment faculty may not be expected to perform the same functions as tenure-eligible faculty. Hence, their type and level of productivity may be considerably different. Second, productivity measures that emphasize the scholarly function of traditional tenure-track faculty provide an incomplete assessment of the productivity of full-time non-tenure-track faculty, who primarily emphasize teaching or other professional activities in their jobs. Third, while many were hired to perform a specific function, they may still be assessed along traditional criteria. Fourth, some full-time non-tenure-track faculty may attempt to be productive in traditional ways because they aspire to tenure-track positions.

Using NSOPF-93 data, we compared the three faculty groups on teaching productivity (table 4.3) and on fourteen different types of scholarly productivity within the previous two years. These included refereed articles, nonrefereed articles, book chapters, presentations, research or technical reports, reviews, textbooks, other books, monographs, fine arts performances, juried and nonjuried creative works, copyrights or patents, and software. Productivity rates for full-time non-tenure-track faculty were lower on all fourteen of these measures.

A summary of scholarly productivity over the last two years and career productivity on six measures is given in tables 4.4 and 4.5. While tenured faculty reported an average of 2.6 refereed articles published in the last two

Table 4.3   Teaching Productivity, by Tenure Status

	Tenured	Tenure-Track	Non-Tenure-Track
Total hours per week teaching for credit	8.81	9.77	10.40
Total classroom credit hours	7.92	8.50	8.42

Source: NSOPF-93.

Table 4.4 Last Two Years' Productivity, by Tenure Status

	Tenured	Tenure-Track	Non-Tenure-Track
Books and chapters	0.89	0.65	0.39
Book reviews	0.61	0.39	0.20
Refereed articles	2.63	2.19	1.31
Presentations and exhibits	5.42	5.65	3.67
Publications	6.76	5.43	3.43
Other reports	2.07	1.61	1.11

Source: NSOPF-93.

years, full-time non-tenure-track faculty had published an average of 1.3 articles in the same period. Career averages showed an even greater disparity: tenured faculty had published an average of 22 refereed articles compared to 6.75 for full-time non-tenure-track faculty. Similarly, full-time non-tenure-track faculty had made an average of slightly more than three and a half presentations and exhibits over the previous two years compared to an average of nearly five and a half for tenured and tenure-track faculty. During the previous two years, full-time non-tenure-track faculty were less likely than tenured and tenure-track faculty to have completed refereed articles, book chapters, book reviews, other books, nonrefereed articles, and textbooks. They were also less likely to have produced software, made presentations, or presented fine arts performances. Nevertheless, although the pattern was similar across the different types of productivity, many of the production levels and productivity differences were very small (e.g., patents, software, creative works, monographs, and textbooks).

Regardless of tenure status, faculty overwhelmingly agreed that teaching effectiveness should be the primary criterion for promotion at their institu-

Table 4.5 Career Productivity, by Tenure Status

	Tenured	Tenure-Track	Non-Tenure-Track
Books and chapters	4.24	1.39	1.21
Book reviews	4.99	1.28	1.01
Refereed articles	22.17	6.91	6.75
Presentations and exhibits	45.52	27.20	19.37
Publications	49.99	19.42	16.46
Other reports	14.87	6.57	5.57

Source: NSOPF-93.

tion. Full-time non-tenure-track faculty (84.7%) were most likely to agree with this statement, followed by tenure-track (72.5%) and tenured (68.8%) faculty. Not surprisingly, the reverse was true when faculty were asked if research should be the primary criterion: 43.4 percent of tenured faculty agreed with this statement, followed by 39.3 percent of tenure-track faculty and 31 percent of full-time non-tenure-track faculty. More than half of all groups, however, agreed that research was rewarded more than teaching at their institutions. These responses seem consistent with the role demands and level of job security of the three different types of faculty.

Our conversations with full-time non-tenure-track faculty help to clarify the reasons for the productivity differences we found. Interest and workload appear to be two key distinguishing influences. As a full-time term-appointment faculty member in languages told us, she is "more interested in teaching than research. [This is] why I am in a lecturer position." The heavy teaching loads of many full-time non-tenure-track faculty also make scholarly productivity difficult. For example, a lecturer in speech and hearing told us that she is "working twice as hard as when [I] was in a tenured position. Tenure-track people have more discretionary time." A senior lecturer in physics reported a similar situation. The tenured faculty in his department teach one course per semester. He teaches two courses and does all the assignments for fifty to sixty teaching assistants. In contrast to his tenured colleagues, however, he does no research. The need to complete tasks not addressed by tenure-eligible faculty may also help to explain some of the productivity differences between full-time term-appointment and tenure-class faculty. A full-time lecturer in ethnic studies told us that "a lot of lecturers have unofficial duties forced upon them . . . A lot of lecturers pick up whatever others won't do."

Our findings concerning traditional measures of faculty scholarly productivity reveal that full-time faculty off the tenure track do not measure up to their tenure-track counterparts in this realm. This does not suggest that FTNTT faculty are not productive, contributing members of the academic profession. Rather, the findings suggest that traditional productivity measures are inadequate, and probably inappropriate, in judging either the quantity or the quality of the professional contributions of many full-time non-tenure-track faculty. Institutions wishing to assess the productivity of these faculty need to define evaluation criteria (e.g., numbers of students served, student achievement measures, number of courses designed and delivered, professional portfolios) more consistent with the tasks their non-tenure-track faculty were hired to perform.

How Do They Feel about Their Jobs?

SATISFACTION

According to NSOPF-93 data, faculty were generally happy in their work regardless of their tenure status. More than 80 percent of full-time tenured and non-tenure-track faculty said that they were "very satisfied" or "somewhat satisfied" with their jobs. The satisfaction rate for tenure-track faculty was slightly lower, perhaps reflecting the stress associated with professional adjustment or preparing for tenure review. Full-time term-appointment faculty with doctorates were slightly less satisfied than those without doctorates; the same is true for tenured and tenure-track faculty with doctorates compared with those without doctorates.

Tenured faculty were most satisfied with their job security and the freedom to do outside consulting and least satisfied with time available to keep current in their fields (table 4.6). Full-time term-appointment faculty were the least satisfied with their job security and their opportunity for advancement but were as satisfied as tenured faculty with their workload. Regardless of tenure status, engineering, business, and education faculty reported the highest overall satisfaction, while humanities and fine arts faculty were

Table 4.6 Mean Satisfaction with Job and Career Opportunities, by Tenure Status

	Tenured	Tenure-Track	Non-Tenure-Track
Authority to decide course content	3.76	3.64	3.60
Authority to make other job decisions	3.10	2.97	3.01
Authority to decide courses taught	3.39	3.14	3.14
Time available for advising	3.14	3.00	3.02
Workload	2.90	2.69	2.88
Job security	3.62	2.79	2.54
Advancement opportunities	3.17	2.88	2.39
Time to stay current	2.58	2.34	2.46
Benefits	2.96	2.87	2.96
Salary	2.54	2.39	2.44
Spouse/partner's job opportunities	3.03	2.73	3.01
Overall job satisfaction	3.21	2.99	3.08
Would choose an academic career again	3.54	3.42	3.38

Source: NSOPF-93.

Note: On the four-point job satisfaction scale, 1 = low, 4 = high.

the least satisfied. These findings come as no surprise. Full-time faculty in term-appointment positions have limited job security and no opportunity for career advancement at many institutions. In contrast, their satisfaction with their workload suggests that they are as content with their actual jobs and work assignments as are their tenure-track colleagues.

Faculty were asked to use a four point scale (1 = very poor, 4 = very good) to rate their satisfaction with ten noninstructional aspects of their jobs. Full-time non-tenure-track faculty exhibited their greatest dissatisfaction on these items. Although their ratings of salary, benefits, and the time to stay current did not differ greatly from tenured and tenure-track faculty, they were more dissatisfied with other aspects of their jobs. They were notably less satisfied than tenured and tenure-track faculty with their authority to decide course content and to make other job decisions. This, of course, reflects their status as temporary employees, which sometimes precludes full-time term-appointment faculty from decisionmaking on curriculum, course planning and scheduling, space allocation, and other job-related matters.

Full-time term-appointment faculty in English and foreign languages (two fields that use a large number of these faculty to teach introductory courses) were less satisfied than other full-time non-tenure-track faculty with their job security, opportunities for advancement, and salary. These findings are consistent with the employment conditions of many FTNTT faculty in these fields. Their work can be student intensive, demanding, and monotonous. At the same time, the ample supply of qualified candidates for teaching positions in English and foreign languages limits job security and advancement opportunities and keeps salaries modest at best.

Using the same four-point scale, faculty were asked to rate the support they received in terms of twelve instruction-related factors (table 4.7). In general, tenured faculty were most positive about these factors and tenure-track faculty were least positive. Much of the tenure-track faculty's dissatisfaction centered on basic research equipment, laboratory support, availability of research assistants, personal computers, and library holdings. They also expressed the greatest dissatisfaction with AV equipment, classroom space, studio space, and secretarial support. Full-time non-tenure-track faculty were generally happier than the other two groups with teaching support, specifically AV equipment and classroom space. Interestingly, full-time term-appointment faculty were the most positive about secretarial support but least positive about office space.

From the perspective of the full-time non-tenure-track faculty, some of

Table 4.7   Mean Satisfaction with Institutional Support, by Tenure Status

	Tenured	Tenure-Track	Non-Tenure-Track
Basic research equipment	2.78	2.74	2.77
Laboratory space and supplies	2.70	2.64	2.75
Availability of research assistants	2.31	2.15	2.26
Personal computers	3.00	2.94	2.97
Centralized computer facilities	3.10	2.90	2.85
Computer networks with other institutions	2.99	2.77	2.63
Audiovisual equipment	2.97	2.85	3.05
Classroom space	2.82	2.75	2.97
Office space	2.89	2.77	2.71
Studio/performance space	2.73	2.60	2.69
Secretarial support	2.79	2.56	2.81
Library holdings	2.86	2.63	2.87

Source: NSOPF-93.

Note: On the four-point job satisfaction scale, 1 = low, 4 = high.

these findings are easy to interpret. Others are more anomalous. Full-time non-tenure-track faculty are probably less critical of research support because most are not expected to conduct research as part of their formal job responsibilities. In contrast, tenure-track faculty often need research support to compete successfully for tenure and promotion. The low rating that FTNTT faculty give to office space is also understandable. Since they are technically temporary faculty, they often are assigned the least desirable office space and equipment. For example, a professor at a master's-level university told us that as a full-time non-tenure-track person he inherited a bad computer and no printer. In contrast, his tenure-track colleague, who was hired at the same time, got a good computer and a printer. The higher level of full-time term-appointment faculty satisfaction with teaching support, classroom space, and secretarial support is more difficult to explain. Perhaps due to their less stable, transient status, these faculty members are more easily pleased with whatever support they do receive.

Our campus visits helped clarify the sources of satisfaction and dissatisfaction among full-time non-tenure-track faculty. A lecturer in languages at a research university reported, "I could see myself staying forever." Not having to do research was a comfortable fit with her family responsibilities. A senior lecturer in psychology at the same university told us she was doing exactly what she wanted to do. She did not want to do what is required to get tenure in her department and was happy with the freedom she had in her full-time non-tenure-eligible faculty position to do as she wished. "I'm beneath the radar screen," she observed. At the same time, this lecturer was unhappy with the opportunities for growth, salary, and status that her job provided, and she was thinking of looking for an administrative appointment. A senior lecturer in chemistry at a research institution saw her options somewhat differently. She had a fair amount of flexibility in her lecturer position, which satisfied one of her primary career needs. She believed that the lecturer post offered "a lot of dynamic possibilities." Hence, she did not see it as a dead end. Nevertheless, she too stated that she might not be able to find all that she wants in a lecturer appointment and might eventually pursue a staff position in higher education.

Concerns with security, status, and opportunities for advancement seemed to influence the job satisfaction of a number of full-time non-tenure-track faculty that we interviewed. For instance, a faculty member in business stated that he saw his rolling term appointment as "a short-term gig." Although he noted that he was pretty well satisfied otherwise, he did not want to be a term-appointment professor for seven or eight years and then have to leave and compete for tenure elsewhere. A science and technology professor made a similar assessment. Generally, he was satisfied with his career but felt contracts should be lengthened as a faculty member's years of service increase. The nature of the security concerns of full-time non-tenure-track faculty was succinctly conveyed in one short statement from a physical science professor in a research university. "I do have a certain 'tenure envy' for my colleagues who do not have to cope with this [reappointment] uncertainty."

The professional status and career advancement concerns that full-time non-tenure-eligible faculty shared with us are interrelated issues. A lecturer in biology at a research institution told us that he did not have enough opportunity to develop and advance, so he was "a little unhappy with [my institution]." A lecturer in English at a different research university described his position as "a dead end." He viewed his full-time term appointment as too brief to permit the types of achievement necessary for professional advancement. A senior lecturer in mathematics at a research university who planned to stay at her institution said that "this [term faculty appointment] is very much my career." At the same time she argued, "I am not comfortable with the title anymore. The status issue of lecturers versus professors bothers me. The fact is in the university there is a large difference between a lecturer and a professor." She thought that there should be some kind of advanced title for lecturers that conveyed equal status with professors. Similarly, a senior lecturer in English asserted, "I have more standing outside the university than I do inside." She saw lecturers as a type of "subfaculty."

Almost 90 percent of the faculty in each group agreed that if they had it to do over again they would choose an academic career. The general pattern of these findings is not surprising. One would expect the most secure faculty to feel most positive about their careers in academe and to wish to choose such a career path again. What is surprising is the high level of commitment that full-time non-tenure-track faculty showed toward the academic career. It is quite remarkable that so many faculty who are not eligible for tenure, the traditional sign of full membership in the academic profession, would choose again to pursue a career in higher education.

In spite of the relatively high level of overall satisfaction among non-tenure-track faculty revealed in the NSOPF-93 findings, our campus interviews uncovered a considerable degree of variation. It was apparent from these personal accounts that many factors enhance or diminish the satisfaction of full-time non-tenure-track faculty. The nature of the work itself and the job's fit with their interests and personal circumstances were sources of satisfaction for many of the FTNTT faculty we interviewed. In contrast, the limited security, lower status, and absence of professional advancement opportunities associated with many term-appointment positions reduced satisfaction with some aspects of life off the tenure track. Institutions should be cognizant of the factors that have an adverse effect on faculty satisfaction and take steps to minimize their negative impact. Failure to respond to the reasons for the dissatisfaction that we repeatedly heard about could lead to rapid turnover or, worse yet, to disgruntled faculty with low morale.

CONCERNS ABOUT SPOUSE'S OR PARTNER'S OPPORTUNITIES

When assessing satisfaction with job opportunities for their spouses or partners, full-time non-tenure-track faculty were more similar to tenured than to tenure-track faculty. Tenured faculty were the most satisfied with their spouse's or partner's opportunities (75.9%), followed by full-time non-tenure-track faculty (73.4%) and tenure-track faculty (63.3%). More than half (53.6%) the tenure-track faculty rated job opportunities for their spouse or partner as a "very important" factor in a decision to change jobs, compared with 46.5 percent of term-appointment faculty and 43.8 percent of tenured faculty. Tenure-track faculty, then, were the least satisfied with their spouse's or partner's opportunities and the most likely to consider changing jobs to improve those opportunities. Many FTNTT faculty find academic employment after their spouse has already taken a job. This probably accounts for their relatively high level of satisfaction with job opportunities for their partners. In contrast, tenure-track faculty often bring a job-seeking spouse with them when they accept an academic post.

Like their tenure-eligible colleagues, however, some full-time term-appointment faculty did express concerns about employment opportunities for their spouses. For example, a full-time non-tenure-track education faculty member reported that he turned down some tenure-track job offers because they were "usually at small colleges in rural areas where my wife did not want to be." Not surprisingly, both he and his wife wanted opportunities for her to work as well. Unlike tenure-track or tenured faculty, however, full-time non-tenure-track faculty tended to be more concerned with their own job opportunities than those of their spouses. As we noted above, in many cases they were accompanying a spouse who had already found employment in the area or they were geographically bound by their spouse's work. Many of the full-time term-appointment faculty we interviewed told us that they came to their present location with their spouse or partner and were not in a position to move. A lecturer in an applied field at a West Coast institution illustrates the geographic constraints that many full-time non-tenure-track faculty live within. She said that her husband is in the film business, "so we are not going anywhere." Many full-time faculty in non-tenure-eligible positions were aware that these personal restrictions limited their career flexibility and might impede their ability to negotiate favorable work assignments and compensation packages.

CONCERNS ABOUT CHANGING JOBS

When faculty were asked to think about how likely it was that they would leave their job within three years, some interesting differences were evident among the three tenure categories. Regardless of tenure status, faculty reported that the most likely reason for them to leave would be to accept a full-time job in a different institution. Tenure-track faculty had the highest percentage (64.4%) of those who reported that it was "somewhat likely" or "very likely" that they would leave for this reason, followed by full-time non-tenure-track faculty (51.8%) and tenured faculty (33.2%). Full-time non-tenure-track faculty were much more likely to leave for a full-time job outside academe (40.9%) than either tenured (14.7%) or tenure-track (35.6%) faculty. The likelihood of any faculty leaving for a part-time job in or out of academe was less than 20 percent, but full-time term-appointment faculty saw this as a more likely option for themselves than did tenured or tenure-track faculty. Not surprisingly, tenured faculty considered themselves more likely to retire within the next three years than the other two groups.

This response pattern reflects the career circumstances of tenured, tenure-track, and full-time non-tenure-track faculty. Of the three groups, full-time term-appointment faculty have the least job security. Hence, they are the group most likely to consider alternatives outside higher education. A senior lecturer at a research university provided a good example of this behavior. Although she regularly taught enormous classes at the university, she maintained a private psychology practice on the side "because my job security varies with whoever is chair."

Faculty were also asked to rate the importance of fourteen factors in making a decision to leave. Here again FTNTT faculty differ from their tenure-class colleagues. The opportunity for a tenured position was rated as "very important" by only 39.9 percent of full-time non-tenure-track faculty, while 62.9 percent of tenured faculty and 65 percent of tenure-track faculty considered it "very important." Full-time faculty in non-tenure-eligible positions attached more importance to freedom from pressure to publish, teaching opportunities, and administrative opportunities (though this was a low priority) than did tenured and tenure-track faculty. Full-time term appointment faculty were considerably less interested in research facilities and opportunities.

These responses suggest that many full-time non-tenure-track faculty do not fit the standard academic model. Fewer of them appear to be seeking the traditional lifelong tenure-track position, and many prefer more specialized or more distinctive teaching and administrative roles than the typical faculty functions of teaching, research, and service may allow.

Four Types of Full-Time Non-Tenure-Track-Faculty

While there are clear differences (and similarities) between full-time non-tenure-track faculty in four-year institutions and their tenured or tenure-track colleagues, there are large variations within FTNTT faculty as well. Our analysis of the NSOPF-93 data resulted in the identification of four distinct types of full-time non-tenure-track faculty: teachers, researchers, administrators, and "other academic professionals," who hold clinical or practitioner-type positions (table 4.8).

The variations appear to be related to two major factors: role (or primary activity) and educational attainment (whether the person holds the doctorate). Some faculty within each of the four groups hold the doctorate and

Table 4.8 Some Characteristics of the Four Types of Full-Time
Non-Tenure-Track Faculty

	Teachers	Researchers	Administrators	Other Academic Professionals
Percentage of FTNTT population	64.00	9.80	11.10	15.10
Demographics				
Percentage with doctorate	31.80	72.40	31.70	13.40
Mean age	44.30	42.70	46.80	42.00
Percentage minority	14.40	19.80	13.60	16.70
Percentage women	52.50	30.50	45.60	40.40
Percentage married	72.80	80.90	75.80	67.80
Percentage with children	60.40	75.00	65.20	66.10
Mean publications (last 2 years)				
Refereed journal articles	0.62	5.42	0.68	2.06
Nonrefereed journal articles	0.30	0.97	0.49	0.50
Mean publications (career)				
Refereed journal articles	2.89	30.81	4.21	9.44
Nonrefereed journal articles	1.49	4.03	3.30	1.98
Workload				
Mean hours worked per week	49.77	55.20	53.77	55.55
Mean teaching hours per week	11.72	3.62	5.62	7.80
Mean number of students	91.76	72.77	50.31	77.88
Mean number of credit classes	3.06	1.45	1.61	1.88
Mean number of committees	1.04	1.37	1.80	0.44
Satisfaction (1 = low, 4 = high)				
Overall satisfaction	3.05	3.08	3.27	3.06
Would choose an academic career again	3.44	3.22	3.44	3.17

Source: NSOPF-93.

others do not. Full-time non-tenure-track faculty who differ in role and educational attainment also differ in workload, job satisfaction, and scholarly productivity.

Virtually all full-time non-tenure-track faculty fit into one of our four categories. These four groups clearly differ from one another in terms of their roles and responsibilities. They also differ demographically, in productivity, and in the degree to which they are satisfied with their positions in higher education. Likewise, there are notable differences within each group that seem to stem from their educational attainment. Among full-time non-tenure-track faculty, only about 32 percent of the teachers and administrators and 14 percent of the other academic professionals hold the doctorate. Conversely, 72 percent of the researchers have a doctorate. Those with the doctorate differ from those without the doctorate particularly in terms of their job satisfaction and scholarly productivity. Full-time non-tenure-track faculty with a doctorate bear a strong resemblance to their tenured and tenure-track colleagues and are likely to be less satisfied to be off the tenure track than those without a doctorate. Those without the doctorate are more satisfied with their jobs and appear to have found a particular niche within their institutions that suits them well.

While the majority of full-time non-tenure-track faculty see their primary activity as teaching (64%), substantial percentages of them see their major activity as research (9.8%) or as administration (11.1%). A fourth group of full-time term-appointment faculty see their major role as some other professional activity (15.1%). These individuals work as practitioners, clinicians, or specialists, in addition to fulfilling their teaching duties.

The Teachers

Full-time non-tenure-track faculty whose primary activity is teaching form the largest group of term-appointment faculty (64%). They spend about two-thirds of their time teaching and the remainder in research and administration and other professional activities. As stated above, less than one-third of the teachers have a doctorate. They teach more credit courses and more students than the other three full-time non-tenure-track groups. They teach more undergraduate courses but fewer graduate courses. The teachers work fewer hours per week, but they teach more hours per week than other term-appointment faculty. The number of hours that they regularly schedule per week for student contact and the number of hours of informal contact with students are about at the average for full-time term-appointment faculty. They serve on the fewest number of committees of the four types of full-time non-tenure-track faculty. These findings suggest that full-time non-tenure-track teachers are more narrowly focused and perhaps less well integrated into the lives of their units or institutions when compared with tenure-class faculty.

More than half the teachers are women. Females (48%) are less likely than males (54.3%) to have a doctorate. About 86 percent of teachers are white. Whites are slightly more likely to be teachers than minority faculty, particularly those with a doctorate. Teachers are the second oldest of the four types.

Teachers are the least likely of the four groups to publish in either refereed or nonrefereed journals. On average, they have published less than one article in the last two years. Teachers with the doctorate are twice as likely as those without the doctorate to publish journal articles in refereed journals but have similar publication rates in nonrefereed journals. Teachers also tend to have the lowest productivity in terms of book chapters and technical reports. Although they averaged around two presentations over the two-year period, this was the lowest of the four groups. In each case those with the doctorate outperformed those who did not have the doctorate. Teachers are above average in terms of fine arts exhibitions, but in this case those without the doctorate outperformed those who had the doctorate; this is probably due to the large number of fine arts teachers who hold the M.F.A., traditionally considered the terminal degree for a working artist.

Our interviews produced similar findings. Due to their heavy teaching loads, many full-time term-appointment faculty we interviewed told us they had little time or energy left over for scholarly activities. The higher levels of scholarship for full-time term-appointment faculty with doctorates suggest that they have been more fully socialized and prepared to conduct scholarship.

Teachers with the doctorate appear to be the least satisfied of all four groups with their working conditions (table 4.9). They gave particularly low

Table 4.9   Teachers' Job Satisfaction, by Educational Attainment

	No Doctorate	Doctorate
Authority to decide course content	3.64	3.59
Authority to make other job decisions	3.01	2.92
Authority to decide courses taught	3.12	3.08
Time available for advising	3.09	3.05
Workload	2.95	2.77
Job security	2.50	2.34
Advancement opportunities	2.32	2.29
Time to stay current	2.48	2.29
Benefits	2.90	2.87
Salary	2.36	2.38
Spouse or partner's job opportunities	2.99	2.87
Overall job satisfaction	3.09	2.96
Would choose an academic career again	3.45	3.42
Would leave for another institution	1.71	1.90
Would leave for opportunity for tenure	2.12	2.37
Would leave for a job outside academe	1.56	1.47

Source: NSOPF-93.

Note: On the four-point job satisfaction scale, 1 = low, 4 = high.

satisfaction ratings to job security, opportunities for advancement, time available to keep current, salary, benefits, job opportunities for their spouse or partner, authority to make job decisions, and the quality of their undergraduate students. Nevertheless, when asked if they would choose an academic career again, they rated themselves as relatively likely to do so. The most important factor in a decision to change jobs would be job security, followed by benefits and quality of instructional facilities. They would attach more importance than teachers without a doctorate to research opportunities and research facilities.

Teachers without the doctorate are generally more satisfied with their working conditions than teachers with the doctorate; the one exception is salary. They are the least satisfied of all groups with their salaries. However, they would be equally as likely as their colleagues with doctorates to choose an academic career again. The most important factor in a decision to change jobs would be benefits, followed by job security, quality of instructional facilities, and salary.

These findings on satisfaction reveal an interesting distinction within the full-time non-tenure-track teacher group. The doctoral-level teachers may aspire to regular tenure-track positions and for this reason feel a higher level of dissatisfaction with their professional circumstances. In contrast, non-doctoral full-time term-appointment teachers may view their professional situation quite positively.

We met full-time non-tenure-track teachers at each type of college and university we visited. Although we were struck by the level of diversity among the teachers we interviewed, most share a dominant commitment to their instructional role. Typically, FTNTT teachers devote limited amounts of time to scholarship and service roles, partially because the demands of their teaching duties do not leave much time for other professional tasks. We also found that many full-time term-appointment teachers genuinely prefer the instructional aspects of faculty life over other traditional academic roles. Naturally, the roles teachers fill on their campuses vary greatly according to their academic field and the type of institution where they work. In virtually all cases, though, they make their principal contribution through their work in the classroom.

Individual cases help to clarify the attributes and professional work experiences of full-time non-tenure-track teachers. For example, Lynn Kramer is a full-time term-appointment teacher at an undergraduate liberal arts institution. The specialized teaching post she holds, designed to meet distinctive needs at her school, is about forty years old. She teaches six chemistry laboratory sections per term and supervises teaching assistants. She has a doctorate in chemistry but found she did not like doing research. Hence, she made a conscious decision to take a teaching-oriented position and turned down a tenure-track job offer at a prestigious institution. She observed that college teaching provides a good fit with her family as well as her professional interests. In her department she has total responsibility for the lab curriculum and feels like an integral part of the chemistry team, even though the position does not allow time to do research. "I love my job. I feel like I make a big difference in the lives of chemistry majors" sums up Lynn's feelings about her teaching role at this college.

Wanda Martin, a management professor at a doctoral university, is another example of a full-time non-tenure-track teacher. Wanda moved to her present location when her husband was transferred. She described teaching as her preferred career choice and reported that she did not want to be a researcher. Her full-time non-tenure-track post offers "a perfect path for [my] career goals," Wanda observed. The full-time term-appointment positions in her school emphasize teaching and service instead of research. Hence, her role is less varied than that of tenure-track faculty. She reported that she teaches an unusually heavy load each semester compared with the normal load for tenure-track faculty in her department.

Betty Lewis is a full-time non-tenure-track senior lecturer in English and writing at a research university. She made a conscious choice to "pursue teaching, not research" and terminated her formal education with the Master of Philosophy degree. She fits the full-time non-tenure-eligible teacher model closely. She noted that she was fortunate to get a teaching appointment and has been working at the same institution for fifteen years. In her program, the primary expectation is that lecturers teach writing and supervise and train teaching assistants. Betty teaches five courses per year. She pointedly stated that as a full-time non-tenure-track lecturer she appreciates the freedom not to be involved in other aspects of the life of her department and college. Indeed, she considers it a privilege of her job not to be required to be on committees. She feels free to say "no thank you" to anybody. At the same time, she and her writing colleagues noted that the opportunity to participate in the intellectual life of the university is a benefit of their positions. She reminded us that "some lecturers have made the choice to be here." Her concluding comment suggests that many full-time non-tenure-eligible teachers prefer their posts to more traditional academic positions. They are not just fall-back jobs for those who did not get standard tenure-track appointments.

These brief profiles complement our findings from the NSOPF-93 survey data. The faculty in these positions tend to be teaching-oriented and devote the majority of their time to instruction-related activities. Their roles are typically more narrowly focused than those of their tenure-track colleagues, who must perform teaching, research, and service concurrently. Nevertheless, the full-time non-tenure-track teachers we studied fill very important roles at their institutions, roles that frequently are consistent with their personal professional inclinations to be college teachers.

The Researchers

Full-time non-tenure-track researchers spend more than half their time doing research, about one-fourth of their time teaching, and the remainder in administration and other professional activities. They have been in their jobs, on average, longer than the full-time non-tenure-track faculty in any of the other groups (about seven and one-half years). Although researchers without the doctorate are above average (for FTNTT faculty) in the number of regularly scheduled office hours they hold per week (11.6) to meet with students, researchers with the doctorate are below average in the number of regularly scheduled hours per week (5.8). Researchers with the doctorate are above average (compared to other types of FTNTT faculty) in the number of committees (1.57) on which they serve.

Only about 30 percent of the researchers are female, the lowest percentage of women among the four groups. The researchers have the largest percentage (20%) of minority faculty of the four groups and are relatively young ($M = 42.7$).

The average number of refereed journal articles published by full-time term-appointment faculty during the past two years was 1.31. The researchers account for the vast bulk of these. They averaged 5.42 publications in the past two years as compared with .62 for the teachers and .61 for the administrators. Surprisingly, researchers without the doctorate published more refereed journal articles (6.83) than researchers with the doctorate (4.88). Researchers were also more likely to publish journal articles in nonrefereed journals: those with the doctorate averaged .91, while those without the doctorate averaged 1.13. They were also more likely to publish chapters, monographs, and technical reports than any other group and to have made presentations in the last two years, with an average of five. The high level of productivity of full-time term-appointment faculty researchers measured by traditional academic standards is not surprising. Unlike the expectations held for the three other types of non-tenure-track faculty, scholarship and writing are a central part of the researcher's role. In contrast, they were the least likely of the four groups to complete creative works, either juried or not, or to publish books, or to have exhibitions in the fine arts.

Researchers with the doctorate had the lowest overall satisfaction rating of any group (table 4.10). They were particularly unhappy with their job security, their opportunities for advancement, their authority to decide which courses they teach, and their time available to advise students. The most important factors in a decision to change jobs would be job security and quality of research facilities, followed by opportunity for professional advancement and benefits. They gave the highest rating of any group to the opportunity for tenure as a factor in the decision to change jobs. Interestingly, they gave a relatively low rating to the likelihood that they would choose an academic career again.

Researchers without the doctorate had the highest overall satisfaction rating of any group of non-tenure-track faculty. They were most satisfied with their benefits but least satisfied with their job security and salary. The most important factors in a decision to change jobs would be job security, geographic location, benefits, and salary. They were more likely than re-

Table 4.10   Researchers' Job Satisfaction, by Educational Attainment

	No Doctorate	Doctorate
Authority to decide course content	3.41	3.35
Authority to make other job decisions	3.36	2.97
Authority to decide courses taught	3.43	2.78
Time available for advising	3.01	2.75
Workload	3.06	2.90
Job security	2.36	2.17
Advancement opportunities	3.04	2.14
Time to stay current	2.86	2.49
Benefits	3.31	3.18
Salary	2.62	2.51
Spouse or partner's job opportunities	3.06	3.02
Overall job satisfaction	3.53	2.91
Would choose an academic career again	3.42	3.15
Would leave for another institution	1.31	1.89
Would leave for opportunity for tenure	2.19	2.45
Would leave for a job outside academe	1.38	1.64

Source: NSOPF-93.

Note: On the four-point job satisfaction scale, 1 = low, 4 = high.

searchers with a doctorate to say they would choose an academic career again.

The lower satisfaction levels of full-time non-tenure-track researchers with the doctorate make sense if we recognize that many in this group are tenure-track "wannabes." Their sources of dissatisfaction suggest that they want traditional tenure-track appointments with all the security and opportunities for advancement that these posts provide. Though many of the full-time term-appointment faculty we have classified as teachers, administrators, and other academic professionals may prefer alternatives to the standard academic career, our data suggest that full-time non-tenure-track researchers in general would be most satisfied with traditional tenure-track positions.

Our campus visits concentrated on full-time non-tenure-track faculty whose major responsibility was instruction. For this reason, we interviewed very few FTNTT faculty who were primarily or exclusively researchers. We did find full-time term-appointment faculty, however, for whom research was a standard or expected part of their position and others who maintained a research agenda even though it was not part of their formal assignment. Most often the full-time contract faculty we met with active research programs held positions that closely paralleled those of tenure-track faculty. Otherwise, the full-time term-appointment faculty researchers we interviewed tended to use their personal discretionary time rather than their normal work hours to pursue their research interests.

Frank Johnson holds a full-time term appointment in the health sciences at a research university. His position is comparable to a regular tenure-track faculty appointment. He is in his twelfth year at the institution. Frank has essentially the same teaching, research, and service duties as his tenurable and tenured colleagues. He is even evaluated by the same criteria used to assess the performance of tenure-eligible faculty in his area. The research demands made on Frank are significant because he functions like a regular faculty member at a research-oriented institution and because his appointment is dependent upon funding from external research grants and contracts. Hence, he is doubly motivated to engage in writing and publication.

Suzanne Javitz is another full-time contract professor who maintains an active line of research. Suzanne is a visiting assistant professor of languages who has taught at her research university for seven years. With a strong educational pedigree from prestigious research universities and postdoctoral experiences at major universities, she has a strong inclination to perform research. Since she is trying to move from a full-time non-tenure-track to a tenurable appointment, Suzanne knows that she must compile a record of successful scholarship if she is to achieve her goal.

George Stephens is a laboratory lecturer at a primarily undergraduate institution where his formal duties do not require or provide much time for research. Not surprisingly, George reported that he does most of his research during the summer months. At the same time, his institution provides a resource-rich environment for his scholarship and has "always been responsive to [my] requests." In spite of his instruction-intensive position, George states that he has kept up in his field and has done everything that would be required to get tenure [at his or another institution].

Of the non-tenure-track faculty we interviewed, those who are productive scholars combine their scholarly pursuits with other standard faculty responsibilities. Each of those we would classify as researchers appears to share a genuine commitment to advancing knowledge. In addition, they are motivated to various degrees by factors like clear job expectations, the need for outside funding support, and the desire to move to the tenure track.

The Administrators

Full-time non-tenure-track faculty whose primary activity is administration spend more than half their time in administrative work, about one-fourth teaching, and the remainder in research and other professional activities. They serve on more committees than any other group. Administrators and teachers who have the doctorate serve on more committees than other term-appointment faculty. Essentially, these findings show that full-time non-tenure-track faculty administrators are probably better integrated into their institutions than other types of non-tenure-track faculty.

Only 38 percent of the administrators with a doctorate are female, while 49 percent of those without a doctorate are female. About 86 percent of the administrators are white. The administrators are the oldest group of full-time non-tenure-track faculty, and administrators with a doctorate are considerably older than those without.

Full-time non-tenure-track administrators, like teachers, are not as likely as the researchers to have published articles in the last two years in refereed or nonrefereed journals or to have written book chapters. They are more likely than the teachers to have published technical reports, made presentations, and had fine arts exhibitions. Interestingly, administrators without the doctorate produced the largest number of fine arts exhibitions.

Administrators with the doctorate fell into the middle range of satisfaction with their working conditions (table 4.11). They were more satisfied than any other group with their authority to decide which courses they teach. Their only areas of relative dissatisfaction were workload and time to keep current in their fields. This is understandable, given their diverse responsibilities, which bridge faculty and administrative worlds. They were the group most likely to retire within the next three years. If they were to change jobs, the most important factor in the decision would be benefits, followed by geographic location and salary. They were the most likely of all four groups to choose an academic career again.

Administrators without the doctorate were among the most satisfied with their working conditions. They were the most satisfied of all groups with their authority to decide course content. The most important factor for them in a decision to change jobs would be benefits, followed by salary and geographic location. They were relatively likely to choose an academic career again. Perhaps administrators are content with their careers because they have achieved a higher degree of security and influence than many non-tenure-track faculty.

Even more than other full-time non-tenure-track faculty, FTNTT ad-

Table 4.11　Administrators' Job Satisfaction, by Educational Attainment

	No Doctorate	Doctorate
Authority to decide course content	3.78	3.73
Authority to make other job decisions	3.31	3.07
Authority to decide courses taught	3.41	3.52
Time available for advising	3.14	2.92
Workload	2.95	2.72
Job security	2.95	2.74
Advancement opportunities	2.68	2.52
Time to stay current	2.54	2.36
Benefits	3.12	2.91
Salary	2.62	2.60
Spouse or partner's job opportunities	3.33	3.14
Overall job satisfaction	3.36	3.07
Would choose an academic career again	3.43	3.46
Would leave for another institution	1.56	1.80
Would leave for opportunity for tenure	1.76	1.94
Would leave for a job outside academe	1.58	1.40

Source: NSOPF-93.

Note: On the four-point job satisfaction scale, 1 = low, 4 = high.

ministrators usually occupy unique and specialized positions that fill well-defined needs at their institutions. Often these needs are not easily addressed within the traditional roles of tenured and tenure-eligible faculty. In other words, full-time non-tenure-track administrators fill gaps and respond to problems that more traditional faculty are not well equipped to handle.

Sarah Allen is a clear-cut example. She is director of a professional preparation program and a lecturer at a predominantly undergraduate liberal arts institution. She described her position as "totally different from a traditional teaching appointment at the college." "It is in between teaching and administration" and involves a lot of both activities. Unlike normal academic duties, her work is year-round due to her administrative status. It provides no time or support for research. In fact, Sarah observed, she was "not sure the college understands what the administrative aspects of these [part faculty, part administrator] jobs entail." Sarah feels that her untenured status complicates her life as an administrator. "Tenured chairs can say, 'No, I don't think so,'" she reported. Full-time non-tenure-track faculty "don't have that luxury."

Peter Matthews holds a full-time term-appointment faculty post in the social sciences at a research university where his mix of teaching and administrative duties qualifies him for the administrator label. Peter has worked at his institution for twenty-one years. Originally he had an appointment in a health-related field but moved to a full-time non-tenure-track position in a social science department when his department was eliminated. For personal reasons he turned down job offers elsewhere. Peter teaches one large course per term and one other course per year; the rest of his duties are administrative. He coordinates the introductory program in his field. Unlike a traditional faculty appointment at a university, Peter's position comes with no research expectations.

Jackie Lavach holds a similar hybrid full-time non-tenure-track faculty–administrator role at another research university. Her unique post illustrates how full-time contract faculty positions are often used to fill gaps that more traditional faculty positions cannot address adequately. Jackie is a lecturer in biology. She came to the university when her husband accepted a job there, and she has held a series of different appointments at the institution over a ten-year period. She views herself primarily as an academic administrator, although she teaches three courses per year. Her administrative duties are significant. She coordinates the instruction of four courses, hires temporary faculty, and supervises a life sciences computing group for which she coordinates a six-figure budget. She also supervises software development in her area and serves on more than a dozen committees. By any standard, Jackie is an integral and important member of her program area. She observed that the impetus for hiring full-time non-tenure-track faculty and academic administrators (such as herself) is to free regular tenure-track faculty to do research.

Full-time non-tenure-track faculty administrators are not regular administrators in the conventional sense of the word. Their positions represent a curious mix of instructional and administrative responsibilities that reflects a blend of individual talents, disciplinary cultures, and institutional circumstances. Most of the full-time non-tenure-track faculty administrators we interviewed fill specialized needs that tenure-track faculty with research agendas and governance obligations could not easily meet.

Other Academic Professionals

These are full-time non-tenure-track faculty who spend almost half their time in some activity other than teaching, research, or administration. They are in technical fields (e.g., they are programmers, technicians, chemists, engineers), clinical service, or community or public service, or in the arts (e.g., they are hired as subsidized performers, artists-in-residence). On average, they spend about one-fourth of their time teaching. They are above average in the number of hours they work per week but below average in the number of hours they teach per week. They teach an average of slightly less than two credit courses per term. Those without the doctorate teach fewer students for credit, but those with the doctorate teach more students for credit. They average one undergraduate class and one graduate class per term. Those with the doctorate have few scheduled office hours per week (3.6) and few hours of informal contact with students per week (3.0). Those without the doctorate, on the other hand, average almost fifteen hours of regularly scheduled time (14.8) and seven hours (7.1) of informal contact with students per week, an unusually high number. Those with the doctorate serve on an average of 1.4 committees, while those without the doctorate serve on an average of less than one committee (.3).

Forty percent of the other academic professional faculty category are women, but only 30 percent of those with the doctorate are female. Those without the doctorate are also less likely to be white (83% vs. 89%). As a group, the other academic professionals are younger than the rest of the full-time non-tenure-track faculty.

Other academic professional faculty are second only to the researchers in the publication of journal articles in refereed journals, in making presentations, and in writing book chapters. They are about average in publishing journal articles in nonrefereed journals and writing technical reports but below average in having fine arts exhibitions.

Other academic professionals with the doctorate were most satisfied with their authority to decide course content, their spouse or partner's job opportunities, and their authority to make other job decisions (table 4.12). They were least satisfied with their opportunities for advancement and their salary. They were the least likely of all groups to say they would choose an academic career again. This finding seems consistent with the unconventional nature of their work in higher education.

Other academic professionals without the doctorate were most satisfied with their authority to decide course content and to decide which courses they teach. They were least satisfied with their time available to stay current in their fields and their opportunities for advancement.

The full-time non-tenure-track other academic professionals are perhaps the most difficult to describe because of the diverse and idiosyncratic nature of their nonteaching roles. There seems to be a notable difference between those with and without a doctorate. The latter group appears to be more di-

Table 4.12   Other Academic Professionals' Job Satisfaction,
by Educational Attainment

	No Doctorate	Doctorate
Authority to decide course content	3.43	3.43
Authority to make other job decisions	2.83	3.30
Authority to decide courses taught	3.15	3.24
Time available for advising	2.77	2.99
Workload	2.70	3.23
Job security	2.84	3.04
Advancement opportunities	2.54	2.74
Time to stay current	2.44	2.84
Benefits	3.10	2.86
Salary	2.50	2.78
Spouse or partner's job opportunities	2.97	3.40
Overall job satisfaction	3.02	3.31
Would choose an academic career again	3.18	2.07
Would leave for another institution	1.63	1.60
Would leave for opportunity for tenure	1.84	1.82
Would leave for a job outside academe	1.56	1.75

Source: NSOPF-93.

Note: On the four-point job satisfaction scale, 1 = low, 4 = high.

rectly involved with students, whereas the former group seems more involved in governance, perhaps by virtue of the noninstructional functions they perform for their institutions. The gender distinctions between the two types of other academic professional term faculty make this an even more enigmatic group.

Like full-time non-tenure-track faculty with administrative roles, the faculty we classify as other academic professionals supplement their teaching duties with a wide range of professional responsibilities. These other responsibilities do not appear to follow any general patterns. Even within the same disciplines or type of institutions, these other tasks appear idiosyncratic and vary with the backgrounds and skills of the individual faculty members and the distinctive circumstances and needs of their places of employment. Profiles of a few other academic professional full-time non-tenure-track faculty illustrate the diverse tasks these individuals assume.

Helen Bradford is classified as a full-time faculty member at her baccalaureate institution, yet she serves as the associate director of an educational fellows program. Prior to her current appointment, she received a prestigious statewide instructional award for her work as a public school teacher. This honor helped qualify her for her present post. She reported that the university sees her as a practitioner who can go out into the schools and organize conferences. Essentially, she serves as a liaison between her public institution and the K–12 educational system of the state.

Christine Carruthers serves as a field coordinator in social work at her doctoral institution. She views herself as a social work practitioner who "sits in the middle between the program and the field." Christine develops fieldwork sites, interviews students, and places students in the sites. She also does all the administrative work for the fieldwork program and trains all field instructors. In this full-time non-tenure-track position, Christine reported that she has "lots of responsibility and no authority."

Michael Tayloe wears two hats at his research university. He is a lecturer in biology who teaches three courses per year. He is also a minority specialist, assisting with tutoring and outreach efforts. Michael's combination of tasks capitalizes on his unique background in entomology and forestry and his work with a major international organization.

Winifred Vargo holds a very personalized position at her research university. Her title of senior lecturer in mathematics does not adequately convey the range of duties that she has assumed over time. Each year she teaches five courses "no one else teaches." In addition, she is the co-principal investigator on a federally sponsored project working with schoolteachers and coordinates a foundation-supported project to prepare future members of the academic profession. To supplement this work, she noted that she invented for herself other jobs "that need doing." These include an informal lunchtime discussion series and a newsletter about teaching and learning in higher education.

These brief biographies represent a small sample of the roles and responsibilities that full-time non-tenure-track faculty classified as other academic professionals assume. Often these nontraditional faculty tasks stem from very specific staffing needs or programmatic gaps. They also provide stimulating and rewarding professional challenges for some full-time contract faculty. Both institutions and full-time term-appointment faculty can benefit from structuring these types of specialized positions.

While there are other ways to characterize full-time non-tenure-track faculty in four-year institutions (see Chapter 3), there are major differences among these four types of full-time term-appointment faculty. They have different roles and responsibilities; they have different types and levels of productivity; and their satisfaction with their positions in the university or college where they work is different. It would be a serious mistake to think that all full-time non-tenure-track faculty in these institutions are identical or even particularly similar.

Summary

As an abstract concept, the label "full-time non-tenure-track faculty" is not particularly meaningful or useful. Chapter 4 tells us who the full-time non-tenure-track faculty are, where they come from, what they do, and how they feel about their jobs and careers. It shows that these faculty are a diverse group who play many roles in different disciplinary and institutional settings. Full-time non-tenure-track faculty are hired for different reasons and perform different functions within their institutions than their tenured and tenure-track colleagues. They tend to fall into four groups: teachers, researchers, administrators, and other academic professionals. There are noteworthy differences among these groups on almost all measures. We also found differences within these groups based on their educational attainment. Full-time non-tenure-track faculty with a doctorate resemble their tenured and tenure-track colleagues in a number of important ways and are more likely to be dissatisfied with positions that offer no opportunity for tenure. Those without a doctorate are more satisfied with the particular niche they fill in their institutions and often find the different expectations for their positions to be a benefit, not a liability.

The heavier representation of women and minorities among full-time non-tenure-track faculty is especially notable and troublesome. For over three decades many colleges and universities have made a conscious effort to diversify their faculties. The substantial numbers of women and minorities in full-time term-appointment positions suggest that progress toward diversification has been incomplete. Many faculty from underrepresented groups work in employment categories that do not provide all of the professional benefits that traditionally accompany tenure-track appointments. In many cases, due to their full-time non-tenure-track status, women and minorities are disadvantaged or second-class when compared to their tenure-class colleagues. The academic community should monitor this phenomenon and react assertively to ensure that it treats all types of academics fairly and favorably.

This chapter demonstrates that the growing use of full-time faculty off the tenure track is a complex phenomenon that has the potential to affect higher education in many ways. Chapter 5 takes a detailed look at the impact and implications of this major trend in academic staffing.

5 Consequences of Employing Full-Time Non-Tenure-Track Faculty: Institutional and Individual Experiences

In this chapter we examine the perceived and actual consequences of hiring full-time non-tenure-track faculty. We examine these consequences from the perspective of the institutions that use contract systems and the faculty members in those positions. The employment of full-time non-tenure-track faculty provokes vigorous arguments for and against this personnel practice. For this reason, we examine in detail both the positive and the negative outcomes associated with the increased use of faculty in these positions.

Discussions among faculty, administrators, and policymakers about increased use of full-time non-tenure-track faculty in higher education often focus on the negative effects that such arrangements have on faculty and academic traditions. Threats to academic freedom and the lack of job security are two consequences frequently mentioned (Finkin 1996). In contrast, David Breneman, in *Alternatives to Tenure for the Next Generation of Academics*, presents an argument in favor of alternatives to tenure. He believes that carefully crafted alternatives could meet the professional needs of academics while also addressing the needs of institutions for flexibility in programming and in employment relations with faculty in the coming decades (1997). Breneman argues that in view of the changing social and economic context in which colleges and universities operate, higher education must adapt and become more responsive to its environment. He states that young academics are becoming increasingly concerned about tenure as the only viable career option while at the same time institutional leaders and the general public are questioning the efficiency of tenure as an employment strategy. Breneman makes several proposals for the use of term contracts for full-time faculty as viable alternatives to tenure, proposals premised on the will-ingness of all parties to change the conventional faculty-institution em-ployment relationship. In his view, these term contracts would be coupled with economic incentives, such as enhanced salaries, to increase the attrac-tiveness of the contract system. Breneman's proposals are theoretical, and their potential effect on faculty choice of a term contract over a tenure-track appointment is uncertain. This chapter moves beyond Breneman's theoret-ical perspective on full-time non-tenure-track employment to report on the actual experiences of several institutions and many faculty members in this type of position at those institutions.

Consequences for Resource Allocation

In this section we address the benefits and costs to institutions of using full-time term appointments in contrast to tenure-track appointments. The context for this analysis is set forth in detail in Chapters 2 and 3. The two most important reasons that institutional leaders give for hiring full-time non-tenure-track faculty are the need for flexibility in staffing and the abil-ity to respond to financial fluctuations. These reasons are similar to those that Gappa and Leslie identified for the growing use of part-time faculty on college and university campuses (1993). It appears that common objectives are driving higher education's growing use of non-tenure-eligible faculty in full-time and part-time positions.

FLEXIBILITY

Several forms of flexibility result from the use of full-time faculty in non-tenure-track positions. The most obvious is the ability to terminate em-ployment at the end of a contract period or to reassign a faculty member for curricular or enrollment reasons. Differentiated staffing also gives institu-tions greater flexibility to, for example, hire and retain faculty members who are excellent teachers but who would not pass muster under the traditional up-or-out tenure criteria.

The flexibility of full-time non-tenure-track positions can also provide institutions that are trying new curricular offerings with a safety zone until they determine whether enrollment and finances are adequate to support the new endeavor. One master's-level institution we studied offers a prime example of this strategy. The university recently strengthened its general ed-ucation program and added numerous term-appointment positions to staff new general education courses. These positions allow the institution to determine how its new general education initiative works before it makes long-term commitments to tenure-line appointments.

Flexibility sometimes comes at a price, however. In order to make the multiple-year (full-time non-tenure-track) contracts attractive to faculty, a number of institutions have built potentially significant short-term costs into their policies. For example, the policy of one liberal arts college guarantees either an added year of teaching at full salary and benefits or a lump sum payment of from 100 to 125 percent of a year's salary if a FTNTT contract is not to be renewed.

ECONOMIC BENEFITS

Not surprisingly, the economic benefits for the institutions that employ full-time non-tenure-track faculty vary significantly based on the terms and conditions of their employment. The institution's purposes for utilizing non-tenure-track personnel shape both those terms and conditions and the benefits achieved.

Many institutions that utilize full-time non-tenure-track faculty positions either assign those faculty heavier teaching loads than they assign to tenure-eligible faculty or pay them lower salaries. Either way, institutions are receiving more credit hours of instruction per dollar invested than they do with tenured or tenure-track faculty. For example, an academic administrator at a public research university told us his institution over the next decade will utilize full-time faculty in non-tenure-eligible positions who will carry heavier teaching loads than tenure-track faculty. This strategy will enable the institution to accommodate a state-mandated enrollment increase in the face of a limit on state appropriations.

A number of administrators we interviewed believe that the use of full-time non-tenure-track faculty who fulfill just one of the traditional faculty roles, primarily teaching, is an economical use of limited resources. Stated another way, duties and roles can be assigned to these faculty that could be viewed as an uneconomical use of the time and talents of tenure-track faculty. Among these functions are laboratory supervision, coordinating the work of teaching assistants, teaching basic writing and language courses, and teaching large lecture courses to lower-division students. In many cases such duties do not necessitate the same level of academic preparation required of faculty who teach upper-division and graduate-level courses, conduct research, and compete for tenure. According to one academic vice-president,

[There is] recognition that some of the work of higher education is best done through differentiated staffing. Colleges have evolved personnel structures that allow staffing flexibility. The typical faculty appointment with strong emphasis on research, etc., is often not suited well to the university's teaching functions, to undergraduate education, to foreign language instruction. It is better finding people who teach languages well. [This] may not be a good use of tenure-track faculty. The university would be in serious trouble if it relied only on tenured faculty to get its work done.

This vice-president predicted that research universities will increasingly move to a differentiated staffing model but that eventually a proportional balance between the numbers of full-time tenure-track and non-tenure-track faculty will be struck. He feels that in using non-tenure-track faculty to improve resource utilization the real questions facing institutions concern the degree to which the institutions employ these faculty and how they deal with the issues of faculty status.

Although a large proportion of faculty hired into full-time non-tenure-track positions have the terminal degree in their discipline, many campuses hire faculty with credentials that are not equivalent to those of tenure-eligible faculty. A faculty member's credentials, skills, and abilities may be appropriate to teach specified course levels and subject areas, but the individual does not meet the traditional degree criteria to qualify for a tenure-track position. At many institutions this difference in qualifications and level of instruction provided serves as the rationale for establishing lower base salaries for full-time non-tenure-track faculty than for tenure-eligible faculty. In her study of alternatives to tenure (1996, 7), Gappa found a similar tendency for institutions to use a lower initial base salary for full-time non-tenure-track faculty in teaching appointments.

In describing full-time non-tenure-track lecturers at his liberal arts college, a tenured professor of philosophy said, "Lecturers are unusually excellent or good at some things but something is usually missing in their credentials. If you got rid of them you would have to kill yourself to get someone as good." He went on to say that this "enables the [institution] to hire extremely valuable people without standard credentials. 'If the Music Department could hire Leonard Bernstein, you would be crazy not to.'" According to this respondent, the opportunity to hire a nontraditionally qualified faculty member into a non-tenure-track position brings benefits that far outweigh the "costs" of a faculty member who lacks traditional faculty credentials.

Institutions paying lower salaries to full-time non-tenure-track faculty can either acquire more faculty positions from the same amount of total compensation or realize significant savings on each full-time position filled. For example, we learned that one of our institutions paid full-time non-tenure-track faculty 85 percent of what it paid tenure-track faculty. If that institution's average annual compensation (salary and benefits) was $75,000 for full-time tenured/tenure-track faculty, its comparable expense for full-time non-tenure-track faculty would be about $63,750. For each $1,000,000 of compensation invested in tenure-track faculty the institution derives 13.3 full-time equivalent (FTE) faculty positions, while for non-tenure-track faculty the figure is 15.7 FTE faculty positions. Viewed from another perspective, for every 13.3 tenure-track positions the institutions spends $1,000,000, while for 13.3 non-tenure-track positions the expenditure is $850,000.

Financial savings realized by employing full-time faculty in non-tenure-track positions at lower salaries rather than tenured and tenure-eligible faculty are a persuasive factor for many of the institutions that employ non-tenure-eligible faculty. The chair of an English department told us, "It is cheaper to hire [full-time] non-tenure-track faculty. We pay them approximately $30,000 to teach four courses, and pay a tenure-track assistant professor $45,000 for three or four courses."

A chair of economics at another research university summarized one of the advantages of hiring full-time non-tenure-track lecturers as follows: "Lecturers are cheaper, and once in a while you get someone who is a spectacular teacher. Senior lecturers earn about $45,000 for 5–6 courses per year. Assistant professors [of economics] today get approximately $58,000 to teach four courses. An assistant professor will be spending 50 percent of his/her time on research. Senior lecturers are more expensive than temporary faculty but considerably cheaper than tenure-track faculty."

It is important to note that full-time non-tenure-track and tenure-class faculty at many institutions do not perform exactly the same functions. The former may teach more classes than the latter, but many are less involved in governance, scholarship, and professional service. Simple comparisons based on the costs of tenure-track and non-tenure-track faculty overstate the compensation savings that accompany the use of lower-salaried FTNTT faculty.

Although administrators at institutions that pay full-time term-appointment faculty lower salaries often commented on the financial advantages of hiring non-tenure-track faculty, some faculty and administrators were dubious about the ethics of the situation. A dean of arts and sciences at a research university stated that such a salary policy "feels like it is a kind of discrimination. We pay them less and work them harder." Similarly, several tenured and full-time non-tenure track faculty members observed that the lower salary and heavier teaching load was an example of the exploitation of the non-tenure-eligible faculty.

Although many institutions reap financial benefits from the use of full-time non-tenure-track faculty, we identified several institutions that are incurring added costs as a result of the terms and conditions of employment that they have established for their full-time contract faculty. In developing alternative employment strategies for faculty, these institutions have determined that certain types of incentives are necessary to encourage faculty to accept full-time employment in non-tenure-track rather than tenure-track positions. These institutional programs address several questions that Breneman (1997) raises in his proposal for the use of economic incentives to create attractive alternatives to tenure: Are faculty willing to accept a wage premium in lieu of the apparent long-term security that tenure implies? Are there other professional rights and benefits that will enhance the attractiveness of a full-time term-appointment system as a viable alternative to tenure? Our study has shown that among a variety of factors that stimulate faculty to pursue, or accept, these non-tenure-track positions, at least two factors that confer added costs on institutions appear to be persuasive to faculty—salary premiums and paid sabbatical leaves.

SALARY PREMIUMS

The first factor, a salary premium, is offered by only a few institutions. One baccalaureate institution's policy on full-time long-term renewable appointments states that "faculty hired on this type of appointment are paid a salary that is somewhat higher than the salary that would be offered to someone hired on the tenure track." According to an administrator at the institution, that differential is approximately 10 percent. If a full-time term-appointment faculty member subsequently seeks and is granted a tenure-track position at the institution, the salary differential is forfeited.

A second institution uses salary premiums for full-time non-tenure-track faculty in specific disciplines. Their salary differential is about 5 percent. Institutions that pay these non-tenure-track faculty a premium salary incentive as an alternative to a tenure-track/tenured appointment incur slightly higher compensation costs per position in exchange for the longer term potential flexibility in faculty staffing that is not generally available through the tenure system. It is evident, however, from the data presented elsewhere in this book that the institutions that pay full-time non-tenure-track faculty less than they pay comparably credentialed tenure-track faculty are more the norm than institutions that pay a salary premium. Among the institutions providing higher salaries to full-time non-tenure-track faculty, it appears that the salary premium serves as an economic quid pro quo for the term-appointment professors for forgoing the security that comes with tenure. Although the higher salaries can be viewed as an economic liability, they function as a benefit because they serve to meet the institutional need for potential flexibility in staffing.

PAID LEAVE OPTIONS

Paid sabbaticals and professional leaves are a second type of investment that some institutions offer to make full-time non-tenure-track positions attractive. Although a limited number of institutions provide professional development support for these faculty, those that do are making an important financial and professional investment not only in the individuals but in the institution's academic programs. We identified two institutions that had significant paid leave programs for full-time non-tenure-eligible faculty. Several other institutions stated that FTNTT faculty were eligible for sabbatical leaves, but the leave possibility did not appear to be a fundamental condition of employment as it did with the two examples we describe in this section.

The same baccalaureate institution that offers a 10 percent wage premium for full-time non-tenure-track faculty also offers sabbatical leaves to those faculty. The faculty appointment letter states: "If the review [sixth year] culminates in a decision by the Chancellor that you will be retained by [this college] and promoted to Associate Professor, you will receive the seventh year off at full pay and benefits, and you will receive an appointment for the next seven year period (beginning after the sabbatical year, i.e., your eighth year at [this college]."

This eligibility for a year off at full pay remains as a benefit every seven years as long as the renewable contract is in effect. This policy differs from the sabbatical leave policy for tenured faculty at the same institution. There is a six-year eligibility requirement for tenured faculty and this program provides full pay for only one semester, or 60 percent of salary for a two-semester leave. The difference in pay for the year-long sabbatical available to term-appointment faculty reflects an investment in these academic person-nel that goes beyond the salary differential.

A master's-level institution we studied has a professional development leave option as the basic incentive for its multiyear contract system. Faculty in pursuit of full-time non-tenure-track continuing status serve a five- to six-year probationary period. After a successful fifth or sixth year review they are eligible for continuing status and are, henceforth, subject to in-depth reviews every five years. There are three development leave options at full salary for full-time non-tenure-track faculty who achieve continuing contract faculty status. The leave options vary in length based on whether faculty members are in their fourth, fifth, or sixth contract year and/or the length of time since their last professional development leave.

The institutional cost for the leave program for the full-time non-tenure-track faculty at this master's-level institution is potentially more expensive than the sabbatical program for tenured faculty, both because the option to take leave arises more frequently and because a summer salary is provided to the continuing contract faculty but not to the tenured faculty. Another variable affecting cost for the institution is the fact that there are more full-time non-tenure-track faculty than tenured faculty. According to one of the campus faculty leaders, the cost of the leave program for the non-tenure-track faculty is marginal because other faculty will teach an overload to cover a necessary course, a course will not be offered, or a low-cost adjunct will be hired to teach a course. It is rare for the institution to hire a full-time replacement for a faculty member on leave.

One benefit from this faculty development leave option is the potential flexibility that it provides, because the five-year review gives the institution a chance to look not only at the faculty member's achievements but also at the continuing need for the position (based on enrollment, finances, and program considerations). A second benefit identified by administrators and several of the tenured and full-time non-tenure-track faculty members is the fact that the contract faculty immerse themselves in scholarship, peda-gogical innovation, or program development activities during their leaves. This directly benefits the institution's academic programs and its students.

On average, the tenured and full-time contract faculty members at this institution carry comparable teaching loads, and their salaries are generally comparable when viewed in the context of rank, qualifications, and experi-ence. It appears that the contract option provides a more generous oppor-tunity for full-time non-tenure-track faculty to remain professionally and intellectually current in their discipline as a trade-off for the long-term security attributed to tenure. The investment in paid leaves for the contract faculty can be construed as an institutional effort to show that the contract positions are long-term commitments. The trade-off for this investment is the potential long-term flexibility in staffing available to the institution.

The above institutional examples of the use of professional development leaves as a condition of employment for full-time term-appointment faculty are in sharp contrast to what we found in the policies and experiences of most other institutions. Among the eighty-six institutions that responded to our survey, only 22 percent indicated that full-time non-tenure-track faculty were eligible for sabbaticals. In contrast, 89 percent of those same institutions provide sabbaticals for tenured faculty.

The professional development leaves for full-time non-tenure-track faculty on multiyear contracts are another quid pro quo for the lack of security resulting from tenure. Faculty value the salary premiums and the opportunity for professional growth and flexibility provided through the leaves, while the institutions benefit from the commitment faculty feel to the institution and the revitalization that faculty achieve through the leaves. Campus leaders stated that the cost of providing the salary premiums and leave programs is offset by the potential flexibility provided in staffing as well as the general current stability in faculty employment they have experienced.

The use of full-time non-tenure-track faculty clearly has economic consequences that institutions should understand and monitor. Depending on the nature of these appointments, non-tenure-track positions may save institutions money, stretch limited financial resources, or actually increase institutional personnel expenses.

Academic Consequences

Full-time non-tenure-track faculty affect the academic programs of their institutions in numerous ways, many of them positive. Others range from positive to negative, often varying with the perspectives of the persons we asked.

Assessing the impact of full-time non-tenure-track faculty on academic programs is challenging because the levels of instruction for which they are hired vary by type of institution, and, based on our interviews, by departments within those institutions. According to the results of our institutional survey, among the baccalaureate institutions, 94 percent stated that they hired full-time non-tenure-track faculty to teach courses across the undergraduate curriculum. In contrast, only 27 percent of the research universities hired them for that purpose while 73 percent restricted them to teaching lower-division undergraduate courses. Master's (86%) and doctoral (83%) institutions also tend to restrict their full-time non-tenure-track faculty to teaching lower-division courses.

Among the institutional administrators we interviewed for this study, there was general agreement that their institution's academic programs and students benefited from the use of full-time non-tenure-track faculty. The nature of the benefits they cited, however, varied based on institutional reasons for having the positions. As noted previously, research universities and doctoral institutions tend to assign faculty in full-time non-tenure-track positions to teach lower-division courses, especially in foreign language, writing, and introductory survey courses. Benefits to these instiutions were generally perceived as freeing tenure-track faculty for upper-division and graduate teaching and for research. The benefits of employing non-tenure-track faculty also included relieving tenured faculty of such responsibilities as training and supervising graduate teaching assistants and supervising laboratory activities in the sciences. In addition, full-time term-appointment faculty often meet highly specialized institutional needs that tenured faculty do not want to assume or that are viewed as an uneconomical use of tenured faculty resources. Coordinating student internships and advising international students are two examples of the specialized duties that some full-time faculty off the tenure track perform.

In institutions that have a primary focus on undergraduate education, full-time non-tenure-track faculty often carry out the same functions as tenure-track faculty. At these institutions emphasis appears to be placed on the instructional contributions and the potential flexibility in staffing that the non-tenure-track faculty provide. A tenured professor in the social sciences at a baccalaureate institution reported that his institution's long-term renewable contract (non-tenure-track) system is driven by a tenure cap mandated by the board of trustees. This renewable contract system was developed by a faculty committee working with the administration and is perceived to be fairer to new faculty than hiring them into a tenure-track position with no chance for tenure because of the cap. The professor said the renewable contract system allows the institution to be competitive in the academic labor market while complying with the tenure cap.

Administrators at the baccalaureate colleges we visited were generally very positive in recounting the teaching benefits derived from their full-time non-tenure-track faculty. They noted that many of these faculty are very committed to teaching and are excellent instructors. Many persons we interviewed during our campus visits viewed the instructional contributions of the full-time non-tenure-track faculty as comparable to those of tenure-track and tenured faculty.

We heard numerous testimonials to the positive academic impact of full-time non-tenure-track faculty. For example, the chair of the French Department at a liberal arts college holds those faculty in her department in high regard as persons dedicated to designing courses and teaching language. Specifically she said, "The French Department would crumble without [the non-tenure-track faculty]. They have specialties and expertise departments rely on that tenured faculty may not have."

A tenured professor in the physical sciences at a master's-level institution views the use of full-time faculty in non-tenure-eligible positions as a positive influence on institutional programs because it brings an influx of new people with new ideas and a high level of motivation. In some cases these faculty do not have traditional academic credentials. This influx of new people with new ideas was an often-cited program benefit for many of the professional fields such as business, law, education, medicine, engineering, and social work. Deans and chairs of professional fields stated that hiring full-time non-tenure-eligible faculty who have extensive experience in the corporate, government, educational, and medical or health care fields enriches the curriculum for students and regular faculty.

A tenured professor in social work at a research university sees the full-time non-tenure-track faculty as providing multiple benefits to the institution in general and to her program area specifically. "[They] strengthen instruction," she observed. "[They] give depth and/or strength in an academic area. [Use of non-tenure-track faculty] lets a program pursue new areas where long-term demand is not known. [We] can try new initiatives when the university is not certain it is long-term."

In large part, these findings parallel Gappa and Leslie's (1993) conclusions about the benefits of employing part-time faculty. Support for undergraduate instruction, distinctive teaching skills, specialized expertise, and the ability to work with special types of students are among the benefits institutions acquire from their non-tenure-track appointments.

Not everyone views the employment of full-time non-tenure-track faculty as beneficial to their institutions' academic programs, however. Many of the administrators and faculty we interviewed from the traditional arts and sciences saw a benefit from the employment of FTNTT faculty to teach undergraduate writing courses, to teach lower-division language courses, and to teach some of the introductory large lecture courses in their disciplines. On the other hand, there were other chairs and tenured faculty who were chagrined about the increasing use of such personnel to teach undergraduate courses. Part of this difference of opinion on the use of full-time non-tenure-track faculty relates to the difference in roles between them and tenure-track/tenured faculty at the same institution. Many of these non-tenure-track faculty are hired with a narrowly defined role, which is "solely to teach." This happens most often in writing programs, foreign language courses, and other introductory-level skills courses but may also occur in other types of lower-division and even some upper-division courses. In contrast, the tenured and tenure-track faculty typically have a more comprehensive role with responsibilities for teaching, scholarship, service, and involvement in governance.

A dean of social sciences at a research university saw a downside to the increasing use of full-time non-tenure-track faculty in cases where a large percentage of upper-division courses were taught by those faculty. Her concern was that students were short-changed because they did not have the advantage of being taught by research faculty. An associate professor in arts and sciences at a research university had a slightly different perspective on the use of faculty hired "just to teach." She said, "In Arts and Sciences, you do research that informs your teaching. It carries over to your classroom. We're a knowledge factory. When you start separating the parts, I begin to question what happens when traditional roles of knowledge production, dissemination, and service are segmented."

Several tenured faculty and department chairs in arts and sciences disciplines expressed a concern about hiring faculty for instruction only, especially when their teaching load was higher than that of tenure-eligible faculty. They strongly implied that faculty who were not research-prepared or research-invested could not be as effective in the classroom as the tenure-eligible faculty member who maintains a research agenda. An associate professor of economics at a research university identified another possible negative effect of hiring a high percentage of full-time non-tenure-track faculty to replace tenure-track positions. She suggested that "overall faculty research productivity within a department suffers when non-research-interested faculty are hired." Her concern was voiced by several more faculty at other similar institutions. The basis of this concern is addressed in the discussion of the impact of non-tenure-track faculty on organizational culture later in this chapter.

Consequences for Students

Does the use of faculty who are deemed to be less permanent than tenure-track faculty have an impact on students that may differ from the impact of these faculty on the academic programs of institutions? According to many administrators, having full-time non-tenure-track faculty who are predominantly committed to teaching and who are recognized for the quality of their instruction is a positive factor in meeting the educational needs of students. Some view the use of these non-tenure-track faculty as beneficial, especially during the first two years of college when the heaviest use of them appears to take place. During our campus visits we learned of full-time non-tenure-track faculty who have developed special expertise in introductory-level instruction and skill in working with entry-level students. Similarly, we met FTNTT faculty who had developed professional specialties in areas such as elementary language pedagogy or science laboratory instruction.

Students may also benefit from exposure to instructors with work experience outside higher education. In the course of our interviews we encountered full-time term-appointment faculty with many years of professional experience in areas like social work, nursing, journalism, business, and industrial technology. These individuals, who often lack a terminal degree, provide a valuable supplement to the theory- and research-based knowledge of more traditional academics. They help students bridge the gap between theory and practice and give students an up-to-date and realistic perspective on the job market.

Nevertheless, a number of tenured faculty and department chairs on several campuses expressed concern about the use of full-time faculty in non-tenure-eligible positions and their relationships with students. A lecturer in religious studies at a liberal arts college summarized this concern when he stated, "[I] sensed a reluctance of students to 'bond' with faculty who are not on the tenure track or tenured because we are not perceived to be long-term at the institution." A lecturer in psychology at the same institution stated it more bluntly when she said, "They don't see us as permanent." These concerns underlie one of the issues that arose at small as well as large institutions. Can full-time non-tenure-track faculty effectively assume roles as mentors to students when their position is seen as tenuous? If the FTNTT faculty member enters into a mentoring relationship or an advisory relationship with students, will the adviser or mentor be available to serve as a source of letters of recommendation for the students when that need arises? These were issues posed by non-tenure-track faculty that they felt they needed to resolve in their dealings with students. Part of the problem involves how tenured faculty perceive the employment security of the full-time non-tenure-track personnel and their willingness to encourage students to seek lecturers as mentors.

The perceived insecurity of lecturer positions also raises concerns about the ability of full-time non-tenure-track faculty to serve as thesis advisers for undergraduates and on program and dissertation committees for graduate students. Several faculty members at baccalaureate institutions indicated a reluctance to serve as thesis advisers because of the insecurity of their position, while other faculty stated that students were unwilling to ask them to serve in that capacity for the same reason. At graduate institutions, the question of full-time faculty in non-tenure-eligible positions serving as graduate program committee members and dissertation advisers appears to be a function of institutional policy, custom, and individual preference. Some institutions bar their full-time non-tenure-track faculty from chairing or serving on students' committees. Some permit it.

Two statements from our respondents summarize many of the observations we heard about full-time non-tenure-track faculty and their relationship to the students they teach. A lecturer in history at a liberal arts college said, "Students are concerned about faculty turnover. They want faculty to stay. That is why they came to a small college [to have relationships with faculty]." A leader in the faculty senate of a public doctoral institution placed his emphasis on coursework and students when he stated that he sees "a lack of continuity for students from faculty on short-term appointments. [There is] less continuity and articulation of coursework."

There appeared to be less concern about full-time faculty in non-tenure-track positions being able to meet the advising and mentoring needs of students when the institution had a long-term contract system for their non-tenure-track faculty and when tenured faculty viewed them as peers. The longer an institution's policies affecting full-time non-tenure-track faculty had been in existence, the more secure the term-appointment faculty seemed to be about their roles. In some circumstances, the advising and mentoring roles of full-time term-appointment faculty were clarified at the departmental level, if not by institution-wide policies. It appeared to us that the willingness of term faculty to assume mentoring roles was a function of their perceived job security.

According to our investigation, students reap positive and negative results from the use of full-time non-tenure-track faculty. Whether they benefit or suffer from their contact with term faculty probably depends on many factors, including faculty employment security, length of appointment, and ability to serve students beyond the classroom.

Impact on Faculty Culture and Collegiality

The impact of full-time non-tenure-track faculty on campus culture and the collegial environment is shaped both by the degree to which campus policies and traditions include or exclude them from various aspects of campus life and by their own predilections for becoming involved and having an impact. There are several dimensions to assessing their actual or perceived impact. The first relates to the degree to which these faculty are involved in departmental and institutional decisionmaking. Are they involved to the same degree as tenure-track and tenured faculty? The involvement, or lack of involvement, in governance assists in understanding the degree to which non-tenure-track faculty are participating members of the campus community.

The second measure of full-time non-tenure-track faculty involvement on campus is the degree to which they collaborate with tenure-track faculty on course and scholarly activities. This seemed to vary significantly across the campuses. Although many of the non-tenure-track faculty we interviewed indicated that they were accepted in their departments and schools and received support in their roles as faculty members, we have little evidence that there was much collaboration between full-time tenure-eligible and non-tenure-track faculty on teaching and research activities. The most common issue faculty and administrators raised with us on the campuses we visited centered on the potential development of two classes (upper and lower) of faculty and what that meant for the culture and collegial environment of a campus.

Faculty and administrators at all twelve of the campuses we visited expressed concerns about the development of two classes of faculty. Non-tenure-eligible faculty and many of their tenured colleagues reported that these class differences relate directly to institutional policies setting forth terms and conditions of non-tenure-track employment. Specific examples of these issues vary somewhat by institution and department. Among the most common topics were differences in titles and ranks and the general lack of opportunity for full-time non-tenure-track faculty to experience professional advancement; lack of, or limited, opportunities for involvement in faculty governance; inequitable treatment in provision of support for professional development; and salaries that are not similar to the salaries of tenure-track faculty with comparable qualifications and years of experience.

It also became evident during our interviews that the perception of two classes of faculty or two faculty cultures was caused not only by explicit actions or institutional policies but also by implicit or inferred differences in faculty quality and status. In a department at one research university, for example, computer upgrades were provided to all tenured and tenure-track faculty, but the full-time non-tenure-track faculty on long-term contracts were given the hand-me-down computers, even though in many cases the computers for the non-tenure-track faculty were necessary for fulfilling assigned instructional responsibilities. At another institution, non-tenure-track faculty were assigned to the end of the faculty line at graduation. Each of these examples reinforces the perception of a two-tier faculty, even though each may be an unintended consequence.

A full-time non-tenure-track female faculty member at a research university said she is treated like a regular faculty member, "but in subtle ways you learn of differences." At the all-college retreat, all non-tenure-track faculty had colored dots on their name tags but did not initially know why. It became clear during the retreat that they were a different category of faculty.

A dean of arts and sciences at a master's-level institution stated that his institution, which uses multiple-year contracts for its full-time non-tenure-track faculty, is making a concerted effort not to have a two-tier system of faculty. However, he feels that a class system will develop because the tenured faculty will accept individuals in full-time non-tenure-track positions whom they will not accept as tenure-track hires. "The practical reality is that they [tenured faculty] do not view [non-tenure-track faculty] as the same." Several factors appear to contribute to this lack of acceptance. The first is that many of the full-time non-tenure-track faculty have a heavy teaching load as their only assignment, therefore research and scholarship are not expected nor supported. At many colleges and universities where research and publication are the coin of the realm, the lack of scholarly publication automatically tags a person as second-rate. The second reason is that many of the full-time non-tenure-track faculty are not hired through a national search. Both factors distinguish full-time non-tenure-track faculty from their tenure-class colleagues and leave the impression that they are members of a lower class of faculty.

A provost at a research university expressed concern that having both tenure-eligible and full-time non-tenure-eligible faculty creates the possibility of a cultural divide between a privileged and an underprivileged class of faculty. He expressed concern that the closer that institutions and departments move to having a cohort of full-time non-tenure-eligible faculty as large as the tenure-eligible cohort, the greater the possibility of cultural problems. He suggested that the concerns, priorities, and activities of the two types of faculty would differ, creating conflict and potentially distorting the mission of his institution.

Tenured faculty concerns about the development of two cultures are also related to the differential roles of tenured and non-tenure-track faculty at their institutions. They cited potential changes in departmental culture at a research university if the faculty included an increasing proportion of faculty committed primarily to teaching (non-tenure-track) in contrast to a majority committed to research and scholarship. A department chair at a research university observed that "hiring lots of [full-time lecturers] skews the intellectual climate. Lecturers see needs focused on teaching, not research. It alters discussion about the long-term future of a program." Another chair at the same institution added, "Since their [non-tenure-track lecturers'] main job is to teach, it sets up a whole different focus of a department." Presenting a broader perspective on the increasing use of full-time non-tenure-track faculty, a dean of a college of arts and sciences at a research university stated that he is concerned that the use of these faculty will erode the professoriate. "It may devalue scholarship [over time]. Use of lecturers raises the status of teaching at the expense of scholarship."

Even among full-time non-tenure-track faculty who want to contribute to the research culture of a department or institution, institutional policy or funding agency policy has the potential to militate against that contribution. At many institutions, and in the policies of many funding agencies, faculty designated as non-tenure-track are excluded from serving as principal investigators or co-principal investigators on projects. As a result, the policies preclude the full-time non-tenure-track faculty from adding to the research mission of the institution in a way that would benefit both the institution and the career of the faculty member. Second-class status is further reinforced as a result of such policies, and the academic community is fragmented further.

Concerns about two classes of faculty were most likely to arise on the topic of involvement in campus governance. For many of the full-time non-tenure-track faculty with whom we spoke, the right to be involved in governance was as important as actually exercising that right. One non-tenure-track faculty member summed up this sentiment when he observed: "Not all of the tenured faculty participate [in governance], but they have the right to do so." A contrasting perspective was expressed by tenured faculty at a number of the institutions when they stated that since full-time non-tenure-track faculty either were not permitted or chose not to be involved in campus governance and committee work, the burden of governance rested with the tenure-track faculty. Other sensitive issues related to the involvement of full-time non-tenure-eligible faculty in governance were evident on several of the campuses. In some cases, during meetings, the chair of the faculty senate or the chair of the department at departmental meetings needed to decide on an issue-by-issue basis those matters upon which the full-time non-tenure-track faculty were eligible to vote. In other circumstances votes by the non-tenure-track faculty were tallied separately from all other faculty.

One of the most critical governance issues for full-time faculty in non-tenure-track positions arises in the limited situations when those non-tenure-track faculty members are responsible for specific aspects of academic programs but are excluded from formal decision making about the program. This situation arises at those institutions that grant governance rights only to tenured and tenure-track faculty but assign program administration or coordinating responsibilities to non-tenure-track faculty. This type of action militates against the development or maintenance of an effective collaborative, collegial environment for all faculty by excluding the individuals most conversant with the programs from participating in decisions about the programs. Such an environment highlights distinctions among faculty based on tenure status, not program knowledge or professional competence.

Questions about the impact on departmental culture of full-time non-tenure-track faculty whose primary focus is on instruction were not as prevalent on baccalaureate campuses or master's-level institutions. This can be attributed to an institutional commitment primarily to instruction. However, on some of these campuses we did hear concerns about retaining an institutional emphasis on high-quality education in the face of an increasing proportion of full-time non-tenure-eligible faculty.

Another dimension of the culture and collegiality issue arose among tenured faculty and many arts and sciences department chairs when discussions focused on faculty recruiting. In this case the discussion centered on the quality of applicant pools for faculty positions when the institution advertises for a non-tenure-track faculty position rather than a tenure-track position. Many chairs and tenured faculty members expect that when their institution is hiring full-time non-tenure-track faculty to fill the same roles that tenure-eligible faculty fill, highly qualified potential applicants who are seeking tenure-eligible positions will self-select out of the applicant pool. Administrators and tenured faculty at some of the institutions we visited indicated that on occasion they had to change advertised faculty positions from non-tenure-eligible to tenure-eligible in competitive disciplines such as the natural sciences in order to identify a high-quality group of applicants from which to choose a new faculty colleague. The perception that only lesser-quality individuals are willing to accept non-tenure-track positions helps to fuel the culture and collegiality problems that emerge in a two-class faculty.

On the other hand, many institutions, because of the oversupply of qualified candidates, have been able to fill vacant full-time non-tenure-eligible positions with individuals who are highly qualified. Even so, there is a perception among tenured faculty and department chairs at many of the institutions we visited that when highly qualified people are employed in non-tenure-eligible positions they do not develop a strong commitment to the institution because they are constantly in the market for a tenure-track position. This constant "market scanning" is viewed as a detriment to developing meaningful relationships with faculty colleagues and in making long-term investments in academic programs and scholarly activities. These investments are deemed necessary for the achievement of departmental and institutional goals and objectives. When an imbalance in institutional commitment separates so-called permanent from temporary faculty, collegiality can suffer further.

Another factor that contributes to the tension on some campuses between full-time tenure-eligible and non-tenure-eligible faculty is the concern that the use of non-tenure-track faculty is a threat to the tenure system. The dean of academic affairs at a liberal arts college told us, "Most faculty who have worked most of their career in a tenure system see this [a formal non-tenure-track contract system] as a development they don't like." A tenured professor in a faculty leadership position at the same institution viewed the increasing use of full-time non-tenure-track personnel as "a devaluing of tenure." At many campuses it was not uncommon to hear faculty and department chairs decrying the substitution of non-tenure-track positions for what "should be" tenure-track slots. The faculty filling those term-appointment positions were in some instances viewed as a different class of academic personnel. We heard perhaps the harshest commentary on non-tenure-track faculty at a research university. A tenured senior professor told us that some regular (tenure-class) faculty are becoming increasingly uncomfortable with the growing use of full-time non-tenure-track faculty. She observed, "Non-tenure-track [faculty] are resented the same way 'scabs' in a UPS strike are resented. [They are a] way for the university to get work done cheaply. Ph.D. students and younger faculty resent these people. Hence, they will resist more equitable treatment for non-tenure-track [faculty]."

At some institutions that have recently implemented a formal multiyear contract system for employing full-time non-tenure-track faculty there were concerns about whether tenure was being phased out. A tenured professor at a master's-level institution expressed the concern that the tenure system at his institution "is being discouraged, at least patently [by the administration]." The basis for this feeling at his institution and several others is the growth in the number of full-time non-tenure-track as opposed to tenure-track positions in the past few years. The increase did not appear to raise as much apprehension at the larger research institutions, although it is a concern in some of their disciplines in which the recruitment of non-tenure-track faculty to teach lower-division courses has grown. This lack of apprehension at the larger, complex institutions may be because many of the departments have few full-time non-tenure-eligible faculty and the relatively large proportions in a few departments are not recognized as a significant issue institution-wide.

Additional factors contribute to the development of two classes of faculty. Among these are the lack of eligibility for professional leave (sabbaticals) for full-time non-tenure-track faculty on many campuses who have long-term contracts or work experience at their institution, and limited opportunity for professional advancement through a system of ranks comparable to those provided to tenure-eligible faculty. Compounding the situation at several campuses, and in specific departments, is the need for the full-time non-tenure-track faculty to share offices, while tenured and tenure-track faculty have individual offices.

All of these factors have the potential to create two classes of faculty and to militate against the maintenance or development of a positive professional culture on a college or university campus. The current treatment of full-time non-tenure-track faculty on many campuses is seen as leading to a clearly defined underprivileged class of faculty. In order to overcome this class system, institutions will need to develop policies that recognize and reward the significant role that these non-tenure-eligible faculty play in assisting the institution in meeting its mission and goals. Our visits have shown us that institutions that view the contributions of these faculty as important and ongoing are attempting to develop policies and practices that may support two or more *types* of faculty, not two or more *classes* of faculty. In a minority of cases the institutions are making bold philosophical and political choices and economic investments to the benefit of their full-time non-tenure-track faculty. These investments recognize the significance of the contributions of their FTNTT faculty to the institution, attempt to overcome the two-class syndrome that has developed between tenure-eligible and non-tenure-eligible faculty on many campuses, and enhance and support the careers of these faculty who are in atypical positions.

Consequences for Faculty Careers

As Chapter 4 documented, faculty members in full-time non-tenure-track positions differ significantly in who they are, where they work, and what they do. They also have many different reasons for accepting their non-tenure-eligible positions. This section describes the perceived impact of full-time employment in non-tenure-eligible positions on faculty careers. Also, we present our observations on how the use of these faculty is affecting the roles and careers of the tenured and tenure-track faculty with whom they work.

As described in Chapter 4, full-time non-tenure-track faculty fall into one of four types: teachers, researchers, administrators, and other academic personnel. Within these four career types, FTNTT faculty tend to be tenure-track hopefuls, non-tenure-track choosers or tenure-track rejecters, persons accompanying a spouse or partner, or alternative- or second-career faculty. In this section we explore these four career paths, classified by a faculty member's expressed reasons for being in their positions. All of the faculty types can follow any of the career paths. The career paths help explain the career aspirations, activities, and satisfaction of full-time non-tenure-track faculty.

TENURE-TRACK HOPEFULS

A large cohort of full-time non-tenure-track faculty includes those individuals whom we classified as *tenure-track hopefuls*. These are faculty who want a tenure-track position but have been unable to obtain one. Gappa and Leslie (1993) found a comparable group among part-time faculty. Obviously, these are individuals dedicated to pursuing an academic career by whatever means necessary. We include in this cohort only those who were actively interested in a tenure-track position and would not have been prevented from accepting one by spousal or other personal constraints. We placed those who had constraints on mobility because they are part of a two-career couple in a separate category (accompanying a spouse or partner).

We found the issue of an oversupply of qualified candidates and a lack of tenure-track positions in many disciplines at almost all of the institutions where we interviewed. Among many of the faculty who wanted tenure-track positions, there was a sense of frustration based on their belief that their non-tenure-track position would not lead to permanent employment or would be a negative factor as they continued to apply for tenure-eligible positions. A female in a full-time lecturer position in English at a research university summarized the sense of frustration expressed by many when she said, "I have been on the market four times and had one terrible [tenure-track] job offer. I am usually beaten out by people on the market longer than me who have books, etc." Because of the heavy teaching loads common among non-tenure-track faculty and the limited support they receive for scholarship and professional development, many conclude that their positions will not enable them to move to a more stable career on the tenure track.

A female lecturer who had been in a full-time non-tenure-eligible position in history for two years at a liberal arts college also summed up the attitudes of many of the tenure-track hopefuls when she said, "I applied everywhere a position was available but the labor market was so tight it made the search difficult. I did turn down a tenure-track position at one university and accepted this position because it was a good fit with my qualifications. I am happy with the current situation but would still like a tenure-track position."

The sense of frustration was especially palpable in our discussions with a large number of tenure-track hopefuls who were fulfilling many roles in full-time non-tenure-eligible positions. The frustrations of these faculty centered around the fact that they were doing the same things as the tenure-track or tenured faculty at the institution but did not have the benefits and security, or potential security, associated with tenure. Some were concerned about receiving a different faculty title or the lack of opportunity for advancement. Others were concerned about the lack of support for research or professional development or the opportunity to be meaningfully involved in governance.

A common feeling among these non-tenure-track faculty was summarized by a tenured humanities faculty member at a liberal arts college. "If these people [lecturers] are good enough to stay on forever [on multiyear contracts], why not give them tenure? These people are very vulnerable."

A second group of tenure-track hopefuls comprise those individuals who were hired into full-time "special role" non-tenure-track positions with primary responsibility for either research, service, or teaching. Many of these persons have primarily instructional roles. Typically, they carry heavier teaching loads than tenure-eligible faculty. For these faculty there is usually no expectation for scholarship and its related role functions. These faculty are less likely than their tenure-eligible colleagues to receive support for professional development or for research activities. A common refrain from numerous faculty filling this type of position is that such a position is a professional dead end.

A common issue raised by the tenure-hopeful faculty is that the longer they remain in the non-tenure-track position, the less marketable they become for a tenure-track position. Part of this concern is directly attributable to the lack of respect they feel that their position has among tenured colleagues at their own and other institutions and to their worry over how they can overcome that perspective in the academic labor market. They are afraid that their non-tenure-track status will be attributed not to market forces but to some flaw in their professional competence or to a lack of ambition.

The second dimension of the problem for those who were hired to carry a heavy teaching load and who received no support for scholarly endeavors outside the classroom was the difficulty in developing and maintaining a set of professional credentials that would make them competitive for tenure-track positions, either at their current institution or in the broader marketplace. Many of the persons we interviewed in this category have resigned themselves to a career track that they did not originally envision for themselves and with which they are not happy. Since they are operating with either full-time fixed term or renewable multiyear contracts in an uncertain environment, long-term security concerns are a continuing part of their life experience.

A full-time political science lecturer who has been at his baccalaureate institution for a number of years summed up his own situation in a question and a statement that reflect the feelings of many tenure-track hopefuls: "When I become expensive, will I become expendable? Every year that I remain in this position makes me less marketable if I want to enter the academic labor market."

Another major subcategory of the tenure-track hopefuls at several of the research universities contains recent Ph.D. graduates who are hired by their own degree-granting institutions. Typically, these are one- or two-year post-doctoral appointments. The positions serve two distinct yet interrelated purposes. First, graduates are given the opportunity to establish academic credentials that ideally will assist them in entering the academic labor market in the near future with teaching experience and the beginnings of a scholarly résumé. Second, these full-time faculty appointees assist the institution in meeting instructional needs with a known person, usually at significantly less cost than if a faculty member from outside the institution had been hired.

Perceptions about the career-launching long-term value of these full-time postdoctoral experiences vary among faculty participants. For example, a lecturer in history at a research university stated that he could not participate in department governance and had no formal research support in his non-tenure-track position. He stated with considerable emotion, "There is no expectation that we will do research in the lecturer position, but I realize that I must do it for career advancement. I view this lecturer post as a transitional phase that I hope will last only a year. This is standard practice in the history department. If I do not get a job, I may consider leaving academia."

A Ph.D. in mathematics participating in a three-year postdoctoral program for recent graduates at another research university contrasts sharply with the relatively negative situation cited above. His postdoctoral program is designed to assist the novice faculty member in establishing academic career credentials through a full-time non-tenure-track position that provides for teaching, research, limited committee work, and student advising. The position includes appointment at the assistant professor rank. This individual feels very positive about the experience and its potential impact on his career.

An academic labor market with an overabundance of applicants for limited tenure-track faculty positions has clearly influenced the careers of the faculty in this tenure-track hopeful category. How many of them eventually acquire the desired tenure-track position will be a function of the condition of the academic labor market and the potential effect of their non-tenure-track status on their competitiveness with new entrants when tenure-track positions become available.

A challenge to the institutions that are benefiting from the current labor market will be to make non-tenure-eligible faculty positions competitive and attractive in future years. In other words, how will institutions that are now able to hire tenure-track aspirants for non-tenure-track positions because of an oversupply of qualified personnel need to change the terms and conditions of employment if the demand for faculty begins to match the supply available? Certainly they will need to respond to the career concerns of these tenure-track aspirants.

Among the many full-time non-tenure-track faculty whom we interviewed, a large number are in those positions by professional and personal choice. Their reasons for the choice varied widely. One group consists of individuals who indicated that they had tried or observed the tenure-track career path. Either they did not find the tenure track to their liking or they did not have a successful experience with it. For example, a lecturer for eight years in chemistry at a liberal arts college stated that she had started in a tenure-track position at a small teaching college but became disenchanted because the demands of a heavy teaching load were "insane." She said, "I applied to [my current institution] on a whim. I had no interest in the job, but was 'wowed' when I got here. Within the department I am treated as an equal by my tenured colleagues. I did not expect to stay, but here I am. My game plan changed when I had kids."

This comment highlights the significance of tenured colleagues' attitudes toward their full-time term-appointment faculty counterparts along with a fulfilling professional role that meets both the professional interests and the personal needs of the non-tenure-eligible faculty member. In this case, children became an important part of the decision to remain at the institution and off the tenure track.

Other faculty members who expressed satisfaction with their non-tenure-eligible positions after experience with the tenure track stated that they have a commitment to teaching. For some, the pressures for research and publication caused them to forgo the tenure system. In several instances full-time non-tenure-track faculty we interviewed were individuals who had achieved tenure at another institution. At some point they had become disillusioned with the pressure for continued publication or other aspects of the tenure track. Some sought a career track with more emphasis on teaching, from which they derive personal and professional satisfaction.

Some of the tenure-track rejecters sought a position off the track right out of graduate school. They made the decision not to pursue a tenure-eligible position because of their observations of the professional lifestyle and pressures faculty faced at their graduate institutions. A full-time lecturer in psychology at a liberal arts college stated that she was taught in graduate school that tenure-track positions are best. She said that she did not necessarily believe that, because "the [full-time] tenure-track faculty I knew were stressed and I do not want that stress." Her current position has given her time off the fast track. This sentiment appeared to be most prevalent among faculty members who expressed a strong commitment to teaching as opposed to a research career.

Although generally satisfied with the opportunity to emphasize teaching and not be held accountable for the other traditional tenure-qualifying criteria, many of the tenure-track rejecters had concerns about their status on campus. Many view themselves as second-class citizens. Titles different from those of tenure-eligible faculty, lack of equitable involvement in governance, lower salaries (in many cases), and the uncertainty of long-term job security each contribute to their perception of secondary status. In many cases, condescending attitudes on the part of tenured colleagues exacerbate the situation. A female lecturer in arts at a baccalaureate college highlights the professional identity issue expressed by some tenure-track rejecters. "[The] title [lecturer] doesn't adequately reflect what I do at this institution. [We] need to convey that we are real faculty. Different titles may do this. [We] would like equity in title and salary. We are real faculty."

Many of the faculty we classify as tenure-track rejecters see their faculty roles as very positive and important. However, they feel that at campuses with a tenure system they may not be viewed the same as their tenure-track colleagues. Interestingly, many of them continue some scholarship in addition to their teaching but do not see it as the *raison d'être* of their career.

Among the non-tenure-track choosers are a number of faculty who are there because they do not have the terminal degree in their discipline, are interested primarily in teaching, and recognize that the full-time non-tenure-track position was the only option available for them to fulfill their professional goals. Many have no desire to go on for the terminal degree. These individuals are most often found teaching writing and introductory language courses, although at some baccalaureate and master's institutions they are fulfilling many of the same duties as tenure-track faculty. Some faculty with terminal degrees are also among the cadre of non-tenure-track choosers. They indicated to us that they have a primary interest in teaching and stated that they have no desire to pursue the tenure track.

The professional interests of many of these individuals who chose to work off the tenure track often related closely to their personal situations, and they highlighted the influence of family circumstances on their decision to choose a non-tenure-track position. These were primarily, but not solely, women. Some stated that the teaching-only requirements meshed well with their personal family needs, including child-rearing. For example, a lecturer in languages told us that not having to do research in her non-tenure-track post was a comfortable fit with her family.

The malleability of non-tenure-track positions is another factor that makes them appealing to some. An accounting professor at a baccalaureate institution is a case in point. She told us she likes her full-time non-tenure-track post because it enables her to continue her work as an accountant. "I need both [teaching and accounting practice] to be whole," she observed. Many of the full-time term-appointment faculty positions we learned about were interesting hybrid appointments that were developed with specific institutional needs and individual attributes and goals firmly in mind.

At times geography and prior institutional affiliation play a significant role in the decision to take a full-time non-tenure-track position at a specific college or university. We found faculty at each type of institution who chose their college or university because of its geographic location or because of the institution itself. In some cases it was an alumnus returning; in others someone with family living in the area. The full-time non-tenure-track position was meeting both personal and professional interests and needs for these faculty members.

Many in this non-tenure-track faculty category see a position off the tenure track as "a bypass around tenure's potholes" (Chait and Trower 1997, 17). For a variety of reasons they view the tenure system with some skepticism. Full-time non-tenure-track appointment alternatives permit them to pursue an academic career without the liabilities often associated with the quest for tenure.

ACCOMPANYING SPOUSE OR PARTNER

The career paths of a significant number of the full-time non-tenure-track faculty we met have been shaped by their roles in two-career couples or families. In most but not all cases, the "trailing" or "accompanying" partner was female. In the majority of accompanying partner employment situations we learned about, the spouse who was initially recruited by the institution received a tenured or tenure-track appointment and the accompanying partner received a full-time non-tenure-track position. In some cases the non-tenure-track position was already established and the accompanying partner qualified for the slot. In other cases, the position was created for the partner to ensure that the partner sought for the primary appointment would accept the tenure-track faculty or senior-level administrative position.

The accompanying partner phenomenon is often based on a geographic consideration that becomes part of the employment decisionmaking and, therefore, helps to shape the career paths of those faculty members. In some instances, one spouse or partner receives a position at a college or university or a professional position in the community, and the accompanying partner acquires a full-time non-tenure-track position at a nearby institution. The geographic constraints faced by two-career partnerships or families are especially critical when institutions of higher education are in rural areas or small cities with a limited number of institutions that can provide employment for the accompanying spouse or partner.

We found individuals identified as accompanying partners who were happy with their appointments and felt that the full-time non-tenure-track position met both their professional and personal needs. (They could also be classified as non-tenure-track choosers.) Other "trailing" partners in non-tenure-track positions were committed to acquiring a tenure-track position as soon as possible (i.e., were tenure-track hopefuls). There was a high sense of frustration among many of these tenure-track hopefuls. Some felt their careers were being stifled because their current institution did not provide them with the opportunity to move to a tenure-track position or to convert their current position to tenure status. In many cases they felt that the non-tenure-track role they fulfilled was equivalent to the role of tenure-track or tenured faculty in their department.

A lecturer in literature who has a Ph.D. in his discipline came to a research university when his wife received a tenure-track position at the institution. He stated that he was not hired as the result of a search. Due to his dual-career situation, a full-time non-tenure-track position was created for him. He feels that his institution is exploiting him. He is doing essentially the same things that tenure-track faculty do but is not on track and has a low lecturer's salary. He summed up his situation by saying, "As years go by, the non-tenure-track faculty member [of a dual career couple] becomes increasingly dissatisfied. I have been on the market every year I have been here." His ability to improve his professional life is restricted, however. He stated that in order to move there would also need to be a satisfactory position for his wife.

On the other hand, this lecturer in literature told us that he has been included in the intellectual life of the university in a gratifying way. In addition, his colleagues have been very good about his situation. There has been no "petty discrimination" on their part. His situation, to a large extent, reflects the feelings of the non-tenure-track partner of many dual-career couples. Many described their colleagues and department chairs as supportive but reported that institutional policy sometimes leads to exploitation of the accompanying spouse or partner. The accompanying spouse is vulnerable because he or she has very little chance of leaving unless the tenure-track partner also leaves and, hence, little flexibility to negotiate more favorable employment conditions.

In contrast, a full-time non-tenure-track faculty member in political science who followed her husband to a tenured position in a liberal arts college shows that dual-career non-tenure-track appointments can lead to fulfilling careers. She has benefited from her institution's support of professional development for its lecturers. Through a leave program she was able to return to her research university to complete coursework on her doctorate. She stated that she has a full-time job teaching courses others in the department choose not to teach. With the completion of the doctorate she sees the chance for a tenure-track position, although she feels her position fits her career aspirations nicely at the present time. Dual-career non-tenure-track faculty represent a diverse and complex group. Many feel constrained and exploited, while others are quite content with their distinctive career situation. Colleague and administrator support along with enlightened personnel policies account for some of the difference between dual-career term faculty who are contented and those who are not.

ALTERNATIVE- OR SECOND-CAREER FACULTY

We also interviewed full-time non-tenure-track faculty who had previous work experience or careers in areas such as government, business, industry, K–12 education, technology, medicine, and law. Although we found the second-career faculty predominantly in professional fields, they are also evident in traditional arts and sciences disciplines. For a variety of reasons, including disaffection with the previous career, retirement, and the need for new challenges, these individuals are now full-time non-tenure-track faculty members.

The experience of a faculty member in business at a doctoral institution exemplifies that of many second-career, full-time non-tenure-track faculty members.

> I was in business for twenty-five years and had started my own business in this city. I started to teach part-time for [this institution] about ten years ago. I received good student evaluations and was asked to take this full-time position this year. They wanted someone with experience and academic credentials. I like the environment and the students. I see the

non-track position as a viable career option. Tenure does not mean much to me. I have my businesses on the outside I can fall back on.

This individual is a typical second-career non-tenure-track faculty member. Many institutions bring practitioners with nontraditional credentials to their faculties in selected disciplines to enrich the curriculum and the educational experiences of students. Because of their outside interests and alternative career opportunities, these faculty members usually do not feel the need for the security that tenure provides. The opportunity to interact with students and to pass on to those students their knowledge of the "real world setting" in which their disciplines are applied appears to be a strong motivation for these faculty members.

For some faculty the full-time non-tenure-track appointment was the beginning of a new career that may last for twenty-five years or longer, especially if they can move to the tenure track. These individuals aspire to a position that will require the full range of faculty responsibilities and for which they have the necessary academic qualifications. For example, we interviewed a practicing lawyer who also taught as a part-time adjunct faculty member for a number of years at a doctoral institution before taking a full-time non-tenure-track teaching appointment. She is an example of second-career faculty members who are hopeful that such an appointment will provide access to an eventual tenure-track position. In her first year in a full-time non-tenure-track position, this faculty member feels that she is in a precarious position because she is aiming for a career transition. She says, "I would not have taken the non-track position if there were not a possibility of an eventual tenure-track position [at the institution]. I feel that I have two years to establish my academic credentials. I view this as a long-term career opportunity." She cited two levels of stress in her career change that other career changers who were seeking tenure-track appointments mentioned. These included the stress of trying to acquire an initial tenure-track position, which (if successful) will then be followed by the stress related to acquiring tenure. This law faculty member summed up the stress issue for career changers when she asked, "Where do I stack up against unknown competition?"

For other second-career full-time non-tenure-track faculty members, there is the anticipation of an academic career that will usually last no longer than one to five years. Many have retired from their previous positions and have the desire only to teach and pass on the lessons learned from their experiences for a short period of time.

Summary

Our intent in this chapter was to assess the impact of using full-time non-tenure-track faculty on the colleges and universities where they work. We also sought to clarify how these positions affect the lives and careers of the individuals who fill them. We found that there are both positive and negative consequences for institutions and for the faculty in these positions, just as there are positive and negative consequences for institutions and faculty under tenure systems.

Many factors influence the specific consequences of employing full-time non-tenure-track faculty. The purpose for which they were hired, the roles they play, their professional status, and the resources and support they receive from their institutions each influence their impact on a campus. These faculty can be a critical element of an institution's academic program over the long term or merely temporary substitutes for regular (tenure-track) faculty in times of institutional stress. They can motivate students in the classroom with their distinctive expertise and provide a bridge between academic life and the world of work. Alternatively, they can teach large introductory lecture classes without ever getting to know their students well. They can be engaged in their institution's governance system or never share their knowledge and experience with colleagues who guide policy development and curriculum planning. They can save their institutions substantial amounts of money or cost more than their colleagues who enjoy the benefits of tenure. They can be frustrated in dead end jobs with no clear path to career advancement or they can shape a career within the parameters of term contracts.

Among the findings in this chapter are many factors and problems that are also faced by part-time faculty working on the same campuses. Many part-time faculty face the same frustrations about job insecurity, lack of career development opportunities, salary inequity, and second-class status that we identified among the full-time non-tenure-track faculty. The majority of part-time faculty suffer from the same lack of fair employment policies and practices (Gappa and Leslie 1993) that we identified for the full-time non-tenure-track faculty. Although FTNTT faculty are disadvantaged when compared to their tenure-class colleagues, they are generally in better circumstances than part-time faculty.

The growing use of full-time non-tenure-track faculty is not inherently a negative or a positive trend. The consequences of hiring faculty in full-time non-tenure-track positions largely depend on the quality of the policies that regulate the employment of these faculty and support their professional performance. Institutions must closely monitor their use of faculty in these types of positions to ensure that these academic professionals make a positive contribution to the institutions' programs, students, and overall culture.

Next, Chapter 6 describes what we feel are some exemplary policies that serve to meet the professional needs and support the careers of full-time non-tenure-track faculty. At the same time, these policies can also help higher education institutions achieve staffing flexibility.

6 Exemplary Policies for Full-Time Non-Tenure-Track Faculty

The academic profession is in the midst of a dramatic transformation. Numerous books and reports (Finkelstein et al. 1998; Gappa and Leslie 1993; AAHE New Pathways Project Working Paper Series, 1996–98) document the evolution of membership in and the work of the professoriate. Changes have been necessary to accommodate a more pluralistic society, new technologies, a changing economy, and greatly increased demands for education. In a period of rapid change, policies written to support the work of a predominantly white, full-time, and tenure-eligible faculty are antiquated if not downright harmful. As we move into a new era in higher education, academic personnel policies must be revised and rewritten if they are to shape a work environment that facilitates the effective performance of all persons who fill faculty roles—nontraditional as well as conventional.

Our study of the full-time non-tenure-track faculty phenomenon has revealed both benign neglect and unhealthy ignorance concerning the working conditions and professional needs of these faculty. Likewise, we have discovered both poorly conceived and well-designed policies and practices that directly influence the work and career paths of faculty off the tenure track. We summarize these policies in Chapter 3. The purpose of this chapter is to highlight exemplary academic and personnel policies that, taken together, result in a composite model of a supportive work environment for full-time non-tenure-eligible faculty. Although no institution that we know of has a perfect program to support these faculty, we found progressive policies at a host of schools that employ substantial numbers of them. Many of these policies are similar to those enacted by institutions when employing part-time faculty, documented by Gappa and Leslie (1993). Such policies are even more important to full-time faculty than to part-time faculty, because the former are making a full-time commitment to the institution, often with career hopes in mind.

We do not suggest that all institutions employing full-time faculty on term contracts adopt this model verbatim. Each college or university must devise policies and practices consistent with its own traditions and context. However, we believe this model can serve as a framework for institutions wishing to reexamine and reform their personnel policies concerning full-time non-tenure-track faculty. It can also benefit deans and department chairs wishing to counsel and support these faculty who work in their academic units. Finally, the model can instruct professional associations and other faculty interest groups seeking to promote overall faculty vitality by enhancing conditions in the academic workplace.

Components of a Good Practice Model

We realize that one-size-fits-all solutions are impossible in an enterprise as large and complex as the American system of higher education. The policies we highlight in this chapter must be adapted to accommodate distinctive institutional, disciplinary, and personal circumstances. We believe, however, that institutions wishing to provide a supportive work environment for full-time non-tenure-track faculty should address each of the following thirteen factors as key parts of an overall model of good practice when shaping a comprehensive set of policies to guide the employment of these faculty.

A DEFINED PROBATIONARY PERIOD

Some full-time non-tenure-track appointments are designed to fill specific needs for fixed periods of time. Short-term appointments should be explicitly labeled as such. A one- or two-year fixed-term appointment in such a position does not represent a probationary period where good performance may yield a renewed or an extended contract. Persons who fill temporary visiting or adjunct appointments need to know from the outset that their position has no potential of becoming a long-term appointment through which they might build a career.

In contrast, we believe positions that fill long-term institutional or programmatic needs and are renewable should have a built-in probationary period similar to the pre-tenure phase of a traditional faculty appointment. Such a probationary period permits a college or university to assess the performance of a full-time term-appointment faculty member and make an informed judgment about his or her long-term potential as a professional. A rigorous and clearly defined probationary phase suggests that a contract will not be renewed indefinitely without evidence of satisfactory performance. Typically, contracts during this trial period are issued for one year at a time. Following satisfactory completion of the probationary phase, longer term renewable contracts are usually issued. Such a probationary phase also demonstrates that these faculty, like their tenure-eligible colleagues, are held accountable. Implementation of a probationary period can help to suppress beliefs that full-time non-tenure-track faculty are second-class or, as some say, "subfaculty."

Many institutions employing non-tenure-track faculty in full-time positions have no probationary period. Instead, they continuously reappoint some of the faculty in a haphazard manner with little apparent assessment of the long-term consequences for the faculty member or for the institution. In contrast to this casual approach to employing term-appointment faculty, some institutions build a carefully prescribed probationary phase into such appointments. For example, a liberal arts institution we studied conducts a thorough review of its full-time non-tenure-track faculty in their third year of employment. It reviews these faculty again after five years on the job. This second review is a more rigorous assessment conducted by the college's tenure and promotion committee. The committee applies "essentially the same [standards] as those it uses in considering its recommendations for the granting of tenure and promotion to Associate Professor." Similarly, a master's-level institution we investigated employs the traditional seven-year probationary period for its full-time non-tenure-track faculty. Each year probationary faculty are evaluated by their department chairs in consultation with departmental colleagues and program students. In addition, a faculty review committee solicits input from the university community as a whole when a candidate comes up for appointment status reviews. Once continuing status is achieved, a non-tenure-track professor at the institution is reviewed for continuation at five-year intervals.

A defined probationary period benefits the non-tenure-track faculty member as well as the institution he or she serves. The institution profits from knowing that its faculty measure up to performance criteria over a lengthy period of rigorous scrutiny. The probationary period decreases the likelihood that colleges and universities will continue to employ off-the-tenure-track full-time faculty regardless of the quality of their work, simply because their work is never thoroughly evaluated. Successful performance throughout a probationary period affirms that a full-time term-appointment faculty member is a valued part of the academic team. For this reason, a probationary period including rigorous evaluation can reduce misperceptions that a faculty member is a second-rate professional who, unlike tenure-track colleagues, could not withstand a stringent evaluation process.

EXPLICIT EVALUATION CRITERIA

Numerous institutions with progressive policies that guide full-time non-tenure-track employment provide explicit evaluation criteria for judging faculty performance. Given the distinctive roles that non-tenure-eligible faculty play at many colleges and universities, the standards are often derived directly from the descriptions of the jobs involved. Evaluation criteria for the faculty should be consistent with the requirements of their non-tenure-track posts. Inappropriately applying the criteria employed for judging tenure-class faculty can result in the valuable contributions of full-time non-tenure-eligible faculty being overlooked and can generate unnecessary anxiety and frustration. We believe the use of standards designed to reflect the distinctive aspects of non-tenure-track roles is a constructive practice. Full-time non-tenure-track faculty need to know the basis on which their work will be assessed and what they must do to succeed professionally.

Every institution we studied seems to address the evaluation of full-time non-tenure-track faculty evaluation in its own unique way. The most helpful policies, however, are those that specify clearly how and on what basis these faculty will be assessed. One baccalaureate college we investigated provides a particularly useful model. It addresses the evaluation process in its appointment letter. The letter makes clear that the faculty will be judged on their performance in teaching, professional development, advising students, and participation in departmental service. It explicitly notes that

> the standards to be employed in assessing . . . professional performance [of term faculty] will be those used for all other evaluations in [the] department, except as they pertain to scholarly work and University service.

The faculty handbook of a research university states that

> nontenure-track faculty member[s] will be evaluated annually during the term of employment . . . The evaluation will be based on those duties described under the terms of employment as agreed upon by the individual and supervisor under the general headings of teaching or re-

search or professional service or administrative duties, or some combination thereof.

A master's-level institution where non-tenure-track faculty are often used interchangeably with tenure-eligible faculty follows a similar pattern. Its policy on renewable term appointments [RTAs] states that

supervisors are expected to evaluate RTA faculty using evaluation procedures and criteria determined by the academic unit(s) to which they are assigned and consistent with university appraisal process and policies [specified in the faculty handbook]. At the outset of the [term] faculty member's employment the supervisor is expected to set forth the faculty member's teaching, research and service responsibilities and also to explain the evaluation procedures the supervisor will use thereafter. Annual evaluations will reference these initial statements of expectations and any subsequent revisions of expectations.

Each of the institutions cited here attempts to enhance the evaluation process in two critical ways. First, it links evaluation criteria to the roles these faculty play at the institution. Second, it has a procedure in place to ensure that the faculty know the criteria and the process by which their work will be judged. Clear and detailed statements on evaluation standards can promote the effective performance of this special group of faculty.

MULTIYEAR CONTRACTS FOLLOWING
A PROBATIONARY PERIOD

A long series of short-term, unpredictable appointments creates instability both for individual faculty and for the institutions that employ them. Such erratic employment arrangements make it difficult for a person to make long-term plans or to grow and advance professionally. Likewise, institutions cannot depend on the availability of qualified academic staff when the latter are not offered any employment security. They may leave for more secure employment elsewhere. To address this situation, many institutions that employ full-time non-tenure-track faculty to address long-term programmatic needs offer them multiyear contracts. Generally, such appointments are awarded only after a lengthy probationary period. Multiyear contracts based on careful assessment of institutional needs can minimize periods of employment uncertainty for the institution as well as the faculty member and permit more systematic staff planning.

Colleges and universities define multiyear renewable contracts in a variety of ways. A liberal arts college we studied has an elaborate multiyear contract arrangement. To quote from its faculty handbook, the college's contract system has a threefold purpose:

A. To promote the growth and development of the individual
B. To provide adequate remuneration and recognition for services rendered
C. To provide appropriate and regular opportunities for the discussion of stages of institutional and personal assessment and need.

This "fixed-interval contract" system consists of one-year contracts (for the first three years), one three-year contract, and subsequent five-year contracts that may continue as long as need for the position continues and the faculty member's performance in the position is satisfactory. This type of arrangement responds both to the individual's need for career security and advancement and the institution's need for faculty accountability and staffing flexibility.

A research university's slight variation on this contract pattern offers essentially the same benefits. It appoints full-time term-appointment lecturers to three-year contracts. Senior lecturers receive an initial three-year contract with subsequent reappointments for five-year terms. This arrangement too recognizes and rewards long-term service to the institution by these faculty. It provides a substantial degree of career stability at the same time that it maintains flexibility that the institution can utilize if financial conditions or programmatic needs change over time.

At a few of the institutions we examined, the length of contracts for full-time non-tenure-track appointments was not spelled out in policy manuals or consistently applied by academic administrators. We learned, for example, of cases where the contracts of long-serving full-time term-appointment faculty were renewed for a shorter period at the whim of a new department chair. Unpredictable or inconsistent contract arrangements led to anger, frustration, and a sense of professional powerlessness among some of the non-tenure-track faculty we interviewed. In contrast, a codified contract system offering multiyear contracts after a successful probationary period recognizes that the faculty and the institutions they serve are interdependent. Multiyear contracts acknowledge the concerns of both in a time of rapid change. They can improve faculty morale and commitment at the same time that they respond to valid institutional concerns about an uncertain future.

DEFINED DATES FOR CONTRACT RENEWAL OR TERMINATION

By definition, non-tenure-track appointments provide less security than do tenured positions. Some institutions, however, have developed strategies to reduce the uncertainty and apprehension that sometimes accompany full-time term appointments. One mechanism is to provide a system of defined dates for contract renewal or termination. Adequate notice of renewal can reduce the anxiety generated by term-appointment positions with casual or erratic reappointment procedures. Conversely, adequate notice of nonrenewal or termination can ease the transition to alternative employment by providing ample time for a job search.

Several of the institutions we studied have established clear procedures for informing full-time non-tenure-eligible faculty in a timely manner whether they will be reappointed. Some policies provide clear dates well in advance of contract termination for informing these faculty about their future at the institution. A few policies go even further and ease the transition to another job with generous financial support. Each of the policies we describe below recognizes the institution's responsibility to support the career of the person it hires in a full-time term-appointment position. Each also provides a model other institutions might adapt to meet their distinctive needs.

A master's-granting university we visited makes the decision to extend three-year term contracts during the second semester of the second contract year. If a contract is not renewed at that time, the non-tenure-track faculty member has more than a year to seek alternative employment. Likewise, when a faculty member is terminated for cause prior to the end of the three-year contract period, he or she is notified by March 1 that the contract will end at the conclusion of the first contract year, or by December 15 if the contract will end at the conclusion of the second year. These notification dates reflect the institution's desire to give its full-time term-contract faculty time to seek other employment. They also demonstrate that the university assumes increased responsibility for supporting the career transitions of its non-tenure-track faculty with their increased length of service to the institution.

A research university takes a similar but somewhat more generous approach to the timing of renewal and termination decisions. Its policy states that

> timely notice shall be given of every decision not to reappoint a lecturer, senior lecturer or principal lecturer or to let an appointment lapse. Notice is timely if given one year before the expiration of the term of appointment.

An extension clause with significant financial implications shows this institution's commitment to easing the transition of terminated non-tenure-track faculty.

In order to comply with this provision, it may be necessary to extend a [term faculty position] by an additional appointment of up to one year, designated as a terminal appointment, the decision not to reappoint or to let the appointment lapse notwithstanding.

An undergraduate college we studied has a detailed procedure in place for notifying full-time term-appointment faculty of their nonrenewal and the most generous policy we identified for easing their transition to other employment. First-year appointees are notified of nonrenewal by March 1. Second-year appointees receive their termination notification no later than December 15. These same dates are used for notifying untenured tenure-track faculty that their appointments will not be extended. After three years of service, full-time non-tenure-track faculty who are not reappointed receive a lump sum payment equal to their third year's salary. However, benefits do not continue. A decision to terminate a term appointment after six years of service is followed by a sabbatical the next year with full pay and benefits. After seven or more years with the college, a full-time non-tenure-track professor must be notified by commencement that his or her position will be eliminated. The faculty member receives "either notice of nonrenewal at the end of the next academic year or notice of immediate nonrenewal with a lump sum payment equal to 125% of the then current salary." If termination is due to unsatisfactory performance, the faculty member is placed on conditional status for one year. If performance is still not satisfactory at the end of the conditional year, the non-tenure-track faculty member may be terminated without compensation.

Each of these policies represents an attempt to balance institutional needs for flexibility with individual needs for time and support to make a difficult career transition. By developing specific dates for announcing nonrenewal decisions, these policies increase the level of predictability in the lives of full-time non-tenure-track faculty. The more time there is between a nonrenewal decision and contract expiration, the more opportunity the faculty have to find a satisfactory professional opportunity elsewhere. When colleges and universities develop a system of contract renewal dates and policies that eases the transition to another position, they support faculty morale and enhance commitment to serving the institution well.

AN EQUITABLE SALARY SYSTEM

Some colleges and universities use full-time non-tenure-track faculty positions to preserve programmatic flexibility and to cut personnel costs. At many institutions, faculty off the tenure track are paid considerably less than their tenure-class colleagues. A small number of institutions we researched do not follow this pattern. In the spirit of equality, which is a fundamental value of higher education, these institutions pay their non-tenure-track faculty salaries comparable to those of tenure-track faculty when their qualifications and the work performed are roughly equivalent. For example, the appointment letter for a non-tenure-track position at a baccalaureate-level college describes the parallels between the college's tenure-track and non-tenure-track compensation systems:

> A salary schedule includes annual steps, similar to the pattern used in the career [tenure-track] faculty schedule. We have endeavored to make this compensation system compatible with the career faculty system and to represent the nature of the appointment and to reflect the compensation for comparable positions elsewhere. As a faculty member, you will receive standard faculty benefits.

An appendix to this policy further states that "academic preparation, search procedures, performance standards and compensation are comparable to career faculty teaching similar courses."

Another baccalaureate-level college we studied pays its full-time non-tenure-track faculty about 10 percent more than its tenure-track faculty. This compensation recognizes the equivalent credentials and work of the two groups of faculty. It also recognizes that faculty off the tenure track live with a higher degree of risk. This policy attempts to compensate these faculty for the increased flexibility in staffing they permit the institution to maintain.

We found very few institutions that have a set policy mandating equal pay for equal credentials and equal work regardless of tenure status. Those that have such policies acknowledge the valuable contributions that non-tenure-track faculty make to their academic programs. Furthermore, they make a bold statement about the necessity of treating all faculty fairly. Policies advocating equivalent faculty compensation for equivalent contributions to their institutions are a key factor in preventing the development of two classes of faculty (haves and have nots) in higher education.

AN EQUITABLE FRINGE BENEFIT PROGRAM

Many colleges and universities with well-defined policies for full-time non-tenure-track faculty provide fringe benefits comparable to those of tenure-class faculty. In some cases the policy simply states that full-time term-appointment faculty will have access to the same benefits as all full-time faculty. Other institutions spell out in detail what benefits are available to faculty off the tenure track. A master's-level university we visited reported that its renewable full-time term-appointment faculty "qualify for many economic benefits accorded tenure/tenure-track faculty members. Such benefits include eligibility for education leaves and university-funded grant programs (summer research/teaching grants, technology grants, etc.)." A unionized doctoral-level institution we studied delineates benefits for these full-time faculty in more detail. At this institution, "*the University shall continue to 'pick up' (assume and pay) the employee contribution to the State Teachers Retirement System.*" The collective bargaining agreement also details that the university will provide full-time non-tenure-track faculty with hospitalization, medical and life insurance benefits "as are provided to other full-time University employees."

Access to the complete range of benefits that full-time tenure-class faculty receive recognizes and rewards the contributions to the institution of non-tenure-track faculty. Perhaps more importantly, it affirms their legitimacy as valued members of the faculty and the larger institutional community. Colleges and universities that provide fair fringe benefits to non-tenure-track faculty show that they are committed to meeting the basic personal and professional needs of those faculty. Full benefits help to make the positions more attractive career alternatives.

A SYSTEM OF SEQUENTIAL RANKS

The common attribute of many non-tenure-track positions, irrespective of their titles, is the distinct lack of opportunity to advance in rank and status. In contrast, institutions with career-sensitive policies for full-time non-tenure-track faculty usually provide a system of sequential ranks that acknowledges continuing service, professional achievements, and contributions to one or more institutions. Some schools employ the traditional faculty ranks of assistant, associate, and full professor. These titles are most commonly utilized at colleges and universities that use tenure-class and non-tenure-track faculty interchangeably. A research university we studied that employs faculty off the tenure track to perform specialized roles precedes each of the traditional faculty ranks with the prefix adjunct, visiting, or college. These classifications relate to the duration of the term appointment. "College faculty" positions are indefinitely renewable. In these positions term-appointment faculty, like their tenure-track colleagues, may climb a career ladder.

The full-time non-tenure-track faculty at another research university play predominantly instructional roles. This institution awards these academic staff members faculty status but uses special titles to designate their professional rank. Nevertheless, the university explicitly preserves the career ladder characteristic of traditional faculty appointments. Non-tenure-track faculty at this institution can proceed from the rank of lecturer to senior lecturer and finally to principal lecturer. Like the rank of assistant professor, the lecturer title denotes a beginning or entry-level post. According to the university's policy on lecturer track appointments, "Senior Lecturers are expected to demonstrate exceptional mastery in teaching with a substantial impact on the university's educational mission." Somewhat like the full professor rank, principal lecturer denotes elevation to a capstone status at the institution. According to the lecturer-track policy statement, appointments at the principal lecturer rank "are made only for extraordinary accomplishment in teaching and fundamental contributions to the university's educational mission." Appointments at the principal lecturer rank must be approved by the university's provost, "who may request the opinion of the University Tenure Committee in any individual case." Perhaps most important, the policy states very explicitly that "the ranks of Lecturer, Senior Lecturer and Principal Lecturer shall be regarded as equivalent to those of Assistant Professor, Associate Professor and Professor, respectively." It is clear from this policy on lecturer-track appointments that progression along the lecturer ranks signifies career advancement and increased professional status within the institution.

For several reasons, a clearly defined system of sequential ranks for full-time faculty off the tenure track is a valuable component of a comprehensive policy for these faculty. It recognizes effective performance and long-term service at institutions that employ the faculty over many years. It provides an incentive for professional growth and high-quality performance over time. It helps to minimize the negative status differences that distinguish tenure-class from non-tenure-track faculty and that can prevent them from working together effectively as team members in program planning, curriculum development, and other professional activities.

SUPPORT FOR PROFESSIONAL DEVELOPMENT

Support for ongoing professional development should be a key element of an institution's program to facilitate the work of its full-time non-tenure-track faculty. Such support is especially important for full-time faculty off the tenure track who work for many years and fill critical educational roles at their institutions. Contrary to this continuing need for professional growth opportunities, however, policies that explicitly address professional development support for faculty off the tenure track are relatively rare. Even though many institutions are increasingly dependent on faculty in non-tenure-track positions to teach introductory-level courses and to meet other academic needs, few have developed clear policies to support the professional growth of this component of their academic work force. Indeed, we were often surprised at what little professional development support term-appointment faculty received and how haphazard and unpredictable that support was. As we reported in Chapter 3, professional development support for non-tenure-track faculty often depends on the good will of a dean or department chair and the vagaries of academic budgets.

A doctoral institution we studied is an exception to this pattern. It provides a general statement on the rights of its full-time non-tenure-track faculty to professional development support. The policy states that

> [non-tenure-track faculty] will be eligible to participate in professional development programs and opportunities at the department/campus college and university levels. These shall include, but not necessarily be restricted to, financial support for faculty research through the existing structure, policies and procedures of the University Research Council and the various programs supporting teaching and instructional improvement/enhancement made available through the structure, policies and procedures of the University Teaching Council.

Although this policy does not give precise details on the professional development assistance and funding that the university's non-tenure-track faculty receive, it leaves no doubt that they are entitled to many of the same types of support that tenure-track faculty usually receive.

Two institutions we discussed in Chapter 3 provide exceptionally generous support for the professional development and scholarship of their full-time non-tenure-track faculty. We elaborate on these policies here to clarify the institutions' strategies for supporting the professional growth of term-contract faculty. These ambitious programs acknowledge the institutions' reliance on their off-tenure-track faculty and their commitment to the long-term professional growth of these academic staff members. Each approach can serve as an instructive model for other institutions seeking to maintain a strong, up-to-date faculty team.

One is a liberal arts college. This institution provides support to the non-tenure-track faculty for professional travel and research on the same basis as tenure-eligible faculty. Unlike most institutions that employ term-appointment faculty, the college's sabbatical policy includes non-tenure-track appointments and provides them with a more generous sabbatical package than tenured faculty receive. Tenured faculty may take a year's leave with 60 percent of their salary. Non-tenure-track faculty who have served six or more years at the school may take a year's leave with full pay and benefits. This policy reflects the college's desire to help its non-tenure-eligible faculty keep current in their fields and its commitment to making its long-term renewable appointments a viable alternative to tenure-track positions.

The other institution with a model program for supporting the professional growth of full-time term-appointment faculty is a master's-level university. This institution offers sabbaticals to its tenured faculty every seven years. A tenured faculty member may choose either a one-semester sabbatical at full pay or a one-year sabbatical at half salary. The faculty with continuing status (non-tenure-track but long-term faculty members) at the institution may choose from a wider and somewhat more generous range of leave options. Leave opportunities vary according to the person's years of service to the university. A continuing status faculty member is eligible for

1. one semester of faculty development leave at half salary or a summer of leave (salary negotiable) with every fourth year of service;
2. one semester of faculty development leave at full salary or a one year leave at half salary with every fifth year of service; or
3. one semester of faculty development leave at full salary plus a summer leave at full salary with every sixth year of service.

These two programs to foster the professional growth of full-time non-tenure-track faculty represent the positive end of a spectrum that is weighted more in the opposite direction. Our investigation suggests that comparatively few institutions that employ full-time faculty off the tenure track have defined clear, consistent, and generous policies to allow them to keep up to date in their fields, enhance their teaching, or facilitate their scholarship. The approaches we highlight above may not be consistent with the needs or the resources of other institutions with non-tenure-track faculty. Strategies tailored to the circumstances of individual institutions are the most appropriate response. Above all, we believe that colleges and universities have an obligation to support the professional development of all their faculty who serve over a long period. Not to do so deprives term-appointment faculty members of the growth opportunities required to respond to a dynamic and demanding educational environment. Over time, inadequate support for professional development can diminish both non-tenure-track faculty and the institutions they serve.

Meaningful engagement in program planning and decision making is an indication of the status and respect that full-time non-tenure-track faculty receive on their campuses. As experts in their fields and experienced educators they have valuable perspectives to offer, yet many institutional policies overlook or intentionally exclude these faculty from governance and other forms of institutional service. We believe this is a mistake. A comprehensive policy for faculty off the tenure track should include a purposeful yet realistic role in the governance process.

The extent of their governance role will vary with the functions the non-tenure-track faculty fill on their campuses. At institutions where they function interchangeably with tenure-class faculty, faculty members off the tenure track often engage in all aspects of governance with the exception of participation in tenure decisions. For example, a master's-level institution we studied treats its renewable term-contract faculty as full academic citizens in nearly all aspects of its governance system. According to its renewable term-appointment policy, "they are . . . eligible for appointment to university, college, and department/school committees, as well as membership on the faculty senate. They enjoy the same voting rights as tenured/tenure track faculty."

Some institutions advocate a more focused, hence limited governance role for full-time non-tenure-track faculty that relates most directly to the specific roles they play at the school. The collective bargaining agreement of a unionized university relieves these faculty from the obligation to participate in institution-wide governance. The policy states that "inasmuch as . . . [non-tenure-track faculty] members are employed . . . primarily to provide instructional services . . . , they have no required committee or other service obligations beyond those directly related to their instructional responsibilities." The policy does, however, outline a governance role for these faculty that is voluntary and more closely related to the work that they perform. It states that full-time non-tenure-track faculty "shall have the opportunity to participate in governance roles at the department/school and/or campus levels, including eligibility for committee assignments and other opportunities."

An undergraduate college also defines a substantive governance role for its full-time non-tenure-track faculty but further narrows its focus. Its standard non-tenure-track appointment letter states that term faculty "will be expected to share in the governing of the department." The institution puts teeth in this expectation by including "participation in departmental service" as one of the four criteria by which the non-tenure-track faculty will be evaluated.

Some formal policies on the role of full-time non-tenure-track faculty in governance, although well intentioned, may reinforce the second-class status of these faculty members. For example, the policy of one research university we studied states that "the tenured and tenure-track faculty in employing units of the university will decide which types and ranks of non-tenure-track faculty may vote on (*a*) routine departmental matters, and (*b*) policy matters. Should a question arise whether an issue is 'routine' or 'policy,' the tenured and tenure-track faculty will decide." At another research university, the dean of arts and sciences must decide on a case-by-case basis whether the full-time non-tenure-track lecturers may vote on any given issue. Policies such as these, implemented on a situational basis, preclude a shared understanding of the roles and status of non-tenure-track faculty. Ideally, some common (perhaps institution-wide) vision and shared policy on the governance role of term faculty are needed to enhance their professional status and engage them constructively in the work of the institutions they serve.

Including full-time non-tenure-track faculty in appropriate aspects of the governance process capitalizes on their expertise in their fields, professional experience as educators, and unique knowledge of the students they serve. Most importantly, respectfully engaging them in substantive discussions around important issues acknowledges them as full-fledged professionals. We believe a policy that encourages meaningful participation in governance is a key element of a comprehensive plan to minimize harmful status differences between tenure-class and non-tenure-track faculty.

RECOGNITION OF AND REWARD FOR THE CONTRIBUTIONS OF FULL-TIME NON-TENURE-TRACK FACULTY

Many institutions have procedures in place to recognize the diverse achievements of tenure-class faculty. Teaching awards, research citations, and named professorships are but a few examples of the ways colleges and universities call attention to meritorious performance. At institutions where full-time faculty members off the tenure track play significant roles, we believe that comparable forms of recognition are needed. One of our baccalaureate institutions annually awards an outstanding teaching award for which any full-time faculty member is eligible. It has been awarded to non-tenure-track faculty several times in recent years. Although we did not identify many other examples of recognition in our national study, a major research university provides a thought-provoking model that other institutions could adapt. This institution has an academic federation that represents the interests and recognizes the achievements of non-tenure-eligible faculty. The federation awards annually a Distinguished Service Award and an Excellence in Teaching Award to non-tenure-track faculty members. Both come with a $1,000 stipend (Sommer 1994).

The significant efforts and achievements of full-time term faculty should not go unsung while their tenure-class colleagues receive accolades. Forms of recognition applied with rigorous standards are an additional way to acknowledge and legitimize the key roles that non-tenure-track faculty fill on many campuses at the beginning of the twenty-first century.

PROCEDURES FOR PROTECTING ACADEMIC FREEDOM

Tenure is widely viewed as the primary defense of professors' academic freedom. Colleges and universities should implement policy and procedural safeguards to ensure that non-tenure-track faculty, who lack this traditional form of protection, have the academic freedom necessary to fulfill their professional obligations without reservation.

We learned in the course of our study that many institutions assume that academic freedom extends to all of their faculty members. Some institutions state explicitly that full-time non-tenure-track faculty enjoy the benefits of academic freedom. For example, a master's institution we studied states in its renewable term faculty policy, "The university is committed to ensuring academic freedom. [These] faculty will share with tenured/tenure track faculty the same rights to academic freedom." The policy goes on to say, however, that "[renewable term] faculty can be dismissed for cause, immediately or otherwise." Similarly, the collective bargaining agreement of a doctoral university directly extends the right of academic freedom to full-time nontenure-eligible faculty. The agreement's article on academic freedom and responsibility states:

> The parties [university and the non-tenure-track faculty bargaining
> agent] recognize that membership in the academic profession carries
> with it both special rights and also special responsibilities. Accordingly,
> the parties reaffirm their mutual commitment to the concepts of aca
> demic freedom and professional responsibility.

What is missing in both policy statements, however, is any description of the procedures by which academic freedom for term-contract faculty is guaranteed and protected. These are not exceptional cases. We learned that many institutions with large numbers of these faculty have not developed an explicit policy for protecting the professional freedom of this special faculty group.

Some institutions have developed safeguards for academic freedom that may be instructive to others concerned about this aspect of the non-tenure-track faculty issue. A baccalaureate institution we studied has a strategy in place for protecting the academic freedom of long-term non-tenure-track faculty. According to this policy,

> Beginning in the eighth year of full-time service to the College . . . if an individual is not renewed on grounds of need and/or performance and the individual believes that the nonrenewal is a violation of legitimate academic freedom and not related to need or performance, an appeal may be made to the Faculty Appeals Committee to consider the reasons for the nonrenewal. In the case of such an appeal, the Dean will present to the Faculty Appeals Committee the evidence used to conclude either that there is no longer a need for this position or that the individual's performance did not meet the standards for renewal. It will then be up to the individual to demonstrate that this argument is without merit and that the nonrenewal is a violation of academic freedom. The Faculty Appeals Committee will report its conclusions to the Chancellor. The Chancellor's decision will be final.

This policy represents a good-faith effort to protect the rights of veteran full-time term-contract faculty, although its effectiveness may be debated. The academic freedom of term-contract faculty with fewer years of service, however, is notably overlooked by this policy.

By definition, full-time non-tenure-track faculty need not be renewed when their contract runs out. There should, however, always be credible programmatic, financial, or professional reasons for such terminations. Non-tenure-track faculty, like their tenured colleagues, should be protected from arbitrary and capricious dismissal. Above all, if they are to function as legitimate members of the academic community, these faculty must be free to express their professional views and exercise their professional judgment without fear of retribution. We recommend that all institutions that employ term-contract faculty develop a formal policy acknowledging academic freedom for these individuals. Likewise, some type of appeal process should be in place at institutions that employ them so that questionable dismissal or nonrenewal decisions may be reviewed by an objective third party. A legitimate system of due process is critical to the academic freedom of tenure-

class faculty and non-tenure-eligible faculty as well. Failure to provide a
strategy for reviewing controversial decisions concerning non-tenure-track
renewals is likely to leave all term-contract faculty feeling anxious and vulnerable.

MONITORING THE USE OF FULL-TIME
NON-TENURE-TRACK FACULTY

Comprehensive policies on the employment of full-time non-tenure-
track faculty should also include

— guidelines covering when, how, and for what purpose persons who perform faculty functions are appointed to non-tenure-eligible positions,
and
— a system for monitoring implementation of policies on non-tenure-
track positions.

Many institutions hire full-time faculty off the tenure track incrementally
and without paying much attention to the philosophy or principles that
should regulate the use of these nontraditional appointments. As their utilization of these faculty positions becomes more common and more routine, colleges and universities should draft clear guidelines that will ensure
that such appointments comply with ethical and professional standards.
Naturally, these guidelines should be consistent with the mission of the
institution. For example, one liberal arts college in our study has crafted
a memorandum of understanding on the employment of full-time non-
tenure-track instructors. This policy has three elements that shape the use
of instructors at this institution:

1. Instructor appointments occur only in departments, schools or
programs where class load requires teaching service greater than can be
accommodated by an appropriate distribution of lower and upper level
teaching assignments among the department's career [tenure-class] faculty. Such load distribution will be agreed upon by the department and
the dean, subject to annual review by the Academic Standards Committee.

2. Because instructors are to be utilized teaching lower level or pre-
requisite courses where teaching skills are of prime importance, academic preparation, search procedures, performance standards, and
compensation are comparable to career faculty teaching similar courses.

3. Instructors' roles, rights, and responsibilities are the same as those
of career faculty as described in this [faculty] code with the exception

that they are not eligible for promotion, do not have tenure, but can be continued with annual contracts beyond 7 years.

This policy guiding the use of certain non-tenure-track positions would not be appropriate for all higher education institutions or all types of such appointments. Nevertheless, it serves as a model for other schools wishing to draft clear statements on the appropriate use of off-track positions.

Institutions that employ full-time faculty in non-tenure-track positions on a regular basis have an obligation to monitor this practice. Higher education institutions check the hiring, promotion, and retirement patterns of their tenure-track faculty. They should be no less systematic about monitoring their faculty off the tenure track. Some colleges and universities keep a record of full-time non-tenure-track appointments primarily to ensure that they do not exceed numerical limits on these types of faculty positions. We believe that this type of oversight is certainly appropriate; however, by itself it is not a sufficient way to monitor how well an institution utilizes and supports its full-time faculty in term-contract positions. Guidelines like those cited above can provide a standard for assessing the appropriateness and impact of a college or university's term-contract faculty positions.

Several institutions we studied routinely monitor their use of full-time non-tenure-track faculty. Some are fairly casual, while others are quite disciplined about the practice. The Faculty Code at the liberal arts college cited above requires that "utilization of non-career [non-tenure-track] faculty positions . . . be periodically reviewed by the Academic Standards Committee." A research university defines the oversight process somewhat more explicitly. According to its policy, each semester the executive vice-president will provide data on non-tenure-track faculty to the chair of the Faculty Senate. Data are presented by job title and rank for all academic units. The Faculty Senate chair presents "these data to the Committee on Committees for analysis and monitoring with respect to [the university's guidelines on non-tenure-track appointments]."

Another research university has devised the most thorough strategy we found for monitoring the use of non-tenure-track faculty. This university has a standing Committee on Lecturer Track Appointments, which includes the provost, who presides, the academic deans, and the chair of the Faculty Organization as ex-officio members. Other committee members must be regular faculty or senior or principal lecturers. "The provost and the chair of the Faculty Organization shall each appoint three members and the chairperson of the faculty of each college shall appoint one member." The Committee on Lecturer Track Appointments has three primary functions. The first is to "review the college policies specifying criteria and procedures regarding appointments, reappointments, and promotions to Lecturer Track positions and submit its recommendations to the provost." The second is to "conduct a triennial review of all Lecturer Track appointments for the sole purpose of ensuring that the functions of these positions satisfy . . . the requirements justifying their discharge by means of Lecturer Track appointments."

Finally, the committee is to

> monitor the general functioning of [the university's] policy on Lecturer Track appointments. To this end, the administration shall provide the committee annually with a summary report on the existing Lecturer Track appointments, as well as with any other relevant and non-privileged information. The committee shall advise the Faculty Senate and the president on any matters concerning the university's policy that may be submitted to it, as well as on those that in its opinion require examination or amendment of this policy.

Obviously, this institution is committed to monitoring its use of non-tenure-track faculty. Its well-defined oversight strategy shows that the university values its full-time non-tenure-eligible faculty and wishes to ensure that they make an effective contribution to the institution. Although the degree of oversight should be consistent with the structure and goals of a given college or university, its importance should be apparent. Without monitoring its non-tenure-track policies and practices on a regular basis, a higher education institution cannot judge whether or how these faculty are enhancing or harming its overall program.

ORIENTATION

A comprehensive package of policies and procedures intended to aid full-time non-tenure-track faculty (such as those discussed above) requires careful dissemination and interpretation. An orientation program for new faculty can ease their integration into the academic community and into their particular roles within the institution. Orientation is no less important for non-tenure-track faculty than for tenure-track faculty. Orientation programs serve to acquaint faculty members with the culture and mission of the institution, institutional resources, the goals and operation of the department within which the faculty member is employed, and the faculty member's role within that department. An orientation program should also educate the full-time term-contract faculty about the policies and procedures directly relevant to their non-tenure-eligible status.

Faculty and administrators we interviewed had specific ideas about what should be addressed when orienting the non-tenure-track faculty. These included introductions to the various resources available to assist faculty in the fulfillment of their roles such as information on library services, teaching resource centers, technology support services, and how to acquire necessary supplies and materials. Some suggested the faculty handbook as a useful reference to policies and procedures that affect the terms and conditions of non-tenure-track faculty employment. Supplemental orientation at the departmental level should be structured to introduce non-tenure-eligible faculty to the department's mission and mores and to integrate them with their tenure-track colleagues.

Orientation of full-time non-tenure-track faculty should also include presentations on the types of resources that an institution provides to support faculty professional development. Information of this type is best provided over a period of time, once new faculty members have gotten past the initial stress of beginning a new job.

The specific components of faculty orientation programs vary considerably across institutions, as do the structures of the programs. Several of the institutions we studied debated whether non-tenure-track faculty should be included with tenure-track faculty in orientation programs or whether they should be oriented separately. Several administrators indicated that the roles of the two types of faculty were sufficiently distinct that they should be oriented separately. A dean of arts and sciences at a research university stated that the full-time non-tenure-track faculty members are not included in the institution-wide orientation but that they do participate in the advising training program at the school level. At this institution, orientation of non-tenure-track faculty is viewed as a departmental responsibility. At many of the institutions that exclude full-time non-tenure-track faculty from orientation programs for tenure-track faculty, there is at best a hit-or-miss approach to socializing the non-track personnel, even at the departmental level.

Two master's-level institutions we studied provide a more systematic approach to non-tenure-track faculty orientation. These programs include both full-time tenure-track and non-tenure-track faculty and extend beyond the first several weeks of the first semester. In both examples the orientation is designed to introduce new faculty to the institutional mission, resources for professional development, and the criteria and process employed in evaluation. Both programs appear to emphasize continuous contact with fellow faculty. They also provide a mechanism for faculty to raise questions with department chairs and faculty leaders about professional issues.

Several institutions provide a senior faculty mentor to assist new full-time term-contract faculty members with their initial adjustment process. Mentors to non-tenure-track faculty should understand the roles and functions of these faculty and be willing to support them in the development of their careers. One of our site visit baccalaureate institutions recently initiated a mentor program pairing new full-time faculty (tenure-track and non-tenure-track) with a senior colleague from a different department in order to prevent the potential among new colleagues (the mentor and the new faculty member) for competition for common resources. Such a strategy also connects colleagues who will not subsequently be in a position to judge one another's performance in reappointment or promotion decisions.

Our study identified a few institutions where well-conceived orientation programs attempted to integrate full-time non-tenure-track faculty into the campus environment to the same degree as their tenure-track colleagues. Such programs typically lasted for a semester or more in order to enhance the socialization process. Regrettably, many institutions employ a haphazard approach to the orientation of these faculty. Others treat new term-contract faculty primarily with benign neglect. If full-time non-tenure-track faculty are going to play increasingly significant roles on college and university campuses, more attention must be paid to the means by which they are introduced and integrated into the academic community.

Implementing Policies and Practices to Support Full-Time Non-Tenure-Track Faculty

The personnel policies and practices we have recommended above to support full-time non-tenure-track faculty cannot be developed in isolation from other faculty personnel policies and procedures. The employment of full-time non-tenure-track faculty must be undertaken as part of a comprehensive institutional faculty staffing plan. In the absence of such a plan it is extremely difficult to monitor, regulate, and reward the contributions of faculty off the tenure track.

The faculty staffing plan and the role of the full-time non-tenure-track faculty in that plan should relate the roles of the several types of faculty directly to the institutional mission. The plan should ask, How do these faculty—their skills, experiences, and interests—contribute to the fulfillment of curricular requirements for students? How do their workload and specialized assignments assist in meeting the needs of students and their tenure-track faculty colleagues? These are examples of the types of questions that should be addressed in a staffing plan. Answers to such questions can help determine the numbers and qualifications of the non-tenure-track and tenure-track faculty the institution needs.

Concurrent with the development of a faculty staffing plan, institutions should review their faculty personnel policies to be certain that they are consistent with changing environmental conditions and support the work of the faculty. We learned from our campus visits that many institutions have clear policies in place for tenure-track faculty but lack thoughtful and supportive policies for full-time non-tenure-track faculty. The thirteen recommendations we set forth above are intended to aid institutions as they work to create the type of supportive work environment necessary to attract and retain high-quality faculty in these positions.

The policies developed to manage and support non-tenure-track faculty should be based on the concepts of equity, fairness, and the ethical treatment of professionals. These policies must reflect the needs and resources of the institution and the professional and personal needs and expectations of the faculty. We identified a number of institutions that have developed exemplary policies that integrate non-tenure-track faculty as full-fledged members of the academic community and that have addressed issues fundamental to the establishment of effective professorial careers. We also identified many institutions that have not. At too many colleges and universities, policies and standard practices seem to place the full-time non-tenure-track faculty at a distinct disadvantage, economically and professionally.

In the development and implementation of policies affecting full-time non-tenure-track faculty, it is very important that all faculty and administrators, and especially department chairs, understand these policies and administer them consistently and equitably across departmental lines. In our site visits, especially at the larger and more complex institutions, we found a lack of common understanding of the institutional policies affecting non-tenure-track faculty. This was the case among department chairs as well as other faculty and administrators. The ethical treatment of full-time non-tenure-track faculty can only be attained through fair, equitable, and clearly articulated and consistently administered policies that control the terms and conditions of the employment of this growing segment of the professoriate.

Earlier in this book we discussed the significant role that department chairpersons play in the professional lives of faculty in general and non-tenure-track faculty in particular. We believe that the department chairperson's role in supporting the work of full-time non-tenure-track faculty cannot be overemphasized. At many institutions we visited, we learned how department chairpersons made life easier or more difficult for full-time faculty off the tenure track. We heard about department heads who define work assignments, locate financial resources, or interpret policies liberally to make the work lives of full-time term-contract faculty engaging and rewarding. Even when clear policies concerning these faculty are in place, a certain amount of discretion is required to mesh individual circumstances with institutional needs. In most cases, the department chairperson is in the best position to balance the goals of consistent policy administration and sensitivity to individual differences. This task is especially important for integrating FTNTT faculty, who often occupy less conventional or less clearly defined roles than their tenure-class colleagues.

Summary

Faculty personnel policies have generally not kept pace with the rapid changes occurring in the professoriate. Policies designed to support the work of full-time, tenure-eligible faculty who probably will spend their entire professional career in higher education are not necessarily appropriate for full-time faculty off the tenure track. Colleges and universities employing non-tenure-track faculty need to reexamine their personnel policies in light of this staffing trend. Some standard faculty policies may need to be adapted to meet their needs. Likewise, some new policies consistent with the distinctive roles they play may have to be developed to support both their work and their long-term career development.

We have yet to identify a higher education institution that has developed an ideal package of personnel policies for full-time non-tenure-track faculty. However, we have found numerous schools with enlightened ideas for enhancing the work and careers of the faculty they employ off the tenure track. Taken together, these progressive practices form a thirteen-part template that can guide other colleges and universities as they design policies and practices to meet the needs of their term faculty members. By supporting the work of their non-tenure-track faculty they are simultaneously strengthening their academic program and the institution as a whole. In addition to serving institutional needs, the progressive policies and practices will serve to integrate non-tenure-track faculty into the academic community and provide term contracts that are a viable alternative upon which to build a career.

In our Best Practices Model (table 6.1) we have identified the thirteen policy areas that we recommend institutions specifically address in developing a comprehensive program to support their full-time non-tenure-track faculty. Together these policies form a composite model of best practices we uncovered in our national study of FTNTT faculty. We discussed each policy area in depth earlier in this chapter. Table 6.1 relates each of the policy areas to an institutional responsibility or goal for non-tenure-track faculty. For example, we strongly recommend that a defined probationary period be established for faculty on non-tenure-track appointments. The period should be set forth in the contract the institution has with the faculty member. This defined period sets contractual expectations of employment and assists the faculty member in planning his or her professional activities and career development. The defined probationary period serves as a companion policy to be used in conjunction with the explicit evaluation criteria in effect for assessing effectiveness and accomplishment in support of renewal or termination. The remaining items cited under contractual arrangements are necessary, we believe, to remove much of the contractual uncertainty that concerns full-time non-tenure-track faculty as well as deans and department chairs. It appears to us that each of these items is fundamental to providing fair and equitable employment conditions under a contract system.

The policy areas identified under the community integration column represent the topics we believe are important to the integration of non-tenure-track faculty into their academic community. For instance, the use of multiyear contracts after a defined probationary period recognizes valuable faculty contributions to their institution and provides sufficient time for them to participate actively in the academic community. Involvement in governance, progression through a system of academic ranks, and support for professional development, to name a few policy items, facilitate integration into the academic community and signify increased involvement.

The items identified in the professional development column are crucial, we believe, to maintaining a competent and academically vital full-time non-tenure-track faculty cohort. The items relevant to professional development demonstrate to the faculty that the institution values their contributions. They also communicate the institution's desire that faculty progress professionally in their careers. In addition, these items place the professional

Table 6.1 A Best Practices Model for the Employment of Full-Time Non-Tenure-Track Faculty

Terms and Conditions of Employment	Purpose			
	Contractual Arrangements	Community Integration	Professional Development	Oversight Monitoring
Defined probationary period	X		X	
Multiyear appointments following probation	X	X	X	
Defined dates for contract renewal or termination	X			X
Explicit evaluation criteria	X		X	X
Equitable salary system	X			X
Equitable fringe benefit system	X			X
System of sequential ranks	X	X	X	
Support for professional development		X	X	
Involvement in governance and curriculum development		X		
Recognition and reward for contributions		X	X	X
Protection of academic freedom	X	X	X	X
Orientation		X	X	
Oversight and monitoring of use of non-track faculty		X		X

development of the non-tenure-track faculty on a comparable level with the professional development of tenure-track faculty.

The final column relates to our strong recommendation that institutions set up mechanisms to monitor the employment of non-tenure-track faculty. We feel that the items listed need to be monitored to assess faculty quality and faculty working conditions. In Appendix E we include an inventory of questions related to our policy and practice recommendations. These questions and Table 6.1 are designed to guide institutions as they review policies and procedures affecting the work and careers of full-time non-tenure-track faculty.

7   The Future: An Action Agenda

J ohn Hickman's article "Adjunct U," published in the *New Repub-lic* (Hickman 1998, 14), suggests that the growing use of faculty off the tenure track (both full-time and part-time) is no longer purely an in-house concern. According to the *New Republic* byline discussing Hickman's article, "The contracting out fad [i.e., hiring part-time and full-time term-contract faculty] has hit university faculties, and that's bad news for professors—and their students" (5). Articles in the popular press indicate that shifting academic employment patterns have become a topic for discussion among a much wider audience as well, including potential students, parents, public policymakers, and the general public. Inevitably, this trend raises questions about higher education's stability, efficiency, and quality among education consumers and others who support and benefit from a healthy and dynamic educational system. Of course, colleges and universities should not base their policies and priorities on quick, and perhaps superficial, analyses in national magazines. Reports like that in the *New Republic*, how-ever, add evidence that the trend we examine in this book is major, signifi-cant, and worthy of attention both within and beyond campus boundaries. Ultimately, the future of the American higher education system is being shaped by this important development.

Changes in academic staffing appear to be a part of a much larger trend. Kanter (1989) wrote more than a decade ago about dramatic changes in cor-porate work and careers. Her chapter "From Climbing to Hopping: The Contingent Job and the Post-Entrepreneurial Career" gives compelling ev-idence of the shift from stable, single-institution careers with long-term se-curity to short-term contingent jobs and nonlinear career paths covering many institutions. The same turbulent environment that has transformed corporations and corporate work over the past two decades is transforming higher education as well.

The changes we observe in academic staffing patterns reflect a major and perhaps a permanent transition in the American academic profession. We believe that policy adjustments to accommodate these changes are an appropriate first step. Each of the exemplary policies we highlight in Chapter 6 would enhance the work lives and careers of full-time faculty off the tenure track. Ultimately what is required, however, is more than fine-tuning of conventional institutional policies and practices that influence faculty work and career development. A comprehensive approach addressing all thirteen components of the Best Practices Model is necessary to meet the evolving needs of FTNTT faculty and their institutions.

As we move into the new century, it is time to rethink the nature of faculty work, the content of faculty roles, and the relationship of faculty to each other and the institutions that employ them. By encouraging colleges and universities to integrate non-tenure-track faculty fully, we are asking them to expand and diversify their definition of what it means to be a faculty member. We believe that higher education and its many consumers will be better served by a more flexible approach to faculty work and the faculty career.

Aberration or Long-term Change?

Evidence suggests that the increasing use of full-time non-tenure-track faculty is a lasting trend. In earlier chapters we presented data showing a significant increase in the employment of full-time faculty off the tenure track between 1975 and 1993. The increase is evident both in the sheer numbers of these faculty members (from 81,010 in 1975 to 148,929 in 1993) and as a percentage of all full-time faculty (from 18.6% in 1975 to 27.3% in 1993) (Benjamin 1997). Will the proportion of full-time faculty employed in non-tenure-track positions continue to grow? According to the institutions that responded to our national survey, the answer is yes. Slightly more than half (50.6%) of our respondents expected that the percentage of non-tenure-track faculty would remain the same at their institution over the next five years. Slightly more than 37 percent predicted a net increase in FTNTT faculty. Only 12 percent anticipated a net decrease.

The factors that led to an increase in the employment of part-time and full-time non-tenure-track faculty over the past quarter century will most likely fuel even more contingent faculty appointments. As we noted in Chapter 2, many variables make the future of higher education difficult to predict. Shifting enrollment patterns, emerging technologies, increased opportunities for distance education, growing demands for accountability, and increased competition for funding and students all contribute to organizational uncertainty. This uncertainty in a dynamic environment may enhance the appeal of full-time non-tenure-track positions over tenure-track appointments.

A Time of Transition

Significant trends both within and outside of higher education strongly suggest that the academic community must reexamine faculty work and consider restructuring faculty roles. We are cognizant that colleges and universities are not-for-profit enterprises and should not blindly adopt corporate values and practices. Proper deference must, of course, be given to the unique mission and attributes of the higher education enterprise. But like many well-established and highly successful American corporations that have been challenged by new technologies and global competition, higher education institutions cannot ignore changing realities in the outside world.

The higher education community has begun to recognize that the staffing changes we highlight in this book reflect more than the responses of individual campuses to their own distinctive financial conditions or enrollment patterns. Rather, the changes reflect a gradual shift in the demands society places upon colleges and universities and the accommodations institutions must make to fulfill their evolving missions. A recent issue of *Daedalus* (1997) examined forces contributing to change in the American academic profession. Similarly, the ongoing Faculty Roles and Rewards/New Pathways dialogue, sponsored by the American Association for Higher Education, is searching for new ways to align faculty roles more closely with the shifting needs and expectations of the larger society. Each of these initiatives emerges from a growing sense that the uniform three-part model of faculty work is no longer adequate to meet the tasks at hand. A standard that asks all faculty to make a lifelong commitment to the profession, fill essentially the same teaching, research, and service roles, and comply with fixed and rigid standards to achieve tenure fails to provide the flexibility necessary for institutions to function in a rapidly changing world.

We heard this observation on many of the campuses we visited. The conventional model of an academic career now dominant throughout higher education makes it difficult for faculty to tailor their careers to capitalize on special interests or expertise or to accommodate distinctive personal circumstances. Likewise, the conventional model of faculty life makes it difficult for institutions to hire faculty to meet particular instructional needs or to bring in instructors with valuable experience and expertise but nontraditional academic credentials.

The overrepresentation of women and minorities in full-time non-tenure-track positions throughout higher education (see Chapter 4) is another symptom of the disconnection between the standard academic model and new realities—societal, educational, institutional, and personal. An academic staffing model designed primarily with traditional Caucasian male professors in mind will not be a comfortable fit for women and minorities, who bring a host of different experiences and concerns to campus. In a rapidly changing education environment, such a model will not meet the needs of evolving institutions very well either. If colleges and universities truly wish to offer equal opportunity and diversify their faculties, they must be willing to expand their definition of faculty work and adapt their expectations and policies to reach out to a larger portion of our complex society. If higher education refuses to adjust the standard faculty model, women, minorities, and other persons who "don't fit the mold" will remain on the periphery of the academy. The whole educational enterprise will suffer as a consequence.

We are not recommending that the standard model of the academic career be eliminated or that tenure be abolished. Our study has led us to conclude, however, that carefully designed alternatives to supplement the standard model are needed to accommodate the needs both of a more diverse academic profession and of institutions attempting to balance complex and sometimes competing demands from society. This view is consistent with the opinions of other investigators who have studied trends related to academic tenure. Breneman (1997), Chait and Trower (1997), and Gappa (1996) all suggest that a flexible, multifaceted faculty appointment system is necessary in a dynamic period of rapid change. A consistent theme emerges from these independent investigations. A policy that locks all faculty into one standard tenure-based employment system is incompatible with emerging conditions and needs in the twenty-first century. The growing employment of part-time faculty and full-time non-tenure-track faculty is part of the same development. It is an aspect of the larger contingent staffing pattern that Kanter (1989) sees as a response to a turbulent environment in which all complex organizations now reside.

The challenge for higher education is to revise its standard operating procedures without violating its fundamental values or threatening the intellectual culture that has contributed so much to the nation's welfare. We believe that colleges and universities can broaden their definition of faculty, support the work and careers of all who perform faculty functions, and at the same time preserve basic academic integrity. Most of the evidence at hand points to inevitable changes within higher education and within the academic profession. The academic community has a choice in this matter. It can react piecemeal to miscellaneous developments related to faculty as they emerge. Alternatively, it can design a coordinated strategy for reshaping faculty roles and responsibilities to bring them in line with new realities. Next, we propose a road map of sorts to help colleges and universities prepare to meet their future academic staffing needs.

Which Path to the Future?

Clearly, we have come to a crossroads in faculty staffing. We may either add more faculty on the periphery of the academy or expand our view of what faculty are and what work they do. We propose taking an affirmative approach that recognizes significant, and probably long-term, changes in higher education and the academic profession. In our view, it is time to set the stage for a diversified but fully integrated faculty work force. Gappa and Leslie (1993), who conducted a national study of part-time faculty, arrived at a similar conclusion.

If the academic profession is to function effectively, all types of faculty (including part-time and full-time non-tenure-track) must be genuine partners in the academic enterprise. A system that confines key segments of the faculty to second-class status and excludes them from professional development resources, decision-making opportunities, and full service roles unnaturally constrains faculty vitality and deprives institutions of valuable professional resources. It is time to acknowledge that the traditional faculty model does not meet all of the educational and institutional needs of today. We believe higher education will benefit if faculty fill different roles at their institutions without being relegated to different professional classes.

Perhaps, like the Catholic Church finally accommodating the discoveries of Galileo or the American auto industry finally acknowledging that it has foreign competition, higher education must adopt institutional policies and practices to acknowledge the reality that is already in place. Many colleges and universities have developed differentiated faculty positions inconsistent with the standard faculty model. They have done this to address critical, and frequently ongoing, academic challenges not adequately resolved by traditional tenure-track appointments. These new types of faculty positions include laboratory instructor, academic skills instructor, clinical education specialist, and professors of practice, among others. Many of the individuals who occupy these types of positions perform a bridging function, fulfilling both traditional faculty roles and administrative or service roles. In spite of the valuable functions these persons perform at their institutions, most of the non-tenure-track faculty we met in our study view themselves as a lower form of faculty. Some described themselves as necessary evils when financial constraints or enrollment uncertainties prevent institutions from making commitments to tenure-eligible, potentially permanent, or "real," faculty.

In contrast, we view these new types of faculty positions as a positive development overall. They bring the academic profession more in line with the educational needs of society and the realities of the higher education enterprise in the early twenty-first century.

The picture we have observed is not entirely positive or healthy, however. Our study showed that the way many institutions structure faculty roles and career advancement today is often not compatible with key life issues confronted by one or both genders. It is also not consistent with the restructured family roles and relationships increasingly common at the start of the new century. Likewise, the academic personnel policies and practices of many colleges and universities have not kept pace with new educational strategies, applications of advanced instructional technologies, or the institutions' changing academic staffing patterns.

The academic profession has evolved over the course of higher education history with the adoption of new institutional missions and functions, the development of new organizational structures, and the diversification of higher education's constituencies. Since the mid-1800s, college instructors have changed from stern disciplinarians whose primary purpose was to develop student character to subject-matter specialists who extend the boundaries of knowledge. In the process, the academic profession was born and professors became semi-autonomous, self-regulating professionals who shared in the governance of their institutions. The growth of the full-time non-tenure-track faculty suggests that the academic profession is in the midst of another significant transition. The majority of faculty still occupy positions defined by the standard teaching, research, and service model. Concurrently, however, many institutions are hiring faculty to fill positions that do not fit neatly into this standard model of faculty work. Obviously, the triumvirate of teaching, research, and service rolled into one generic and universal academic position fails to meet all the needs we are asking faculty to fill. Likewise, for some potential faculty, this traditional type of position is too rigid to accommodate their personal life circumstances or professional interests and ambitions.

Over a decade ago, Ernest Lynton and Sandra Elman, in *New Priorities for the University* (1987), called for a redefinition of institutional missions and faculty roles. Ernest Boyer, in *Scholarship Reconsidered* (1990), called for similar reforms of the scholarly role of faculty. Many other reform advocates (e.g., AAHE New Pathways: Faculty Careers and Employment for the Twenty-first Century) have been encouraging the academy to reexamine its purpose and roles and its ways of doing business. This includes the way it defines, utilizes, and evaluates its faculty. We believe it is time for colleges and universities to acknowledge new circumstances and redefine what it means by the word *faculty*. By recognizing and rewarding the contributions of all the academic staff members who perform instructional, scholarly, and service roles in some capacity, institutions will be building an integrated, healthier, and more effective academic community.

Three Steps to Reform: An Action Agenda

The reforms we advocate raise an obvious question. How can institutions achieve a more diversified yet integrated faculty work force? We believe that three steps are necessary to achieve this objective: (1) academic staff planning, (2) investment in nontraditional faculty resources, and (3) moving non-tenure-track faculty from the periphery to the center of the institution.

ACADEMIC STAFF PLANNING

Institutions should employ full-time non-tenure-track faculty thoughtfully and systematically to achieve specific, clearly defined objectives. Too often, the use of non-tenure-eligible faculty seems to be growing incrementally and erratically. Many such appointments are added on a case-by-case basis and are not guided by any overarching purpose. In contrast to this haphazard approach, institutions should identify specific purposes or circumstances where hiring faculty according to nontraditional employment models is appropriate. For example, we can see a strong case for hiring faculty to specialize in introductory-level instruction in areas such as languages, composition, and laboratory sciences. Similarly, with increased demands that higher education link theory more effectively with practice, hiring "professors of practice" with valuable skills based on work in their professional fields makes a lot of sense. Also, "bridge appointments" linking instructional and administrative duties or instructional and outreach roles could meet emerging needs that are not easily addressed by persons occupying exclusively faculty or administrative positions. These examples represent only the tip of the academic staffing iceberg. Many other types of appointments could be devised to meet changing educational circumstances and needs.

Effective utilization of a more diversified faculty work force would require institutions to develop systematic faculty staffing plans and to monitor the implementation of these plans. Careful academic staff planning that includes full-time and part-time non-tenure-track as well as tenure-class faculty is necessary to ensure that all types of faculty are effectively and fairly utilized in fulfilling an institution's core mission. This recommendation parallels advice that Gappa and Leslie (1993) offered concerning part-time faculty. Staff planning that overlooks one or more major segments of the academic work force cannot adequately prepare an institution to hire and retain the staff it needs. Gappa and Leslie argue that part-time faculty should be included in an institution's overall faculty staffing plan. Likewise, they recommend that part-time faculty should be consulted during the academic staff planning process. We concur with these suggestions but would expand them to include full-time non-tenure-track faculty and all other types of faculty who do not fit the traditional model of faculty life.

Monitoring the implementation of an academic staffing plan is especially important because non-tenure-track faculty (full-time and part-time) are often called upon to meet emerging needs and fill fluid roles. Effective monitoring requires institutions to maintain and update a comprehensive data base on their non-tenure-track faculty work force. Many institutions lack current, consistent, and accessible data on faculty off the tenure track. At best, they possess only a partial picture of their faculty staffing situation and may base policy and resource allocation decisions on incomplete data and inaccurate impressions of who the faculty are and what they do. Failure to monitor and update faculty staffing plans regularly could lead to unbalanced, rigid staffing arrangements that are unresponsive to changing circumstances in an institution's service area.

INVESTMENT IN NONTRADITIONAL FACULTY RESOURCES

A fully integrated faculty work force also requires investment in nontraditional faculty resources. In the past, most institutions have restricted their investments in faculty capital to persons they believed would be permanent members of the community. Faculty who occupied any types of temporary, non-tenure-eligible positions were considered a poor investment of limited discretionary funds. Today the evidence showing that full-time non-tenure-track faculty often fill long-term institutional needs coupled with the statistics showing that many of these faculty work at the same institution for many years belies the wisdom of such a policy.

Several steps are necessary to remove limitations on support for faculty who do not fit the conventional model of who a faculty member is. First and most important, perhaps, academic leaders and institutional policies must acknowledge publicly that nontraditional faculty fill essential roles and are valued members of the institutional community. Such statements should also acknowledge that these faculty resources, like all others, must be nurtured over time in order to maintain their value. In other words, colleges and universities that employ faculty in nontraditional roles or on nontraditional contracts have an obligation to replenish the professional capital of everyone who works in a faculty capacity. Granted, the level of support for faculty should be consistent with the role they play at the institution. For institutions to deny any responsibility to support the development of nontraditional faculty (full-time or part-time), however, affirms the notion that these faculty are second-class, lesser faculty compared to their tenure-track colleagues. This is a perception that institutions would be wise to eradicate.

Several forms of professional development support can help to integrate full-time non-tenure-track faculty and enhance their overall performance. First, as we discussed in Chapter 6, it is important to orient term faculty to their new situation. Too often full-time faculty off the tenure track are left to their own devices when they join an institution on a term contract. Some institutions include these term-appointment faculty in brief generic orientation programs for all new faculty. Alternatively, orientation may occur informally at the department level under the guidance of a supportive chairperson. Given their complex status and the distinctive roles that full-time non-tenure-track faculty often play, these approaches seem too casual to be effective. Faculty who join an institution in a nontraditional capacity need information on instructional resources, the roles they will play, evaluation standards, faculty rights and responsibilities, and any other factors that will affect their performance. They also need instruction in institutional values, mores, and traditions to ease their integration into their department, their school, and the larger institutional community.

Linking full-time non-tenure-track faculty with established faculty mentors can also ease the transition to their new situation by supplementing a formal orientation program and tailoring it to the individual. An orientation program that addresses both generic faculty concerns and those distinctive to non-tenure-track faculty should provide a solid foundation for a successful career at an institution, whether one's tenure is brief or long-term.

Full integration of full-time non-tenure-track faculty also means that they should be able to participate in all professional development programs relevant to their defined duties and long-term professional growth. This does not mean that the faculty with very specialized positions should have carte blanche access to all types of professional development programs. We do believe, however, that such programs should be more inclusive than exclusive. For example, faculty who have teaching duties should be eligible to participate in workshops on course planning and effective instructional strategies. Likewise, they should be eligible to use instructional development centers and other forms of support for teaching improvement. Ability to participate in grant competitions for research funds or to use library and computing resources for scholarship is also fundamental to functioning as a full-fledged professional or member of an academic community. Again, appropriate limitations on participation may be imposed, but arbitrary restrictions that ignore the legitimate professional needs of these faculty are detrimental to full faculty integration, not to mention their morale. They also overlook the well-being of institutions that rely on up-to-date, vital faculty to deliver high-quality education and to preserve institutional integrity.

Recognizing the contributions of full-time non-tenure-track faculty is another form of investment that legitimizes their membership in the academic community. Most higher education institutions recognize the achievements and valuable contributions of tenure-class faculty with a host of awards and honors for meritorious performance. Likewise, nontraditional faculty off the tenure track should be eligible for teaching, scholarship, service, and other awards, depending on the functions they perform for their college or university. In some cases this means that special awards should be available for faculty playing unusually distinctive roles. In other cases, nontraditional faculty should be eligible for the very same honors as tenure-class faculty. After all, good teaching is good teaching and valuable service is valuable service. Why should awards to recognize meritorious performance in such areas be limited only to one type of faculty member? Perhaps there are appropriate reasons in some cases, but inclusion rather than exclusion should be the general rule. When all faculty know that they have the potential to be recognized for their good work, they are more likely to feel a part of and committed to the same community.

Full-time non-tenure-track faculty, like their tenure-eligible colleagues, should have opportunities for professional recognition and professional growth. According to Kanter (1989), "professional opportunity is inherently less limited" than advancement opportunity in a traditional corporate structure because "'growth' is not dependent on either widening the pyramid or heightening the hierarchy ... Professional opportunity involves setting high performance standards and incentives to master them" (313). Non-tenure-track positions should have a built-in opportunity structure that supports professional improvement and recognizes noteworthy achievements and contributions. Institutions that employ nontraditional faculty need to ensure that a flexible and diversified opportunity structure is in place for these valuable members of their academic team.

FROM THE PERIPHERY TO THE CENTER

We believe that full-time faculty off the tenure track should be completely integrated into the academic community. At the same time, we recognize that change in higher education occurs slowly and deliberately. Major reform of the academic profession will not, and perhaps should not, occur overnight. We urge colleges and universities to begin the process of adapting their faculty staffing at a pace that is consistent with their history, traditions, and distinctive circumstances. This process should recognize changing realities, however. New policies should not be based on out-of-date institutional customs or an abstract ideal of what a college or university professor should be.

Developing clear, consistent, and fair policies to support the work and career advancement of full-time non-tenure-track faculty represents a progressive first step. The ultimate goal of this deliberate process should be a diverse but fully integrated academic work force. To continue down the current haphazard path, adding more subfaculty on the periphery of the academy to fulfill important and permanent educational and institutional functions, will aggravate class differences within higher education. Such a process will inevitably lead to a fragmented, demoralized, and perhaps hostile work force. Much recent education and business literature (e.g., Austin and Baldwin 1991; Bennis and Biederman 1997; Kanter 1983) sings the praises of teamwork, collaborative problem solving, and community building. To continue to move toward a two-class faculty with privileged and underprivileged members runs counter to the insights we have gained from decades of study of productive corporate practices and effective educational strategies.

By enhancing the status of full-time non-tenure-eligible faculty, supporting their work, and fostering their long-term professional development, colleges and universities can build a vital community responsive to the changing needs of a dynamic society. We believe this goal will not be fully achieved, however, until the academic community takes two very important steps. One, it must acknowledge that the academic profession contains different types of faculty, all of whom perform important functions that are critical to the higher education enterprise. Two, it must reject arbitrary status distinctions that benefit some faculty members while stigmatizing others regardless of their professional credentials, the quality of their work, and the value of their contributions.

Moving full-time non-tenure-track faculty from the periphery to the center of a college or university means actively engaging these faculty in the core operations of the institution. Several actions are required to achieve this goal. First, these faculty should be encouraged to participate in course and curriculum planning at a level that is appropriate to their expertise and academic functions. For instance, the term-contract faculty who teach introductory-level courses should have a role in planning these courses. They should also help to coordinate introductory courses with more advanced offerings.

Second, full-time non-tenure-track faculty should participate in shared governance according to their ability to contribute. Under no circumstances should they be summarily excluded from governance activities that directly concern their duties or affect their well-being. This principle may have to be implemented on an institution-by-institution or case-by-case basis to make it workable. What is most important is that these important members of the faculty have a place at the table and a voice in decisions that will affect them or their students where they have directly relevant expertise or experience. To exclude them arbitrarily from the governance process deprives their programs, departments, and institutions of key insights only they are qualified to provide.

Third, full-time non-tenure-track faculty should be welcome to participate as equals in social and professional activities that help to nurture an academic community. Often persons classified as "temporary" are excluded from mailing lists that automatically invite regular members of a department or college to meaningful social and academic functions such as convocations, graduation ceremonies, receptions, and parties. Any actions or inaction that designates them as different and less important may bruise egos and damage the sense of community that is so important to a healthy academic environment. Including these nontraditional faculty in formal and informal social and academic events is another way to integrate them completely into the life of an institution.

Fourth, full-time non-tenure-track faculty should enjoy the same right to academic freedom as their tenured and tenure-track colleagues. They will never be respected as full-fledged academic professionals if procedures are not in place at their college or university to protect their academic freedom. If the basic rights of some members of the faculty are compromised, the faculty as a whole is compromised. In the process, an institution's integrity and its academic program are diminished.

Other barriers, intangible but very real, may prevent non-tenure-track faculty from moving into the mainstream of academic life. Institutions wishing to enhance the status of full-time term-contract faculty must attack each of these barriers aggressively. Ignorance, prejudice, and suspicion form one barrier that excludes them from full membership in the academic community. While investigating the growing non-tenure-track faculty phenomenon, we found that many "regular" faculty and administrators do not know much about them—who they are, what qualifications they possess, or what work they do. In some cases, we found concern that the hiring of full-time non-tenure-track faculty was part of a larger scheme to eliminate or weaken an institution's tenure system. We believe that clear communication is necessary to eliminate fears and prejudices that diminish the status and contributions of non-tenure-track faculty. Without accessible information and open dialogue, harmful mythologies will persist or even grow and the academic community will be harmed in the process.

Rigid tradition derived from an intractable institutional culture is another barrier to the integration of faculty on and off the tenure track. Traditions that dictate specific faculty roles or activities and exclude others lock all faculty onto a track that can inhibit growth and professional vitality. Mandating that all introductory-level courses be taught by Ph.D.'s, for example, may squander individual talents and institutional resources needlessly. Similarly, an expectation that all faculty must conduct original research in their area of specialization along with other duties may divert some faculty from more appropriate and more fulfilling tasks. Inflexible class scheduling, unstoppable tenure clocks, and competitive departmental cultures are other examples of conditions that may foster academic segregation into distinct classes by discouraging women, minorities, and other nontraditional candidates from aspiring to positions on the tenure track. In an era of rapid change, all higher education institutions must be vigilant to internal cultural norms that preclude effective responses to new educational challenges. Making room for nontraditional types of faculty may actually enhance the work of regular faculty by enabling them to concentrate in areas where they can make the greatest contribution.

An informal but very obvious two-class faculty system is a third intangible barrier that prevents full faculty integration on campuses today. We know of no higher education institution that has intentionally created a two-class faculty through official policy. Nevertheless, faculty and administrators on many campuses we studied spoke freely about the two-class system that currently exists. Gappa and Leslie (1993) identified the same phenomenon in their study of part-time faculty. On many college and university campuses, the higher class is composed of "legitimate" or "real" professors who function in all respects according to the standard faculty model. The lower class consists of faculty who do not fit the conventional model in some way and, hence, are perceived to be less valuable, less influential, and more dispensable. Both part-time and full-time non-tenure-track faculty are often found within this lower class. The two-class system that pervades higher education today excludes full-time non-tenure-track faculty from fully utilizing their expertise and talents. In the process, it prevents colleges and universities from capitalizing on the full range of resources term faculty possess. As a result, the education enterprise is diminished. Colleges and universities wishing to integrate their faculty work force in the interest of institutional effectiveness must attack the two-class faculty system. Failure to eliminate class differences will eat away at the fragile collegiality that is critical to creative curriculum design, effective program management, shared governance, and other important professorial functions.

The academic community by design includes many pressure points that create tension and foster fragmentation. Disciplinary differences alone can damage the academic community if they are not addressed with great diplomatic skill. The emergence of two faculty classes defined by tenure eligibility adds another source of tension to the traditional mix. Just as racial integration was advanced in the 1960s to preserve our nation, integration of differing types of faculty is needed to strengthen higher education and prepare it to meet the needs of a rapidly changing society.

Key Players in Reform

Several groups have key roles to play in order to achieve a fully integrated faculty. Each must take some initiative to move full-time non-tenure-eligible faculty into the academic mainstream. Next, we discuss the actions we believe each group should play in this process. Ideally, the efforts of these constituencies should be closely coordinated to maximize their efforts and to speed positive changes in the academic profession.

FULL-TIME NON-TENURE-TRACK FACULTY

Current and potential full-time faculty off the tenure track must look out for their own best interests. Applicants for these positions should assess the merits of such posts by reviewing personnel policies at the institutions where they are applying. They should also speak with current faculty in non-tenure-track positions as well as deans and department chairs who supervise and regulate these appointments. Gathering facts on full-time non-tenure-track positions, institutional policies, and an institution's culture will help applicants make informed, rational decisions. If the details do not add up to a supportive work environment that offers growth opportunities, the candidate must decide whether the available position represents a positive career move.

Persons already working in full-time non-tenure-track posts should not accept the status quo passively but should focus attention on their circumstances and needs by communicating with academic leaders and representative faculty assemblies. It is naive to believe that higher authorities will always look out for the best interests of these faculty. Many issues and interest groups compete for the attention of provosts, deans, and faculty senates. Incumbent term faculty must keep their interests on the radar screens of those officials or groups responsible for faculty well-being. If their numbers are sufficient, term-contract faculty may choose to form an association to represent their unique interests on and off campus.

DEANS AND DEPARTMENT CHAIRS

Deans and department chairs must play active roles if full-time non-tenure-track faculty are to become integral parts of the academic community. First, they must communicate to tenure-class faculty how important non-tenure-track faculty are to vital institutional operations. Deans and department chairs also must ensure that these faculty are adequately oriented to their roles and new institution. Perhaps most important, these academic leaders have primary responsibility for ensuring that non-tenure-eligible faculty are treated fairly and equitably when compared to tenure-eligible faculty. They should provide comparable compensation for work that is essentially equivalent to the functions that tenure-class faculty perform. They should reserve appropriate resources for the professional development of term-contract faculty. They should also monitor work assignments to be certain that non-tenure-track faculty receive stimulating assignments that involve reasonable workloads. Finally, they should make sure that evaluation criteria are realistic, accurately reflecting the roles these faculty fill at the institution.

REPRESENTATIVE FACULTY ASSEMBLIES

Senates, assemblies, or other faculty governance bodies should monitor the welfare of all faculty, including those off the tenure track. Such groups should ask senior academic administrators to provide regular reports on academic staffing patterns and should be prepared to raise questions when traditional faculty staffing arrangements are replaced with new policies and practices. To protect the fragile academic community, representative governing bodies should support policies that provide equivalent compensation and resources for comparable contributions to the academy. Maintaining a healthy institutional culture should be the primary objective of organizations that represent the interests of all faculty.

SENIOR ADMINISTRATIVE LEADERS

Senior administrative leaders have an especially important role to play in the successful integration of full-time non-tenure-track faculty. They can most effectively focus their institution's attention on the FTNTT faculty issue and its related subissues. Bringing up the non-tenure-track faculty topic in speeches, press conferences, and committee deliberations can promote action on non-tenure-track faculty issues throughout an institution. Ensuring that adequate resources flow to support the work of full-time faculty off the tenure track also sends an important message about the value of this growing faculty component. Senior administrative leaders such as presidents and provosts are also in the best position to monitor the use of full-time non-tenure-track faculty at the institution-wide level. They have the best vantage point from which to ensure fair and equitable treatment of faculty in non-tenure-eligible positions as well as consistent administration of policies and procedures. Senior-level administrators are also well positioned to initiate policies and practices still needed to regulate and support the work of their institutions' full-time faculty who work off the tenure track. By focusing attention on these faculty and promoting their professional well-being, senior administrators can help to upgrade the status of this important component of the academic work force.

PROFESSIONAL ASSOCIATIONS INCLUDING THE AAUP

The full-time non-tenure-track faculty phenomenon is clearly too large to be addressed solely at the institutional level. Several other types of organizations should also participate in efforts to raise the status and enhance the contributions of faculty off the tenure track. Discipline-based professional associations such as the Modern Language Association should study, and perhaps take a stand on, the growing employment of full-time non-tenure-track faculty. Data-based policy statements on the proper utilization and proper working conditions of these faculty would nourish the national dialogue on this significant issue. We believe that statements advocating a return to the status quo of exclusive tenure-track hiring would be naive and probably counterproductive. Associations must be willing to acknowledge the changing climate within which colleges and universities must operate. The proper response to these changing realities is by no means certain, however. Professional associations could play a significant role in shaping enlightened policies to guide full-time non-tenure-track appointments and other types of faculty employment in the new century.

The American Association of University Professors (AAUP) can play an especially valuable role in confronting the full-time non-tenure-track faculty phenomenon constructively. To perform this function, the AAUP must be willing to represent the interests of all faculty, not just the tenure-eligible component. We recognize that the AAUP views the tenure system as the best defense of academic freedom, and we agree with that view in large part. However, academic employment trends for the foreseeable future suggest that a mix of tenure-eligible and non-tenure-track appointments will be the norm on American campuses. The AAUP has already begun to provide leadership for institutions wrestling with full-time non-tenure-track faculty issues. It presents a set of important recommendations in *Non-Tenure-Track and Part-Time Faculty: Guidelines for Good Practice* (AAUP n.d.). The statement acknowledges this new reality in faculty staffing and offers employment standards for full-time term-appointment faculty.

GOVERNING AND COORDINATING AGENCIES

We found a bewildering absence of consistent practice in our national study of full-time non-tenure-track faculty. Even on the same campus, we learned that policies were often interpreted and applied in dramatically different ways. For this reason, we believe that multicampus governing boards and statewide coordinating agencies can also play an important role in shaping uniform understanding and equitable practice with regard to term faculty. These organizations can advance the cause of full-time non-tenure-track faculty by bringing key people together to develop statements on the appropriate use of and proper workplace conditions for them. They can also focus attention on the needs of these faculty by developing uniform definitions of term-appointment positions and by requesting reports on the numbers of these nontraditional faculty and the functions they perform at their institutions.

Over a period of decades, policies concerning tenure-track faculty positions have achieved a degree of consistency in the different sectors of American higher education. No comparable consensus has yet occurred concerning full-time non-tenure-track appointments. Agencies that serve to coordinate the functions of higher education can promote this search for shared understanding and equitable practice by fostering discussion across campuses and by drafting common definitions and standards.

GRADUATE SCHOOLS

We feel that having one in four full-time faculty in a non-tenure-track position in American higher education is significant. If this development is essentially creating a major new faculty career track, what are the implications for the graduate preparation of this growing segment of the professoriate? Should the professional preparation of faculty who desire or who have available to them only non-tenure-track positions be different from the preparation of those who desire only a tenure-track career? Or should graduate schools be more honest and forthright about the fact that the academic labor market is changing and that career satisfaction can be achieved in more than one type of academic employment?

We believe that graduate schools also have a major role to play in guiding the transformation taking place in the academic profession. Traditionally, graduate programs have ignored employment issues entirely. Many have implicitly assumed that their students would follow the standard path into tenure-track positions. Considerable evidence reveals that it is no longer safe to assume that newly minted Ph.D.'s will find a suitable post on the tenure track (Wilson 1998). For this reason, we believe that graduate schools have a role to play in preparing their students for alternative careers both within and outside of higher education.

Certainly, graduate institutions should make their students aware of the changing academic employment situation. They should also help to prepare them for the new types of employment opportunities, including full-time non-tenure-track positions. In addition to formal academic instruction, graduate schools should consider providing workshops, seminars, and internships to introduce students to new types of faculty appointments. Graduate students should know about instructional positions that focus primarily on introductory-level teaching, positions that bridge instruction and administration, and other types of new hybrid academic appointments before they read about them in *Chronicle* employment announcements. By helping to prepare their students for a broader range of employment options, graduate schools can ease the transition to nontraditional faculty careers, elevate the status of full-time non-tenure-track faculty positions, and strengthen higher education in the process.

In Search of a Larger Vision

The increased employment of full-time faculty in non-tenure-eligible positions has been an erratic, incremental process. Rarely has a larger vision or clear and comprehensive policy guided this development, yet this gradual shift to contingent faculty appointments has begun to transform faculty functions and the academic profession as a whole. It is time to move discussion of this development from the departmental offices or academic conference rooms where individual staffing decisions are made. At the beginning of the new century, it is time for a larger and more open dialogue on faculty roles and the structure of faculty careers. The full-time non-tenure-track faculty issue must be part of a larger conversation on the future of the academic profession. We hope that this book helps to inform that discussion.

In our opinion, full-time faculty off the tenure track have been ignored for too long. We believe that it is time to take an affirmative stand in support of those who fill these roles. We hope to do this by clarifying who these faculty are and by highlighting the valuable contributions that they make to higher education. It is also important to clarify their status within the academic community and to communicate their distinctive professional development needs. By painting a detailed picture of this growing component of the professoriate and by recommending appropriate new policies and practices to support full-time non-tenure-track faculty, we hope to strengthen the academic profession as a whole.

As we conclude this investigation of the growing use of non-tenure-track faculty, we remember the wise counsel of one term-appointment faculty member whom we interviewed late in our project. Her advice was to "label us by what we are, not by what we are not." The phrase *non-tenure-track faculty* inevitably places this valuable group of academics in a negative light. By fully integrating this growing group into their institutions and the higher education community as a whole, we can erase the stigma many of these faculty feel. By acknowledging their contributions fully and by defining their roles affirmatively, we can strengthen the entire academic community and move higher education into a new era of responsive and effective service to society. Many positive titles could be used to convey the valuable roles that faculty off the tenure track perform in higher education. Depending on the role played by the faculty member, any of a number of titles might be appropriate for faculty who work outside the dominant model: clinical professor, professor of practice, laboratory professor, and service professor, for example. Whatever titles institutions choose to utilize, they should leave no doubt that full-time faculty off the tenure track fill important roles and make valuable contributions to education.

Kanter (1989) sees a whole new stream of entrepreneurial careers emerging in the corporate world. These are careers unconstrained by rigid hierarchies and traditional institutional practices. These types of careers evolve and advance by "creating new value rather than simply preserving [and complying with] old ways" (318).

The emerging non-tenure-track component of the academic profession may be the professorial counterpart to this corporate development. The diverse hybrid positions we found under the non-tenure-track label demonstrate how easily these positions can be molded to meet specialized institutional needs and to accommodate unique personal circumstances. If colleges and universities define full-time faculty positions off the tenure track as avenues of professional opportunity and as positions where educational problems can be addressed creatively in an entrepreneurial spirit, what Kanter calls "newstream" faculty positions may become highly desirable and widely respected. To achieve this objective, however, institutions must be willing to treat nontraditional faculty off the tenure track as first-class members of the academic community.

Appendix A

Colleges and Universities Participating in the Institutional Survey and Site Visits

(An asterisk indicates a site visit.)

Research I

Carnegie Mellon University
Columbia University
*Cornell University
Michigan State University
New Mexico State University—Main Campus
North Carolina State University
*University of California at Los Angeles
University of Colorado at Boulder
University of Florida
University of Hawaii
University of Iowa
University of Miami
*University of Minnesota
University of Nebraska at Lincoln
University of North Carolina at Chapel Hill
University of Pittsburgh at Pittsburgh
University of Tennessee at Knoxville
University of Virginia
*University of Washington
Virginia Polytechnic Institute and State University

Research II

George Washington University
Northeastern University
Ohio University
Saint Louis University
Southern Illinois University at Carbondale
University of South Carolina at Columbia

Doctoral I

Ball State University
College of William and Mary
*Georgia State University
University of Alabama
University of Denver
University of Toledo

Doctoral II

*Cleveland State University
DePaul University
University of Central Florida
University of Colorado at Denver
University of Montana

Master's I

Azusa Pacific University
California Lutheran University
College of Charleston
East Carolina University
Francis Marion University
Ithaca College
*James Madison University
*Shenandoah University
Southeast Missouri State University
Springfield College (Mass.)
University of North Alabama

University of Portland (Oreg.)
University of Wisconsin at Whitewater
Villanova University
*Webster University

Master's II

Mary Washington College
Philadelphia College of Textiles and Science

Baccalaureate

*Bryn Mawr College
Bucknell University
Centre College of Kentucky
Coe College
Colgate University
College of the Holy Cross
Colorado College
Columbia College of Missouri
Columbia College of South Carolina
East Texas Baptist University
Eastern Mennonite University
Goucher College
Hampshire College
Hartwick College
Hastings College
Haverford College
Hollins College
Illinois Wesleyan University
King's College
Macalester College
Mount Olive College
Northland College
Olivet College
Randolph-Macon Woman's College
*Rhodes College
Spring Arbor College
*University of North Carolina at Asheville

University of Puget Sound
University of the South
Wellesley College
Wingate University
Wittenberg University

Appendix B

Institutional Survey Concerning Non-Tenure-Track Faculty

This questionnaire has been designed to obtain information about full-time non-tenure-track faculty on college and university campuses. In this phase of the study we are attempting to gather information about the number of faculty filling these positions and the institutional policies that affect the faculty employed in full-time non-tenure-track positions. A subsequent phase of the study will involve on-campus interviews with faculty and administrators at a sample of institutions.

In responding to the questions about full-time instructional faculty, include only those members of the instruction/research staff who are employed full-time (as defined by the institution) and whose major (more than 50%) regular assignment is instruction, including those with released time for research. We are utilizing the definition of eligible faculty that is used by the National Center for Education Statistics in its Integrated Postsecondary Education Data System (IPEDS). Also to be included are:

- full-time instructional faculty on sabbatical leave
- full-time replacements for instructional faculty on leave
- chairs of departments who hold full-time faculty rank, and who have no other administrative duties

Not to be included are:

- instructional faculty on leave without pay
- instructional faculty employed part-time
- military personnel who teach only ROTC courses
- graduate teaching assistants

Your participation in the study by completing this survey instrument is deeply appreciated.

Institution: _____

1. During the Fall Term 1991, what was the number of full-time instructional faculty at your institution in each of the following categories? (Please use data from your institution's 1991–1992 Institutional IPEDS Report, Part A, in responding to this question.)

	Tenured	On Tenure Track	Not on Tenure Track
a. 9/10-month contracts			
(1) Men	___	___	___
(2) Women	___	___	___
(3) Total	___	___	___
b. 11/12-month contracts			
(1) Men	___	___	___
(2) Women	___	___	___
(3) Total	___	___	___
Grand Total (a3 plus b3)	___	___	___

2. During the Fall Term 1995, what was the number of full-time instructional faculty at your institution in each of the following categories? (Please use data from your institution's 1995–1996 Institutional IPEDS Report, Part A, in responding to this question.)

	Tenured	On Tenure Track	Not on Tenure Track
a. 9/10-month contracts			
(1) Men	___	___	___
(2) Women	___	___	___
(3) Total	___	___	___
b. 11/12-month contracts			
(1) Men	___	___	___
(2) Women	___	___	___
(3) Total	___	___	___
Grand Total (a3 plus b3)	___	___	___

3. Compared to the Fall Term 1995, do you anticipate any changes in the number of full-time instructional faculty in the next five years? (Please check the appropriate places.)

	Net Increase	No Change	Net Decrease
Tenured	____	____	____
Untenured but on track	____	____	____
Non-tenure-track	____	____	____

4. What is (are) the length of contracts of the full-time non-tenure-track instructional faculty appointments made at your institution? Check all that apply and please circle the one most often used.

    a. __ One academic term/semester
    b. __ One academic/calendar year
    c. __ Two to four years (academic or calendar)
    d. __ Five or more years (but specified number)
    e. __ Unspecified number of years

5. What is the maximum number of years that a full-time non-tenure-track faculty member may remain in a full-time non-tenure-track position at your institution? _____

6. On average, when compared with tenured or tenure-track faculty, the teaching load of full-time non-tenure-track faculty is __ the same, __ heavier, __ lighter.

7. Is there a primary level of instruction for which non-tenure-track appointees are hired? (Example: lower-division undergraduate, upper-division undergraduate, etc.)

    a. __ yes   b. __ no
    If yes, what is that level? _____

8. Do full-time tenure-track and non-tenure-track appointments with similar rank and professional experience receive comparable salaries?

    a. __ yes   b. __ no
    If no, are non-tenure-track faculty __ lower, or __ higher?

9. Are there specific disciplines or program areas in which full-time non-tenure-track hires are most likely to be made, or is it a generalized practice across all disciplines or program areas?

    a. __ Yes, specific disciplines (If yes, please check the appropriate items in *c,* below)

    b. __ No, it is generalized

    c. If you answered yes to 9*a,* please check the disciplinary area(s) in which non-tenure-track faculty appointments are most likely to be made at your institution.

    __ (1) Agriculture/Home Economics
    __ (2) Business
    __ (3) Education
    __ (4) Engineering
    __ (5) Fine Arts
    __ (6) Health Sciences
    __ (7) Humanities
    __ (8) Natural Sciences (including Mathematics)
    __ (9) Social Sciences
    __ (10) Other (Please specify)_____

10. Are faculty in full-time non-tenure-track positions eligible for:

    __ Yes __ No *a.* merit salary increases
    __ Yes __ No *b.* full fringe benefits
    __ Yes __ No *c.* academic promotion in rank (excluding tenure)
    __ Yes __ No *d.* service on department committees
    __ Yes __ No *e.* service on the faculty senate

11. Listed below are ways in which institutions provide support for the professional development of faculty. Please respond to the items in column *B* regarding the availability of the activity or funding for tenured and tenure-track faculty, and column *C* in terms of full-time non-tenure-track faculty. Please check the correct response under each letter for both columns.

A	B		C	
	Yes	*No*	*Yes*	*No*
(1) Funds to support professional travel	__	__	__	__

(2) Professional association memberships
     and/or conference registration fees   — — — —
(3) Sabbatical leave (paid)   — — — —
(4) Training to improve research or
     teaching skills   — — — —
(5) Retraining for fields in higher demand   — — — —
(6) Tuition remission   — — — —

12. Are full-time non-tenure-track faculty eligible to vote on:

__ Yes   __ No   *a.* departmental matters (academic)
__ Yes   __ No   *b.* Institutional matters (academic)

13. Does your institution have written faculty personnel policies that govern full-time non-tenure-track faculty appointments/positions that
distinguish them from tenure-track/tenured positions?

__ Yes   __ No

If yes, please send us a copy of the policies. We will also appreciate receiving a copy of your faculty handbook.

14. Would you be willing to have your institution participate in the on-
campus interview phase of this study? This will necessitate providing us
with a list of full-time non-tenure-track faculty from whom we would
randomly select ten to twelve for interviews. We will also request the
names of the department chairs and deans of the non-tenure-track faculty so that we may interview a sample of the administrators and a few
tenured faculty members.

__ Yes   __ No

15. We are interested in receiving any comments or clarification about the
responses you provided to the above questions, or your thoughts about
the increased use of non-tenure-track faculty on college and university
campuses.

Name of person completing the form _____
Date _____
Title _____
Telephone _____

Appendix C

Site Visit Interview Questions

Author's Note: The questions set forth under each of the designated categories of personnel served as a guide for the discussions with these individuals. The researchers did avail themselves of the opportunity to vary from the structured questions at times based on pertinent topics and issues that arose during the discussions, interviewee time constraints, and unique institutional circumstances that were deemed to contribute to the study and its intended purposes.

Academic Vice-Presidents and Academic Deans

1. What are the principal reasons your institution employs full-time faculty in non-tenure-track positions?
2. What are the costs and consequences of hiring non-tenure-track faculty as opposed to hiring tenured or tenure-track faculty members?
3. What has been the pattern of hiring of full-time non-tenure-track faculty over the past five years (increased, stable, decreased)? What do you anticipate in the next five years?
4. How does your department/institution recruit non-tenure-track faculty? Compare the necessary employment qualifications of the faculty your institution hires on the tenure track and off the tenure track.
5. How does your institution/department support the professional development of tenure-track and non-tenure-track faculty?
6. Are there any resources, services, or benefits available to tenured or tenure-track faculty that are not available to full-time non-tenure-track faculty?
7. How are non-tenure-track faculty oriented to your campus/department?

8. Are there any particular issues concerning non-tenure-track faculty appointments you believe this study should examine in depth?

Department Chairs

1. What are the principal reasons your institution employs full-time faculty in non-tenure-track positions?
2. What are the costs and consequences of hiring non-tenure-track faculty as opposed to hiring tenured or tenure-track faculty members?
3. What percentage of your institution's/department's faculty are in non-tenure-track positions? What fields employ the most and least non-tenure-track faculty?
4. How do the non-tenure-track faculty participate in decision-making governance in your department/institution? Do they participate in the social activities of your department/institution?
5. How does your department/institution recruit non-tenure-track faculty? Compare the necessary employment qualifications of the faculty your institution hires on the tenure track and off the tenure track.
6. How does your institution/department support the professional development of tenure-track and non-tenure-track faculty?
7. Are there any resources, services, or benefits available to tenured or tenure-track faculty that are not available to full-time non-tenure-track faculty?
8. How are non-tenure-track faculty oriented to your campus/department?
9. How are non-tenure-track faculty in your department/institution evaluated?
10. Are there any particular issues concerning non-tenure-track faculty appointments you believe this study should examine in depth?

Tenured and Tenure-Track Faculty

1. Tell me about yourself. What is your educational background and professional experience? How long have you been a faculty member at this institution?
2. What attracted you to be a faculty member? How did you enter the profession?
3. Your institution hires full-time faculty members who are not on the tenure track. How do you feel these colleagues contribute to meeting

the institutional mission? How do you feel they fit into the department and assist in meeting departmental instructional, research, and service objectives and goals?

4. Do you work directly with any non-tenure-track colleagues on instructional, research/publication, or service activities?

5. Do faculty in non-tenure-track positions function any differently than tenured or tenure-track faculty?

6. What are the positive or negative consequences for the institution of utilizing a non-tenure-track system?

Non-Tenure-Track Faculty

1. Tell me about yourself. What is your educational background and professional experience? What has been your teaching experience prior to accepting your current position?

2. What attracted you to be a faculty member? How did you enter the profession?

3. Describe your current position. Why are you in a non-tenure-track position?

4. What are some of the challenges you face in your current position? Does your institution support your professional development? Do you have opportunities for professional development?

5. How satisfied are you with your current work situation? (How do you feel about your relationship with the institution and colleagues? Describe your participation and involvement in your department. Are you involved in school/institutional governance activities?)

6. What are some of the key decisions you have made that led you to this point in your career? How satisfied are you with your career?

7. What are you attempting to accomplish in terms of your career? What are your career goals?

8. Are there any particular issues concerning a non-tenure-track appointment you believe a study of this sort should explore in depth?

Appendix D

Topical Areas Addressed in the Review of Institutional Policies Affecting Full-Time Non-Tenure-Track Faculty

The following topical areas were established as the framework for reviewing the content and comprehensiveness of policies (acquired from surveyed institutions) governing the terms and conditions of employment of full-time non-tenure-track faculty. The review involved determining whether these topics were included in institutional policies, as well as the nature of the policy statements.

1. Role definition
2. Hiring practices
3. Employment qualifications
4. Length of contracts and renewal standards
5. Evaluation standards and requirements
6. Compensation
7. Workload
8. Governance
9. Protection of academic freedom
10. Professional development support

Appendix E

A Framework for Institutional Self-Assessment of Personnel Policies and Practices Affecting Full-Time Non-Tenure-Track Faculty

This framework, set forth in the form of an inventory of questions, is designed to assist institutions in assessing how well their policies and practices concerning full-time non-tenure-track faculty meet defined institutional needs and the thirteen policy recommendations set forth in Chapter 6 of this book. The inventory poses questions that institutional policy makers need to address in order to assess the viability and integrity of the policies and practices governing the employment of non-tenure-eligible faculty.

A. The Purpose and Procedures for Hiring Full-Time Non-Tenure-Track Faculty

Questions in this section examine how full-time non-tenure-track faculty fit into an institution's larger faculty staffing goals, plans, and procedures.

1. Does the institution have a comprehensive faculty staffing plan?
   a. If so, is the use of full-time non-track faculty set forth as part of that plan?
   b. If there is no faculty staffing plan, how are decisions made in regard to whether a new or vacant position will be tenure-track or non-tenure-track?

2. Has the institution clearly articulated the reasons for hiring non-track faculty?

3. Will non-track faculty have the opportunity for continuous employment at the institution if their productivity is satisfactory? (I.e., will faculty have the opportunity to pursue a career at the institution if the need for the non-tenure-track position continues?) Does this opportunity vary by discipline or faculty role?

4. What qualifications are required for employment as a full-time non-track faculty member?

   a. Do the qualifications vary by specific position, discipline, and length of contract?

   b. If so, at what level of campus leadership are those decisions made?

   c. Are full-time non-tenure-track faculty expected to have qualifications comparable to those of faculty holding tenure-eligible positions when the position descriptions are similar?

5. Do the policies and procedures that apply to the recruitment of faculty for tenure-eligible positions also apply to full-time non-tenure-track positions? If not, how do they differ, and what is the rationale for any differences?

B. Contractual Arrangements

The questions posed in this section deal with policy areas directly related to the contractual relationship between non-tenure-track faculty members and the institution.

1. Are full-time non-tenure-track faculty issued a contract that sets forth the beginning and end dates of their appointment?

2. Has a clearly defined position description been articulated for each non-track faculty position?

3. Have explicit evaluation criteria derived from the position description been established for each non-track position?

4. Has a defined probationary period been established for non-track faculty during which productivity and performance are assessed?

5. Does this assessment serve as the basis for the decision to renew or terminate the appointment?

6. Has the institution established specific dates for contract renewal or termination for non-track faculty members?

    a. Are the dates related to the number of years of employment of the non-tenure-track faculty members?

    b. Is the relationship between dates of notification and years of service similar to those recommended by the AAUP?

    c. If not, what is the rationale for the schedule for notification of renewal or termination?

    d. If not, do the dates allow sufficient time for transition to another career opportunity?

7. Are multiyear contract appointments available for full-time non-tenure-track faculty after successful completion of the probationary period?

    a. Are these multiyear appointments of such length (i.e., five to seven years) that a successful faculty member is afforded employment security within the bounds of the institution's purpose for utilizing non-tenure-track faculty?

    b. In the absence of contracts at least five years in length, does the institution offer the potential for rolling or renewable contracts through which the contract is automatically extended each year based on program need and satisfactory performance by the faculty member?

8. Does the institution have an equitable salary system for non-track faculty?

    a. Is the salary scale for non-track faculty comparable to that for tenure-eligible faculty when qualifications, duties, and years of service are comparable?

    b. Are non-tenure-track faculty eligible for salary increases (merit and basic) comparable to those of tenure-track faculty when productivity and achievement are comparable?

9. Are the fringe benefits for non-tenure-track faculty comparable to those of tenure-track faculty? (This question applies directly to items such as pension plan, health insurance, life insurance, etc.)

10. Is there a written policy that protects academic freedom for non-tenure-track faculty comparable to that provided tenured faculty?

    a. Does the policy provide an appeals and grievance process for the non-track faculty equivalent to that provided tenured faculty?

11. Is there a system of sequential academic ranks for full-time non-tenure-track faculty that is the same as, or comparable to, the academic rank structure for tenure-eligible faculty in order to reward the professional growth and contributions of the non-track faculty?

C. Integration into the Campus Community

The questions in this section are designed to assess the degree to which non-tenure-track faculty members are integrated into the academic, intellectual, and social fabric of the campus community.

1. Is there a formal orientation program for new full-time non-tenure-track faculty? Is there an orientation program for new tenure-eligible faculty?
    a. Are the programs comparable in purpose and content?
    b. Does the program also address issues and concerns unique to non-tenure-track status?
    c. Do the programs attempt to socialize the faculty into the institution's culture and mission?
    d. Is there an attempt to educate faculty about the resources available to them in support of their roles and responsibilities?
    e. Is the orientation program an activity that is confined to a short period of time at the beginning of the first semester, or does it include activities that take place over the first semester or academic year?
2. Are non-tenure-track faculty provided with the opportunity to be involved in campus and departmental governance activities?
    a. Is their role in governance clearly articulated in policies at the institution and department levels?
    b. Are the topics from which they are excluded from participation, if at all, clearly articulated in the policy documents?
    c. Are department chairs and faculty leaders oriented to the governance policies so that policies are implemented in a fair and consistent manner?
    d. Is governance participation credited in merit salary decisions?
3. Are non-track faculty eligible for support for professional development in a manner consistent with their role and contributions to the institution and their needs for professional growth and career progression?
    a. Are their opportunities for professional development comparable to those of tenure-eligible faculty?
    b. Are their professional development opportunities funded at levels comparable to such support for tenure-track faculty?
4. Are full-time non-tenure-track faculty eligible for recognition and re-

wards for their professional achievements and contributions to the campus? (I.e., are they eligible for teaching awards, service awards, and research awards if the institution provides such forms of recognition to tenure-eligible faculty?)

D. Oversight and Monitoring

The questions included in this section are designed to assist in monitoring the use of full-time non-tenure-track faculty in keeping with the institution's purpose for such hires, staffing plans, and institutional policies and procedures.

1. Does the institution have a single office that has responsibility for monitoring the numbers of faculty employed in full-time non-tenure-track positions?
2. Is there a mechanism in place that provides for a periodic review of policies that affect the terms and conditions of employment of full-time non-tenure-track faculty?
    a. Who has responsibility for conducting such a review?
    b. Do non-track faculty have a role in the review?
3. What type of monitoring is conducted to ascertain that the policies and procedures governing the employment of full-time non-track faculty are consistently and equitably implemented?
4. Is there a periodic review of all full-time non-tenure-track faculty positions to assess whether the positions are functioning in keeping with the reasons and justifications that were used to request and support their creation?

The amount and structure of oversight and monitoring of non-tenure-track faculty must be consistent with the size and complexity of the institution and the magnitude of the employment of non-track faculty.

References

Academe Today. 1996. "State Appropriations for Higher Education." *Chronicle of Higher Education*, December 2.

The Almanac Of Higher Education, 1991. 1991. Chicago: University of Chicago Press.

American Association of University Professors. 1995a. "1940 Statement of Principles on Academic Freedom and Tenure with 1970 Interpretive Comments." In *Policy Documents and Reports*, 7–10. Washington, D.C.: AAUP.

———. 1995b. "The Status of Non-Tenure-Track Faculty." In *Policy Documents and Reports*, 72–81. Washington, D.C.: AAUP.

———. N.d. *Non-Tenure-Track and Part-Time Faculty: Guidelines for Good Practice*. Washington, D.C.: AAUP.

Austin, Ann E., and Roger G. Baldwin. 1991. *Faculty Collaboration: Enhancing the Quality of Scholarship and Teaching*. ASHE-ERIC Higher Education Report, vol. 20, no. 7. Washington, D.C.: School of Education and Human Development, George Washington University.

Benjamin, Ernst. 1997. "Changing Distribution of Faculty by Tenure Status and Gender." Memorandum to AAUP Executive Committee, January 29.

Bennis, Warren G., and Patricia W. Biederman. 1997. *Organizing Genius: The Secrets of Creative Collaboration*. Reading, Mass.: Addison-Wesley.

Bland, Carole J., and William H. Bergquist. 1997. *The Vitality of Senior Faculty Members: Snow on the Roof—Fire in the Furnace*. ASHE-ERIC Higher Education Report, vol. 25, no. 7. Washington, D.C.: Graduate School of Education and Human Development, George Washington University.

Bok, Derek. 1992. "Reclaiming the Public Trust." *Change* 24 (July/August): 13–19.

Bowen, Howard R., and Jack H. Schuster. 1986. *American Professors: A National Resource Imperiled*. New York: Oxford University Press.

Bowen, William G., and Julie Ann Sosa. 1989. *Prospects for Faculty in the Arts and Sciences*. Princeton, N.J.: Princeton University Press.

Boyer, Ernest L. 1987. *College: The Undergraduate Experience in America*. New York: Harper and Row.

———. 1990. *Scholarship Reconsidered: Priorities of the Professoriate*. Princeton, N.J.: Princeton University Press.

Breneman, David W. 1997. *Alternatives to Tenure for the Next Generation of Academics*. New Pathways Working Paper Series, Inquiry no. 14. Washington, D.C.: American Association for Higher Education.

Capelli, Peter, Laurie Bassi, Harry Katz, David Knoke, Paul Osterman, and Michael Useem. 1997. *Change at Work: Trends That Are Transforming the Business of Business.* Washington, D.C.: National Policy Association.

Carter, Deborah J., and Eileen M. O'Brien. 1993. *Employment and Hiring Patterns forFaculty of Color.* ACE Research Briefs, vol. 4, no. 6. Washington, D.C.: American Council on Education.

Chait, Richard P., and Andrew T. Ford. 1982. *Beyond Traditional Tenure.* San Francisco: Jossey-Bass.

Chait, Richard P., and Cathy A. Trower. 1997. *Where Tenure Does Not Reign: Colleges with Contract Systems.* New Pathways Working Paper Series, Inquiry no. 3. Washington, D.C.: American Association for Higher Education.

The Chronicle of Higher Education 1997–1998 Almanac Issue. 1997. August 29.

Chronister, Jay L., and Thomas R. Kepple, Jr. 1987. *Incentive Early Retirement Programs for Faculty: Innovative Responses to a Changing Environment.* ASHE-ERIC Higher Education Report, no. 1, Washington, D.C.: Association for the Study of Higher Education.

Clery, Suzanne B., and John B. Lee. 1998. "Faculty Salaries: 1996–97." In *The NEA 1998 Almanac of Higher Education,* 11–27. Washington, D.C.: National Education Association.

Daedalus. 1997. Issue devoted to "The American Academic Profession." 126(4).

El-Khawas, Elaine. 1992. *Campus Trends, 1992.* Higher Education Panel Report, no. 82. Washington, D.C.: American Council on Education.

———. 1995. *Campus Trends, 1995.* Higher Education Panel Report, no. 85. Washington, D.C.: American Council on Education.

El-Khawas, Elaine, and Linda Knopp. 1996. *Campus Trends, 1996.* Higher Education Panel Report, no. 86. Washington, D.C.: American Council on Education.

Fairweather, James S. 1996. *Faculty Work and Public Trust: Restoring the Value of Teaching and Public Service in American Academic Life.* Boston: Allyn and Bacon.

Finkelstein, Martin J., Robert K. Seal, and Jack H. Schuster. 1998. *The New Academic Generation: A Profession in Transition.* Baltimore: Johns Hopkins University Press.

Finkin, Matthew W., ed. 1996. *The Case for Tenure.* Ithaca: Cornell University Press.

Finn, Chester F., Jr. 1998. "Today's Academic Market Requires a New Taxonomy of Colleges." Opinion. *Chronicle of Higher Education,* January 9.

Frances, Carol. 1998. "Higher Education: Enrollment Trends and Staffing Needs." *Research Dialogues,* no. 55. New York: Teachers Insurance Annuity Association–College Retirement Equities Fund.

Gappa, Judith M. 1996. *Off the Tenure Track: Six Models for Full-Time, Nontenurable Appointments.* New Pathways Working Paper Series, Inquiry no. 10. Washington, D.C.: American Association for Higher Education.

Gappa, Judith M., and David W. Leslie. 1993. *The Invisible Faculty: Improving the Status of Part-Timers in Higher Education.* San Francisco: Jossey-Bass.

Gumport, Patricia J. 1997. "Public Universities as Academic Workplaces." *Daedalus* 126 (4): 113–36.

Hammond, P. Brett, and Harriet P. Morgan, eds. 1991. *Ending Mandatory Retirement for Tenured Faculty.* Washington, D.C.: National Academy Press.

Harper, Elizabeth P. 1997. *A Study of Full-Time Non-Tenure-Track Faculty in Higher Education: Results of the Institutional Survey.* Charlottesville, Va.: Center for the Study of Higher Education, University of Virginia.

Heydinger, Richard B., and Hasan Simsek. 1992. *An Agenda for Reshaping Faculty Productivity.* Denver: Education Commission of the States.

Hickman, John N. 1998. "Adjunct U." *New Republic,* December 7, 14–16.

Holden, Karen C. 1985. "Maintaining Faculty Vitality through Early Retirement Options." In *Faculty Vitality and Institutional Productivity: Critical Perspectives for Higher Education,* edited by Shirley M. Clark and Darrell R. Lewis. New York: Teachers College Press.

Honeyman, David S., and Megan Bruhn. 1996. "The Financing of Higher Education." In *A Struggle to Survive: Funding Higher Education in the Next Century,* edited by David S. Honeyman, James L. Wattenbarger, and Kathleen C. Westbrook, 1–28. Thousands Oaks, Calif.: Corwin Press.

Hutcheson, Philo. 1998. "Tenure: Traditions, Policies, and Practices." *Review of Higher Education,* 21 (3): 303–13.

Introduction to the Open University. 1998. www.open.ac.uk.

Jaschik, Scott. 1991. "State Funds for Higher Education Drop in Year; First Decline since Survey Began Thirty-Three Years Ago." *Chronicle of Higher Education,* November 6.

———. 1992. "One Percent Decline in State Support for Colleges Thought to Be First Two-Year Drop Ever." *Chronicle of Higher Education,* October 21.

Kanter, Rosabeth Moss. 1983. *The Change Masters: Innovation for Productivity in the American Corporation.* New York: Simon and Schuster.

———. 1989. *When Giants Learn to Dance.* New York: Simon and Schuster.

Leatherman, Courtney. 1996. "More Faculty Question the Value of Tenure." *Chronicle of Higher Education,* October 25.

Levine, Arthur. 1997. "How the Academic Profession Is Changing." *Daedalus* 126 (4): 1–20.

Lynton, Ernest, and Sandra Elman. 1987. *New Priorities for the University.* San Francisco: Jossey-Bass.

Magner, Denise K. 1997. "Job Market for Ph.D.'s Shows First Signs of Improvement." The Faculty. *Chronicle of Higher Education,* January 31.

———. 1998a. "'Postdocs,' Seeing Little Way into the Academic Labor Market, Seek Better Terms in the Lab." The Faculty. *Chronicle of Higher Education,* August 7.

———. 1998b. "Shrinking Job Market for Ph. D.'s Collides with Need for 'Cheap Labor,' Scholars Argue." Today's News. *Chronicle of Higher Education,* November 24.

Massy, William F., and Andrea K. Wilger. 1992. "Productivity in Postsecondary Education: A New Approach." *Educational Evaluation and Policy Analysis* 14 (4): 361–76.

National Commission on the Cost of Higher Education. 1998. *Straight Talk about College Costs and Prices.* Washington, D.C.: American Institutes for Research.

National Education Association. 1998. "Distance Education in Higher Education Institutions." *NEA Update* 4, no. 1. Washington, D.C.: National Education Association Higher Education Research Center.

New York Times. "The Downsizing of America," March 3, 1996.

Ottinger, Cecelia, and Robin Sikula. 1993. *Women in Higher Education: Where Do We Stand?* ACE Research Briefs, vol. 4, no. 2. Washington, D.C.: American Council on Education.

Russell, Alene B. 1992. *Faculty Workload: State and System Perspectives.* Denver: Education Commission of the States.

Sommer, Barbara. 1994. "Recognizing Academe's Other Faculty." *Planning for Higher Education* 22 (summer): 7–10.

Traub, James. 1997. "Drive-Thru U: Higher Education for People Who Mean Business." *New Yorker,* October 20, 27).

U.S. Department of Education. National Center for Education Statistics. 1996. *Institutional Policies and Practices Regarding Faculty in Higher Education.* Rita J. Kirshstein, Nancy Matheson, and Zhongren Jing. NCES 97-080. Washington, D.C.

———. 1997a. *Instructional Faculty and Staff in Higher Education Institutions: Fall 1987 and Fall 1992.* Rita J. Kirshstein, Nancy Matheson, and Zhongren Jing. NCES 97-470. Washington, D.C.

———. 1997b. *Retirement and Other Departure Plans of Instructional Faculty and Staff in Higher Education Institutions.* Jay L. Chronister, Roger G. Baldwin, and Valerie M. Conley. NCES 98-254. Washington, D.C.

———. 1998. *Fall Staff in Postsecondary Institutions, 1995.* Stephen Roey and Rebecca Rak. NCES 98-228. Washington, D.C.

Van Dusen, Gerald C. 1997. *The Virtual Campus: Technology and Reform in Higher Education.* ASHE-ERIC Higher Education Report, vol. 25, no. 5. Washington, D.C.: Graduate School of Education and Human Development, George Washington University.

Wilson, Robin. 1998. "Contracts Replace the Tenure Track for a Growing Number of Professors." The Faculty. *Chronicle of Higher Education,* June 12.

Winston, Gordon C. 1992. "Hostility, Maximization, and The Public Trust." *Change* (July/August): 20–27.

Zumeta, William, and Janet Looney. "1994. State Policy and Budget Developments." In *The NEA 1994 Almanac of Higher Education,* 79–103. Washington, D.C.: National Education Association.

Index

References to tables and figures are indicated by the italicized letters *t* and *f*, respectively. The abbreviation FTNTTF is used for "full-time non-tenure-track faculty."

academic freedom: about, 68–71; protection of, 161–63; recommendations, 185
academic labor market: about, 29–30; challenges, 137–38; FTNTTF at disadvantage, 55; specialized hires, 35–36; trends, 173–74
academic profession: conventional career model, 175–76; forces of change, 175; literature about, 8–9; in transition, 178–79
academic ratchet, 25
academic staff planning, 179–80
accompanying partners, 79, 140–42
action agenda. *See* reform agenda
"Adjunct U" (Hickman), 173
administrators: about, 106–9; characteristics of, 98*t*; job satisfaction by educational attainment, 107*t*; percentages of, 86; in reform roles, 188
advisory relationships, 126–27
age: demographics, 23, 28–29; for mandatory retirement, 17–18
Age Discrimination in Employment Act, 17–18
Allen, Sarah, 108
alternative career faculty, 142–43
alternative career track employment model, 74–75
Alternatives to Tenure for the Next Generation of Academics (Breneman), 114–15

American Association for Higher Education, 9, 175
American Association of University Professors: *Non-Tenure-Track and Part-Time Faculty: Guidelines for Good Practice*, 189; notification standards, 45–46; in reform roles, 189; reports on non-tenure track faculty, 9; tenured faculty standards, 2, 22
American Professors (Bowen and Schuster), 8
appointment policies, 163
appointment trends, 3–4
assessment. *See* evaluation
Association of American Colleges, 22
Austin, Ann E., 183
autonomy. *See* academic freedom
awards, 160–61, 182–83

baccalaureate-level institutions: academic freedom policies, 162; award policies, 160–61; contract issues, 45, 150–51, 153; culture impact, 131; distribution of FTNTTF, 83–84; employment qualifications, 39, 131–32; explicit evaluation criteria, 149; faculty mentoring, 167; gender gap, 79; governance participation, 58*t*, 159–60; instruction levels, 32*t*; non-tenure track choosers, 140; oversight, 164; percentage policies for FTNTTF, 40;

baccalaureate-level institutions (*cont.*)
  probationary periods, 148; professional development support, 157–58;
  ranks, 47–48; salary comparisons,
  50*t;* salary equity, 154; staffing aca-
  demic consequences, 122–24; tenure-
  track hopefuls, 136; workload issues,
  53, 54
bachelor's degree percentages, 81
Baldwin, Roger G., 183
benefits. *See* fringe benefits
Benjamin, Ernst, 3, 174
Bennis, Warren G., 183
Bergquist, William H., 29
best practices model, 171*t*
Beyond Traditional Tenure (Chait and
  Ford), 9–10
Biederman, Patricia W., 183
Bland, Carole J., 29
Bok, Derek, 14
Bowen, Howard R., 8, 23, 25
Bowen, William G., 8–9
Boyer, Ernest L., 15, 179
Bradford, Helen, 111
Breneman, David W., 114–15, 119, 176
bridge appointments, 179–80
Bruhn, Megan, 16
budget considerations, 35

Capelli, Peter, 21
career aspirations: about, 134; accompanying spouse/partner, 140–42; al-
  ternative/second-career faculty, 142–
  43; non-tenure track choosers, 138–
  40; tenure-track hopefuls, 134–38;
  tenure-track rejecters, 138–40
career development. *See also* professional development support: advancement concerns, 94, 128, 133;
  backgrounds, 81; career progression,
  47–49; job satisfaction, 91–95, 98*t*,
  100–101, 104–5, 107, 110, 138–40;
  morale, 49, 54, 95, 151, 153, 182; orientation, 165–67, 181–82; policies to
  support, 183; promotions, 47–49,
  89–90; ranks, 47–49, 82–83, 155–
  56; teaching loads, 54–55; titles, 47–

49, 82–83, 139, 155; two-tier faculty,
  128–34, 181, 186; work histories, 81–
  82
career ladder, 155–56
career productivity, 89*t*
Carruthers, Christine, 111
Carter, Deborah J., 80
Case for Tenure, The (Finkin), 10
case studies: Betty Lewis, teacher, 102;
  Christine Carruthers, other academic
  professional, 111; Frank Johnson, researcher, 105; George Stephens, researcher, 106; Helen Bradford, other
  academic professional, 111; Jackie
  Lavach, administrator, 108–9; Joyce
  Szabo, visiting assistant professor, 5–
  6; Lynn Kramer, teacher, 101–2; Marilyn Thompson, hybrid position, 4–
  5; Michael Tayloe, other academic
  professional, 111; Peter Matthews,
  administrator, 108; Sarah Allen, administrator, 108; Suzanne Javitz, researcher, 105–6; Wanda Martin,
  teacher, 102; Winifred Vargo, other
  academic professional, 111–12
Chait, Richard P., 9–10, 140, 176
child-rearing, 140
Chronicle, 191
Chronister, Jay L., 18
class differences, 128–34
Clery, Suzanne B., 24
clinical teaching, 36
collaboration, 128
collective bargaining, 67, 155, 159, 161
collegiality, 128–34
compensation: salary and benefits, 49–
  52, 154–55; savings in differentiated
  staffing, 118–19
competition: in higher education, 20–
  21; for increased funding, 175
computer sciences faculty, 85
condescension, 139
contingent personnel, 2, 21
continuing need evaluations, 121
contract issues: defined renewal dates,
  151–53; fixed-interval contracts, 151;
  length and renewal policies, 42–47;

multiyear contracts, 150–51; renewability, 150–51
contributions, recognition of, 160–61, 182–83
controversy, and academic freedom, 71
convenience institutions, 20–21
coordinating agencies, in reform, 189–90
corporate leaders, hiring retired, 36, 40
cost considerations: economy of full-time tenure-track faculty, 35; increases, 24–25; in recruitment, 37
credentials: employment qualifications, 38–40; maintaining, 136; nontraditional, 36, 40, 143; and salary equity, 154
culture: faculty culture, 128–34; institutional culture, 73, 185, 188
curriculum development involvement, 159–60, 184

Daedalus, 175
deadwood, 22
deans, in reform roles, 187–88
decisionmaking involvement, 128
degree requirements, 39–40
degree status, 80–81
demographics: age, 23, 28–29; FTNTTF *vs.* tenured and tenure-track, 3; gender, 78–79, 99, 103, 106, 109, 176; minorities, 78, 99, 103, 106, 109; from National Study of Postsecondary Faculty, 78–80; by primary FTNTTF classifications, 98*t;* of students, changing, 26–27; tenure statistics, 23
departmental orientation, 166
department chairs: in contract renewals, 46; in evaluations, 64; in promotion decisions, 49; in reform roles, 187–88; roles in FTNTTF development, 168–69
differential staffing, 118–19, 177–78
disciplines, 84–86
dismissal. *See* termination
dissertation committee participation, 54–55

distance learning, 19, 20, 174
distribution of FTNTTF, 83–84
doctoral degrees: in FTNTTF classifications, 97–99; and job satisfaction, 100*t,* 104*t,* 107*t,* 110*t;* and non-tenure-track choosers, 139; percentages, 80–81; researchers holding, 103–4; surplus, 29–30; teachers holding, 100; time in current position, 80*t*
doctoral institutions: academic freedom policies, 161; contract issues, 42–43; distribution of FTNTTF, 83–84; emphasis shifts, 25; gender gap, 79; governance participation, 57, 58*t;* government support decline, 15–17; instruction levels, 32*t;* percentage policies for FTNTTF, 40; professional development support, 67, 157; ranks, 47; salary comparisons, 50*t;* second-career faculty, 142–43; staffing academic consequences, 123; workload issues, 53
dual-career couples, 141–42
due process, 162–63

economic considerations, 35, 116–17
educational attainment, job satisfaction by: administrators, 107*t;* other academic professionals, 110*t;* researchers, 104*t;* teachers, 100*t*
El-Khawas, Elaine, 16, 17
Elman, Sandra, 179
employment models: about, 71–72; alternative career track, 74–75; integrated, 73–74; marginalized, 72–73
employment of FTNTTF: about, 115; academic community enrichment, 35–36; academic consequences, 122–25; collegiality, 128–34; degree status, 80–81; economic benefits, 116–17; and faculty culture, 128–34; flexibility, 115–16; increases in, 17, 174–75; institutional economies, 35; program areas, 84–86, 85*f;* protection of tenure-track faculty, 34–35; qualifications, 38–40, 131–32; savings in

employment of FTNTTF (*cont.*)
compensation, 118–19; spouse/partner concerns, 95–96; staffing pattern changes, 36, 173–74; student consequences, 126–28

Employment Retirement Income Security Act (ERISA), 17

enrollment: changing student demographics, 26–28; shifting patterns of, 174

equal employment opportunities, 80

ethical standards, 163

ethnic characteristics: of administrators, 106; demographics, 78; diversity, 80; of other academic professionals, 109; of researchers, 103; of teachers, 99

evaluation: about, 60–61; criteria, 62–65; explicit criteria recommendation, 149–50; frequency of, 63; during probationary period, 147–48; procedures, 62–65; purpose and timing, 61–62

exemplary policies. *See* good practice model

faculty: aging of, 28–29; autonomy of, 25–26; conventional career model, 175–76; deadwood, 22; enrollment increase staffing, 28; percentages of FTNTTF allowed, 40–42; personnel policies, 17–18; pressures faced by, 138; two-tier system, 7, 128–34, 139, 181, 186; workload and productivity, 25–26

faculty culture, 128–34

faculty governance bodies, in reform, 188

faculty mentors, 167

Faculty Roles and Rewards/New Pathways, 175

faculty staffing plan, 167–68

faculty turnover concerns, 127

Fairweather, James S., 15

family needs, 140

federal deficit, 16

federal government: funding support decline, 15–17; influence on faculty personnel policies, 17–18

Finkelstein, Martin J., 9, 79, 146

Finkin, Matthew, 10, 114

Finn, Chester, 20

fixed-interval contracts, 151

flexibility, in staffing, 115–16, 154

Ford, Andrew T., 9–10

for-profit education, 2

Frances, Carol, 21, 27–28

fringe benefits: about, 51–52; recommendations, 154–55; savings in differential staffing, 118–19

frustration, of tenure-track hopefuls, 135, 141

full-time non-tenure-track faculty: academic program impact of, 122; appointment trends, 3–4; career productivity, 89*t*; characteristics of, 98*t*; in collaborations, 128; consensus lack on employment conditions, 7–8; degree qualifications, 39–40; distinction from tenure-eligible faculty, 32–33; distribution of, 83–84; expendability of, 7; institutional support satisfaction, 93*t*; integration into academic community, 181–83, 183–86; job and career opportunity satisfaction, 91*t*; last two years' productivity, 89*t*; monitoring use of, 163–65; as percentage of faculty, 40–42; as present study focus, 2–3; primary activities, 86*f*; by private or public institution, 84*f*; by program area, 85*f*; programs and disciplines, 84–86; proportion increase in, 17, 174–75; proportion in differentiated staffing model, 117; by rank, 83*f*; ranks, titles, and promotion, 47–49; recognition of contributions, 160–61, 182–83; salary comparisons, 50*t*; support percentages offered, 66*t*; teaching productivity, 88*t*; tenure eligibility, 38; as threat to tenure system, 132–33

full-time tenure-track faculty: career productivity, 89*t*; collaboration with

FTNTTF, 128; decline in, 23; demographic characteristics, 78*t;* freed by FTNTTF, 123; institutional support satisfaction, 93*t;* job and career opportunity satisfaction, 91*t;* last two years' productivity, 89*t;* primary activities, 86*f;* proportion in differentiated staffing model, 117; protection of, 34–35; by rank, 83*f;* salary comparisons, 50*t;* support percentages offered, 66*t;* teaching productivity, 88*t;* traditional model, 7
funding: government support decline, 15–17; increased competition for, 175

Gappa, Judith M.: advanced degrees of part-time faculty, 81; exemplary policies, 146; *Invisible Faculty,* 2, 9, 77, 146; *Off the Tenure Track,* 9; part-time faculty benefits, 124; recommendations, 177, 180; salaries, 117; staffing issues, 115; tenure-track hopefuls, 134; two-class system, 186; work histories of part-time faculty, 81–82
gender: administrator percentages, 106; other academic professional percentages, 109; researcher percentages, 103; teacher percentages, 99
gender gap, 78–80
geography: and accompanying partner, 141; and recruitment, 37; in tenure-track decisions, 140
ghost faculty, 77
good practice model: about, 147; academic freedom protection, 161–63; benefit program, 154–55; compensation, 153–55; curriculum development involvement, 159–60; defined renewal or termination dates, 151–53; evaluation criteria, 149–50; governance involvement, 159–60; monitoring use of FTNTTF, 163–65; multiyear contracts after probation, 150–51; orientation programs, 165–67; probationary periods, 147–49; pro-

fessional development support, 156–58; recognition of FTNTTF contributions, 160–61; salary equity, 153–54; sequential rank system, 155–56; support policies for FTNTTF, 167–69
governance: participation in, 56, 57–60, 69–70, 159–60; recommendations, 184; and tenure-track hopefuls, 137; in two-tier faculty system, 128, 130–31
governing agencies, in reform, 189–90
graduate schools, in reform, 190–91
grant support, 15, 182
Gumport, Patricia J., 22, 26

Hammond, P. Brett, 18
Harper, Elizabeth P., 26
health coverage benefits, 52
Heydinger, Richard B., 15
Hickman, John, 173
higher education: aging faculty, 28–29; challenges to, 175; changing student demographics, 26–28; competition, 20–21; cost increases, 24–25; current status, 1–2; faculty personnel policies, 17–18; faculty workload and productivity, 25–26; funding resources, 15–17; government support decline, 15–17; outside work experience, 126; public mistrust, 14–15; technical staffing, 19; technology impacts, 18–20; two-class faculty system, 7; workplace transformation, 21–22
hiring practices, 36–38, 131–32
Holden, Karen C., 17
Honeyman, David S., 16
humanities faculty, 84–85
Hutcheson, Philo, 22
hybrid positions, 108–9. *See also* other academic professionals

incentives: paid leave options, 120–22; salary premiums, 119–20
information technology impact, 18–20
institutional culture, 73, 185, 188

insurance benefits, 52, 155
integrated employment model, 73–74
international students, advising, 123
Invisible Faculty (Gappa and Leslie), 2, 9, 77, 146

Jaschik, Scott, 16
Javitz, Suzanne, 105–6
job change concerns, 96–97
job satisfaction: of administrators, 107; with non-tenure-eligible positions, 138–40; of other academic professionals, 110; by primary FTNTTF classifications, 98*t;* of researchers, 104–5; survey data, 91–95; of teachers, 100–101
job security: academic freedom, 68–71, 161–63, 185; compensation, 49–52, 118–19; concerns about, 97; contract length and renewals, 42–47; contract termination, 44–46; due process, 68–69; multiyear contracts, 150; notification of renewals and termination, 45–46; revolving term appointments, 44; rolling contracts, 44; and satisfaction, 92, 94; tenured faculty views of FTNTTF, 127
Johnson, Frank, 105

Kanter, Rosabeth Moss, 173, 176, 183, 192
Kepple, Thomas R., 18
key themes, 7–8
Knopp, Linda, 17
Kramer, Lynn, 101–2

Lavach, Jackie, 108–9
Leatherman, Courtney, 23
leave policies, 66–68, 120–22, 153, 157–58
lecturers: earning potentials, 118; qualifications for, 39
Lee, John B., 24
Leslie, David W.: advanced degrees of part-time faculty, 81; exemplary policies, 146; *Invisible Faculty,* 2, 9, 77,

146; part-time faculty benefits, 124; recommendations, 177, 180; staffing issues, 115; tenure-track hopefuls, 134; two-class system, 186; work histories of part-time faculty, 81–82
Levine, Arthur, 15, 27
Lewis, Betty, 102
longevity. *See* time in position
Looney, Janet, 15, 16
Lynton, Ernest, 179

Magner, Denise K., 29
mandatory retirement ages, 17–18
marginalized employment model, 72–73
market scanning, 132
Martin, Wanda, 102
Massy, William F., 16, 24
master's degree: percentages, 81; teachers holding, 100
master's-level institutions: academic freedom policies, 161; benefit programs, 155; contract issues, 42–43, 44–45; culture impact, 131; distribution of FTNTTF, 83–84; evaluation, 62, 63; explicit evaluation criteria, 150; governance participation, 57, 58*t*, 159; instruction levels, 32*t;* orientation programs, 166–67; probationary periods, 148; professional development leave options, 121–22, 158; salary comparisons, 50*t;* staffing academic consequences, 123, 124; two-tier faculty system, 129; workload issues, 54
Matthews, Peter, 108
mentoring relationships, 126–27
methodology, 10–11
minorities: demographics, 78, 99, 103, 106, 109; overrepresentation as FTNTTF, 176
models. *See* best practices model; employment models; good practice model
Modern Language Association, 189
monotony factor, 54
Morgan, Harriet P., 18

Motorola University, 20
multiyear contracts, 150–51

named professorships, 160
National Study of Postsecondary Faculty, 10, 77
New Academic Generation, The (Finkelstein, Seal, and Schuster), 9
new curricular offerings, testing, 115
New Priorities for the University (Lynton and Elman), 179
niche teaching, 21
nonrenewal notification, 152, 153
Non-Tenure-Track and Part-Time Faculty: Guidelines for Good Practice (AAUP), 189
non-tenure track choosers, 138–40
nontraditional credentials, 36, 40, 143
nontraditional faculty resources, investment in, 180–83
nontraditional students, 27
notifications: nonrenewal, 152, 153; renewals, 45–46; termination, 45–46, 152

O'Brien, Eileen M., 80
office sharing, 133
Off the Tenure Track (Gappa), 9
Old Dominion University, 20
Open University, United Kingdom, 20
orientation programs, 165–67, 181–82
other academic professionals: about, 109–12; characteristics of, 98*t*; job satisfaction by educational attainment, 110*t*; percentages of, 86
Ottinger, Cecilia, 79
outside work experience, 126

partners: and career aspirations, 140–42; concerns about, 95–96; trailing spouses, 79
part-time faculty: benefits, 124; studies of, 2
personal family needs, 140
personnel policies, 17–18, 163–64, 167–68
planning, participation in, 70

policies: academic freedom, 161, 162; appointment, 163; awards, 160–61; career development, 183; contract issues, 42–47; of federal government, 17–18; leave, 66–68, 120–22, 153, 157–58; personnel, 17–18, 163–64, 167–68; roles of FTNTTF, 31–33, 163–64, 183
policy development participation, 70
politics, participation in, 70
postdoctoral programs, 136–37
present study: about, 8–10; key themes, 7–8; method, 10–11; terminology, 12
primary activities, 86–88
prior institutional affiliation, 140
private institutions: distribution of FTNTTF, 84*f*; funding concerns, 16–17; governance participation, 57–60; salary offerings, 50–51
probationary periods, 43, 44, 46, 147–49
productivity, 88–90
professional activity participation, 184–85
professional associations, in reform, 189
professional degree percentages, 81
professional development support: about, 65–68; as exemplary policy, 156–58; impact on faculty culture, 128; leave options, 66–68, 121–22, 157–58; orientation to, 166; recommendations, 181–82; satisfaction with, 92–93; for tenure-track hopefuls, 135, 136
professional meetings, 66
professors of practice, 179
program areas, 84–86, 85*f*
promotion: about, 47–49; advancement concerns, 94, 128, 133; teaching effectiveness as criterion, 89–90
publications: by administrators, 106; as continuing pressure, 138; by other academic professionals, 110; primary FTNTTF classifications, 98*t*; by researchers, 103–4; by teachers, 99–100

rank prefixes, 155
ranks: about, 47–49; sequential system
of, 155–56; statistics, 82–83
recommendations. *See also* best practices model; good practice model; reform agenda: academic freedom, 185;
explicit evaluation criteria, 149–50;
fringe benefits, 154–55; governance,
184; professional development support, 181–82
recruitment practices, 36–38, 131–32
reform advocates, 179
reform agenda: academic staff planning, 179–80; integration of
FTNTTF into academic community,
183–86; investment in nontraditional faculty resources, 180–83
reform key players: about, 186–87;
deans and department chairs, 187;
FTNTTF as, 187; governing and coordinating agencies, 189–90; graduate schools, 190–91; professional associations, 189; representative faculty
assemblies, 188; senior administrative leaders, 188
renewable contracts, 150–51
renewal notifications, 45–46
renewal process, 45–46
research citations, 160
researchers: about, 103–6; characteristics of, 98*t;* job satisfaction by educational attainment, 104*t;* percentages
of, 86
research institutions: accompanying
partners, 141; contract issues, 42–43,
151, 152–53; distribution of
FTNTTF, 83–84; downside of
FTNTTF use, 125; emphasis shifts,
25; employment qualifications, 38–
39; evaluation, 64; explicit evaluation
criteria, 149–50; federal policies in-
fluencing, 18; gender gap, 79; governance participation, 57, 58*t,* 160;
government support decline, 15–17;
instruction levels, 32*t;* orientation
programs, 166; oversight, 164–65;
percentage policies for FTNTTF, 40–

41; postdoctoral appointments, 136–
37; professional development support, 68; ranks, 47, 155; salary comparisons, 50*t;* satisfaction with, 93–
94; staffing academic consequences,
123, 124; tenure-track hopefuls, 135;
threats to tenure system, 132–33;
two-tier faculty system, 129–30;
workload issues, 53, 54
research roles: FTNTTF in, 34; specialized hires, 36; support for, 68; in two-
tier faculty system, 130
research support: lack of, 135, 136; satisfaction with, 93; and tenure-track
hopefuls, 137
resource allocation: about, 115; economic benefits, 116–17; flexibility in
staffing, 115–16; paid leave options,
120–22; salary premiums, 119–20;
savings in compensation, 118–19
respect, lack of, 136
retirement: mandatory, 17–18; patterns
of, 29; phased options, 17
review. *See* evaluation
revolving term appointments, 44
rewards, 160–61. *See also* awards
roles of FTNTTF: as administrators,
106–9; classifications of, 97–99; differing opinions on, 125; institutional
policies, 31–33, 183; instruction levels, 32*t;* as other academic professionals, 109–12; policies governing,
163–64; primary activities, 86–88;
productivity, 88–90; in reform, 187;
as researchers, 34, 103–6; as teachers,
99–103; technical, 19–20; workload
issues, 25–26, 53–56, 98*t*
rolling contracts, 44
Russell, Alene B., 26

sabbatical leaves: following termination,
153; as incentives, 120–22; for professional development, 66–68, 121–
22, 157–58; in two-tier faculty system, 133
salaries: about, 50–51; class differences,
128–29; comparisons, 50*t;* equitable

system of, 153–54; rationale for lower, 117; salary premiums, 119–20; savings in differential staffing, 118–19

satisfaction. *See* job satisfaction

scholarly productivity: of researchers, 106; survey data, 88–90; of teachers, 100–101

scholarship: academic freedom in, 69–70; support of, 157, 158

Scholarship Reconsidered (Boyer), 179

Schuster, Jack H., 8, 9, 23, 25

Seal, Robert K., 9

second-career faculty, 142–43

second-class faculty, 139. *See also* two-tier faculty

security. *See* job security

senior ranks, qualifications, 38–39

short-term appointments, labeled as such, 147

Sikula, Robin, 79

Simsek, Hasan, 15

social activity participation, 184–85

social characteristics, 78–80

Sommer, Barbara, 161

Sosa, Julie Ann, 8–9

specialized hires, 35–36, 136

spouses: and career aspirations, 140–42; concerns about employment of, 95–96; trailing spouse, 79

staff planning, 179–80

standards: ethical, 163; notification, 45–46; for tenured faculty, 2, 22

state government funding, 16–17

"Status of Non-tenure-track Faculty, The" (American Association of University Professors), 9

Stephens, George, 106

stereotypes, 77

student internship coordination, 123

students: culture impact on, 126–28; demographic changes, 26–27; in distance learning, 19; diversity of, 1–2; faculty turnover concerns of, 127; nontraditional students, 27; quality of education, 8; underprepared students, 27–28

Szabo, Joyce, 5–6

Tayloe, Michael, 111

teachers: about, 99–103; characteristics of, 98*t*; job satisfaction by educational attainment, 100*t*; percentages of, 86

teaching: academic freedom in, 69–70; commitment to, 138–39; productivity by tenure status, 88*t*

teaching awards, 160

teaching loads. *See* workloads

technology: impact of, 18–20, 174; in training, 68

temporary contract renewals, 46

tenure alternatives, 114–15

tenure caps, 123

tenured faculty: career productivity, 89*t*; culture concerns, 130; demographic characteristics, 78*t*; freed by FTNTTF, 123; institutional support satisfaction, 93*t*; job and career opportunity satisfaction, 91*t*; last two years' productivity, 89*t*; primary activities, 86*f*; by rank, 83*f*; standards for, 2, 22; support percentages offered, 66*t*; teaching productivity of, 88*t*; threats perceived by, 132–33; views on FTNTTF security, 127

tenure-eligible faculty, 32–33

tenure envy, 94

tenure ratios, 40–42

tenure system: criticism of, 22–23; debate over, 9–10; FTNTTF as threat, 132–33; public mistrust, 15; tenure as defense of academic freedom, 161

tenure-track hopefuls, 134–38, 141

tenure-track rejecters, 138–40

terminal degree requirement, 39–40

termination: arbitrary or capricious, 162; defined dates for, 151–53; notifications, 45–46, 152; with sabbatical leave benefit, 153

terminology, 12

thesis committee participation, 54–55

Thompson, Marilyn, 4–5

time in position, 80*t*, 82, 103

titles, 47–49, 82–83, 139, 155
TOTAL (Turn It Over to a Lecturer) principle, 56
tradition as barrier, 185
trailing spouses, 79, 140–42
training support, 67–68. *See also* professional development support
Traub, James, 20
trends, 3–4, 173–74
Trower, Cathy A., 140, 176
tuition: spiraling costs, 14–15, 17; statistics on, 24
turnover concerns, 127
two-tier faculty, 7, 128–34, 139, 181, 186

underprepared students, 27–28
University of Phoenix, 2, 20

Van Dusen, Gerald C., 18, 19
Vargo, Winifred, 111–12
virtual universities, 20

Western Governors University, 2, 20
Wilger, Andrea K., 16, 24
Wilson, Robin, 190
Winston, Gordon C., 15
women. *See also* gender: demographic characteristics, 78–79; overrepresentation as FTNTTF, 176
workloads: economics of, 116; FTNTTF *vs.* tenured and tenure-track, 53–56; by primary FTNTTF classifications, 98*t*; productivity, 25–26
workplace transformations, 21–22

Zumeta, William, 15, 16